D1826728

POLITICAL ECONOMY OF
MONEY AND FINANCE

Political Economy of Money and Finance

Makoto Itoh
Professor of Economics
Kokugakuin University
Tokyo

and

Costas Lapavitsas
Lecturer in Economics
School of Oriental and African Studies
University of London

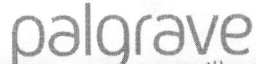

First published in Great Britain 1999 by
MACMILLAN PRESS LTD
Houndmills, Basingstoke, Hampshire RG21 6XS and London
Companies and representatives throughout the world

A catalogue record for this book is available from the British Library.

ISBN 0–333–66521–X hardcover
ISBN 0–333–66522–8 paperback

First published in the United States of America 1999 by
ST. MARTIN'S PRESS, INC.,
Scholarly and Reference Division,
175 Fifth Avenue, New York, N.Y. 10010

ISBN 0–312–21164–3

Library of Congress Cataloging-in-Publication Data
Itō, Makoto, 1936–
Political economy of money and finance / Makoto Itoh and Costas
Lapavitsas.
p. cm.
Includes bibliographical references and index.
ISBN 0–312–21164–3 (cloth)
1. Finance. 2. Economics. I. Lapavitsas, Costas, 1961– .
II. Title.
HG173.I87 1997
332—dc21
97–40502
CIP

This book is printed on paper suitable for recycling and made from fully managed and
sustained forest sources.

Transferred to digital printing 2002
Printed and bound in Great Britain by
Antony Rowe Ltd, Chippenham and Eastbourne

Contents

Introduction

The economic life of the great majority of people across the capitalist world has been haunted by profound insecurity since the early 1970s. A long period of high economic growth followed the Second World War, but ended with an inflationary crisis that ushered in a long economic depression that has lasted to the present day. In the course of the depression, various policies have been implemented to restore stable and harmonious economic growth: Keynesian effective demand management coupled with state welfare provision, floating exchange rates, monetarist control of the supply of money, neoliberal cuts in the marginal rate of income tax and international cooperation in the management of exchange rates. None of these policies have been successful, a failure that has had painful repercussions on the employment and real income of working people and weaker social groups.

The advanced capitalist economies, meanwhile, have undergone continuous restructuring, resulting in a severe intensification of competition in the world market. To regain some vigour, the capitalist world economy appears to be moving towards the reestablishment of a competitive and spontaneously operating international market order. The new competitive conditions are proving very harsh for the livelihood of workers and the weaker members of society. This historical trend has been both cause and effect of the failure of postwar Keynesian economic interventionism, the crumbling of state welfare provision, and the deterioration of workers' legal rights and conditions at work. It is not possible at the moment to tell how and when the restructuring of the capitalist economies will end. One thing, however, is already clear: the euphoria that greeted the collapse of the Soviet bloc and the so-called final victory of capitalism has evaporated. World capitalism is also undergoing a profound historical transformation, often with calamitous implications for the lives of the great majority of people.

It is apparent that a major source of the economic problems of this period has been the instability of money and finance. Moreover the successive economic policies implemented by the major capitalist economies since the beginning of the 1970s seem to have aggravated monetary and financial instability. Why is it so difficult to bring order and harmony to money and finance in contemporary capitalism? The

xi

issue is very complex and the major economic schools of thought tackle it in different ways.

Neoclassical economics (in the manner of classical political economy) treats capitalism as a natural and non-historical social order. Monetary and financial instability is typically attributed to erroneous and misguided management of money and finance by the authorities. If the errors and misconceptions of theory and practice were removed, the underlying natural harmony of the capitalist economy would, presumably, reveal itself. Despite the prevalence of this notion, it has not been possible in practice to devise reliable policies allowing natural harmony to materialise. Nevertheless governments have continued to operate a wide range of monetary and financial policies, reflecting the complexity of the social functions of money and finance in advanced capitalism and revealing the underlying need to exercise some regulation over money and finance. The impact of government monetary and financial policies on the capitalist economy is difficult fully to ascertain, and theoretical debate on the issue is likely to continue in the future. At the same time, the expectation that some judicious mix of policies could restore natural harmony to the capitalist monetary and financial order is highly dubious.

This book is critical of the neoclassical naturalist perspective and adopts a political economy approach. It offers a systematic presentation of the Marxist theory of money and finance by focusing on monetary and financial instability. A characteristic strength of Marxist political economy is its emphasis on the historically specific nature of capitalism. By adopting a broad historical perspective, the Marxist analysis of capitalist monetary and financial instability stresses the following three points.

First, the roots of capitalist monetary and financial instability are to be found not only in market operations (and the influence of the authorities on these) but also within the process of capital accumulation itself. Monetary and financial instability is not caused solely by policy mistakes or by possible defects of the mechanisms of money and finance. In order fully to identify the sources of such instability it is imperative to consider, in their totality, the social relations among real capital accumulation and the operations of money and finance, and to demonstrate their contradictory and often irrational character. It is also important to transcend the narrowly technical treatment of money and finance, typical of so much professional work on the subject, and reveal the broader issues and concerns affecting the lives of working people.

Second, in historical terms the character of monetary and financial instability has been complex and variable. Developed precapitalist markets, permeated by credit relations, have inevitably possessed elements of monetary and financial instability. Capitalism has exhibited additional (and characteristic) instability, arising from the necessary connections between money, finance and real accumulation. In the course of capitalism's historical development, the attributes and consequences of monetary and financial instability have changed greatly. For a full understanding of contemporary monetary and financial instability an appreciation of its historical evolution is necessary. Even at the level of the pure theory of money and finance the continually changing historical context ought not to be neglected.

Third, the critical assessment of rival theories, in their appropriate historical context, is also important for the development of the theory of money and finance. Since the early eighteenth century, several issues of money and finance have been repeatedly debated by economists belonging to different schools of thought. These issues have included the historical origin of money, the logical demonstration of money's emergence, the social and economic functions of money, theoretical determination and practical regulation of the quantity of commodity money and credit money, determination of the exchange value of money (the inverse of the price level), and the role of the discretionary policies of the central bank. All these issues have a bearing on the analysis of contemporary monetary and financial instability. Marxist political economy, because of its analytically founded emphasis on history, is advantageously placed to assess and utilise the insights of the rich theoretical tradition in money and finance.

Money and finance are, in essence, the spontaneously emerging *nexus rerum* of market economies, and of the capitalist economy in particular. Under capitalist social conditions a pyramid of social relations emerges spontaneously, and comprises, in successive layers, commodities, money, the turnover of capitals in competition, commercial credit, the banks, the money market and the central bank. In an anarchical manner, highly integrated monetary and financial social institutions materialise, which admit of a degree of social and political control depending on the historical context. Economists and politicians have historically aimed at lessening the instability of capitalism by using the integrated social mechanisms of credit and finance. The regulation of money and finance, often in relation to the operations of the central bank, has been proposed even by those who believe in the naturally harmonious nature of capitalism.

Towards the middle of the nineteenth century the currency school, the heirs of the Ricardian quantity theory of money, supported the introduction of the Bank Act of 1844 in Britain. This Act was the first attempt by a capitalist state systematically to regulate the supply of money in order to achieve greater economic stability. Contemporary monetarism, whose cornerstone is control of the supply of money, is the modern equivalent of the currency school. There is an evident contradiction between the generally liberal beliefs of this theoretical tradition (particularly its emphasis on the freedom of the market) and its proposal to regulate money. It will become clear in the course of this book that the quantity theory of money has serious theoretical defects, and could never provide the necessary framework for the stabilisation of capitalist money and finance. More compatible with the spirit of economic liberalism is the proposal by contemporary supporters of free banking to abolish the central bank and its monopolistic privileges. It will also be seen in the course of this book that this is not a realistic policy for a capitalist economy.

The banking school, the main opponents of the currency school, exhibited a more profound understanding of the workings of the capitalist credit system and of the functions of capitalist money. There is considerable similarity between the arguments of the banking school and the work of contemporary post-Keynesianism. Despite its greater theoretical sophistication, however, this tradition has not been able to propose a coherent set of policies to effect greater stability in money and finance. Marxist political economy is naturally sympathetic towards the theory of the banking school (including the insights of Keynes himself) and rejects the simplistic arguments of the currency school. At the same time, Marxist political economy also rejects the psychological and subjective elements of Keynesianism, and attempts to construct a socially founded theory of money and finance. The objective labour theory of value, as opposed to the subjective theory of marginal utility, provides necessary analytical guidelines in this respect, although it does not have to be directly applied to the theory of money and finance in all instances. Even more significantly, and again unlike the proposals of the banking school, the Marxist theory of money and finance attempts to locate the ultimate causes of monetary and financial instability within the process of capitalist accumulation itself. Capitalist monetary and financial crises are both inevitable and necessary for capitalist accumulation. Their specific features, on the other hand, depend on the historical and institutional framework within which they materialise. Thus no policies can permanently resolve capitalist monetary and financial instability, though they can significantly ameliorate (or worsen) the effects of crisis, particularly on working people.

A socialist restructuring of the entire economy, including the sphere of money and finance, could provide a final answer to monetary and financial instability. Nevertheless the manner in which a socialist economy would substitute for the social functions of capitalist money and finance by means of consciously organised socialist 'money' and 'credit' is not immediately clear and has to be reexamined. Soviet 'orthodox' Marxism was at fault in this respect, as the last chapter of this work makes clear. In our view it is important to note the historical trend towards the greater socialisation of money and finance as capitalism has evolved. On the one hand this trend indicates the possibility of greater economic democracy in the direction of socialism. This is certainly important for the shape of a future alternative socialist economy. On the other hand the trend alerts us to the inherent flexibility of monetary and financial policies in effecting improvements in the lives of workers and the weakest members of society, even if such policies cannot fully remove capitalist instability.

In the last three decades there has been a veritable renaissance of Anglo-Saxon radical political economy. A peculiar feature of this development has been the relative neglect of money and finance, despite the significant advances that have been made in several other fields, including value theory, the labour process, the analysis of real capital accumulation and the critique of mainstream economics. Few systematic theoretical studies of money and finance from a political economy perspective can be found in the English language. This is all the more paradoxical given the increasing importance of the topic in contemporary capitalism. Japanese political economy, on the other hand, has devoted considerable effort to the theory of money and finance in the postwar period. The Japanese Academic Association for the Study of Credit Theory alone has several hundred members, most of whom broadly belong to the Marxist tradition. Why such a disparity should have arisen between Anglo-Saxon and Japanese political economy is itself an interesting question in the history of economic thought. For the purposes of this work, it is evidently important systematically to present in English some of the fundamental concepts of the radical political economy of money and finance that are familiar in Japan.

In undertaking this task, however, it soon became clear that it was necessary to delve more deeply into the complex interaction of real accumulation with the mechanisms of money and finance. Thus this book endeavours to break new ground on the relationship between the logical and historical genesis of money, the concept and the process of creation of interest-bearing capital, the nature and functions of the central bank, and the historical character of monetary and financial instability in a capitalist economy. At the same time it strives systematically to present some well-established (at least in Japan) aspects of the political economy of money and finance, such as the structure of the capitalist credit system, the distinction between commodity money, fiat money and credit money, and the relationship between the credit system and joint-stock capital.

It also became clear that the monetary and financial analysis offered by several rival theoretical schools had to be presented systematically. The history of ideas is itself a gauge and a reflection of the development of society. At the minimum, a brief overview of the classical political economy of money and credit had to be put forth, acknowledging especially the unjustly forgotten work of Sir James Steuart. It transpires even at a cursory glance that the classical theories of money and credit have a particular resonance with the problems and theories of contemporary capitalism. The world capitalist economy, which is increasingly dominated by the competitive pressures emanating from the world market and exacerbated by the advance of new information technology, is manifesting on a grand scale the monetary and financial problems that have been innate to it since the age of mercantilism and liberalism.

There remained the issue of how extensively to deal with the international aspects of money and finance. Though these are certainly discussed in this book when it is necessary so to do, they have not been investigated separately. A requirement for the full theoretical analysis of international money and finance is that the capitalist world market is first analysed using concepts such as the ones developed in this book. International money and finance as a separate topic are best left for another book.

It is not possible to know at this point how successfully this book achieves its aims. We hope it will be as rewarding to read as it was enjoyable to write. It would be very gratifying if it proved of value in encouraging further cooperative study in the political economy of money and finance. The remarkable instability of our *fin de siècle* has given much urgency to this task.

Acknowledgements

The plan to write this book was conceived in the summer of 1993. In April 1993 Costas Lapavitsas was invited by the University of Tokyo to work there as Associate Professor of Economics for a year, during which time he collaborated with Makoto Itoh on several theoretical issues. It had been a long-standing aim of Makoto Itoh to write a book in English on money and credit, as is stated in the preface of his *Political Economy for Socialism* (1995). He found in Costas Lapavitsas a person with a common theoretical background, and a similarly long-standing research interest in the political economy of money and finance.

In Japan, we took advantage of several meetings and discussions with Michiaki Obata, a colleague at the University of Tokyo, as well as post-graduate students Koji Daikoku, Makoto Nishibe, Kazutoshi Miyazawa and Hideaki Tanaka, who now teach at, respectively, Ryukoku, Hokkaido, Ibaragi and Shiga Universities. Costas Lapavitsas, who speaks and reads Japanese, was also able to visit the University of Tokyo for three months in the summer of 1996, financed by a grant from the European Union, the help of which in writing this book is gratefully acknowledged.

In Britain, Ben Fine, a colleague at SOAS, read most of the draft chapters and made valuable comments, especially regarding the fragmentation of orthodox economics and post-Keynesianism. He was critical of some points, for instance the concept of interest-bearing capital and the process of capitalist crisis. Kiyoshi Nakagawa of Aichi University, who was a visitor at SOAS for more than a year, meticulously read and commented on the drafts of several chapters. Bob Rowthorn of Cambridge University also made useful suggestions, such as to reconsider Nassau Senior's work on determination of the value of commodity money. Alfredo Saad-Filho of South Bank University helped us improve Chapters 2 and 3 and offered penetrating comments on the rest of the material. Arie Arnon of Ben-Gurion University read parts of the manuscript while visiting SOAS.

Several other colleagues at SOAS read parts of the drafts, including Massoud Karshenas, Terry Byres, John Sender, John Weeks, Mushtaq Khan, Rathin Roy, Dic Lo, Sonali Deraniyagala and Graham Dyer. Post-graduate students Sedat Aybar and Bassam Fatouh also contributed comments and ideas. Finally, Nikos Petralias, Giorgos Stamatis and Stavros Mavroudeas of, respectively, the University of Athens, Panteion University and the University of Macedonia in Thessaloniki, read parts of the manuscript. Though final responsibility rests with the authors, we wish to thank all the colleagues and friends who contributed to its improvement.

This book is a joint work for which we both take responsibility. As far as individual authorship can be attributed, Costas Lapavitsas is largely responsible for Chapters 1, 2, 3, 7, 9 and 10, and Makoto Itoh for Chapters 4, 5, 6, 8 and 11.

MAKOTO ITOH
COSTAS LAPAVITSAS

Part I
Classical Foundations

The high period of classical political economy ran roughly from the publication of Adam Smith's *Wealth of Nations* in 1776 to that of John Stuart Mill's *Principles of Political Economy* in 1848. This was also the time when European mercantile capitalism, with its great trading monopolies and chartered companies, finally gave way to industrial capitalism. The dust of more than two centuries has not dimmed the insight into the organisation of society offered by classical economic thought. Still, the classical economists of the high period saw far because they stood on the shoulders of giants: to appreciate classical monetary theory we shall also consider the writings of John Law, David Hume and James Steuart.

Classical political economy emerged against the background of the American and the French Revolutions. It emerged, however, in Britain which had had its own political revolution more than a century earlier. Republicanism, the rights of man, bourgeois taxation and public finance had begun to spread across the world. Equally significantly, the British industrial revolution, already under way by the last quarter of the eighteenth century, had sharply outlined three great classes of modern society: capitalists, workers and landowners. At the heart of classical political economy lay the corresponding division of the annual product of society into profits, wages and ground rent.

In the realm of ideology, classical political economy had to defeat mercantilism, the set of economic ideas that had dominated European economic thought for more than two centuries. Early mercantilism tended to identify national wealth with metallic money, and advocated import controls to prevent money from flowing abroad. Late and more sophisticated mercantilism aimed at manipulating the terms of trade in order to secure a balance of trade surplus and ensure the regular inflow of money. Neither version recognised a spontaneous order in the functioning of the economic system. Rather, the objective of mercantilist thought was to establish rules and conditions for state intervention in economic life. The classical assault on mercantilism established the principle that national wealth, which comprised mostly commodities, did not originate in the surplus of the balance of trade but, above all, in labour. In this connection the question of commodity value inevitably arose. Typically for the mercantilists, value was determined by demand and supply in the sphere of exchange. For the classical political economists, on the other hand, value was determined by the expenditure of labour in production. The labour theory of value provided objective 'cost of production' determination of value, and shifted attention from exchange to production. The theory also had profound implications for monetary analysis since money was typically a produced commodity: gold and silver. Valueless forms of money closely related to the nascent credit system, such as privately issued banknotes, were also heavily used in domestic and international exchanges among capitals.

The German historical school, neoclassicism and Marxism emerged almost simultaneously after classical political economy had run its course.[1] Of the three, Marxist economics is arguably the closest to classical political economy in its theoretical content. Nowhere is this more obvious than in the theory of value. Where the historical school tended to reject all theoretical thought in principle and neoclassicism adopted the subjective theory of marginal utility, Marxism strove to develop the labour theory of value. On the foundation of the labour theory of value, Marx proposed a coherent theory of money and credit, while also criticising the treatment of these issues by the classical school.

1 Classical Political Economy of Money and Credit

The classical theory of money and credit is characterised by the underlying assumption that natural harmony prevails in the operations of the market economy, a harmony that extends to the realm of money and credit. Two distinct traditions can be discerned within classical theory in this respect. On the one hand the quantity theory of money (or the currency school) emphasises the harmonious equilibration of the total quantity of commodity output and the total quantity of commodity money, provided no state or other interference has taken place with the domestic and international operations of the capitalist markets. In this view money is a secondary aspect of capitalist exchange, a 'veil' on real economic activities. Credit money created by banks could upset the presumed harmony, resulting in commodity price disturbances. Thus this tradition supported the introduction of the English Bank Act of 1844 in the hope that the tight quantitative regulation of credit money created by the Bank of England would eradicate capitalist market disturbances.

On the other hand, the tradition of the anti-quantity theory (or the banking school) stresses that harmony also largely prevails in the relation between commodity output and credit money, as long as bank lending and repayment take place along non-speculative lines. In order to sustain this view, the economists of this tradition had to reexamine the role of commodity money in capitalist exchange, and opposed the quantity theory by emphasizing the hoarding and paying functions of money. For this reason the anti-quantity theory tradition has left a more substantial legacy for the analysis of the monetary phenomena of capitalist exchange. At the same time, however, it has left a poor legacy of theoretical and practical recommendations on how to deal with capitalist market disturbances.

In this chapter the antecedents and the main exponents of the two traditions are examined. Section 1.1 deals with the emergence of money, the measurement of commodity values, and the relationship between commodities and money as aggregate quantities. Section 1.2

considers the implications of the operations of the credit system for the forms and functions of money.

1.1 VALUE, COMMODITIES AND MONEY

1.1.1 The Measurement of Value

Among the classical economists,[1] Adam Smith (1776, bk I, ch. 4) offered an early and full discussion of the origin of money. Smith first examined the division of labour, the root cause of increases in labour productivity. Given an elaborate division of labour, producers have to exchange a part of the product of their labour for that of others. The process of direct commodity exchange, however, is frequently 'clogged and embarrassed in its operations' because of the inevitable incompatibility of wants among the producers (ibid., p. 26). Thus a 'prudent' person is forced to keep 'a certain quantity of some one commodity or other, such as he imagined few people would be likely to refuse in exchange for the produce of their industry' (ibid.). Precious metals, since they are imperishable and divisible, are best suited for the purpose. Metallic money initially went by weight, but the costs of weighing and assaying the metal in each transaction, not forgetting the inevitable fraud, led to state-minted coinage based on weight. Soon, however, coin began to circulate 'by tale' rather than weight and so established the nominal price of goods.

Thus Smith theoretically derived money as a commodity that reliably purchases other goods and so overcomes the problems of barter. The nominal price of goods clearly is a measure of their exchangeability. Smith (ibid., p.34) consequently distinguished between 'value in use' and 'value in exchange', and put forth the first authoritative statement of the classical theory of exchange-value, 'Labour, therefore, is the real measure of the exchangeable value of all commodities....The real price of every thing, what every thing really costs to the man who wants to acquire it, is the toil and trouble of acquiring it.' There is considerable ambiguity in Smith's treatment of value, particularly between the labour embodied in a commodity in production and the labour commanded by the commodity in exchange. These two concepts, which Smith used interchangeably, are not identical in thought, and could result in contradictory theoretical conclusions regarding changes in relative prices. Nevertheless, coherently to relate value to labour was an

intellectual breakthrough for Smith, and it became the cornerstone
of the classical theory of value. Smith also engaged in a vain search for
an invariant measure of value in exchange (and mostly identified
it with corn). Since the 'real' price of the money commodity is directly
affected by changes in the conditions of its production, the metal used
for money cannot be this invariant measure. The most that metallic
money can do is establish 'nominal' prices, which vary inversely with
the value of the metal and the metal content of coin.[2]

Other than differentiating between 'real' ('value') and 'nominal'
('money') price, however, Smith had little to say on the accounting
system of nominal prices, and its relation to the value of money and
the value of commodities. Sir James Steuart, a late mercantilist and
unjustly neglected contemporary of Smith,[3] had an important insight
on this issue. Steuart, despite some rather muddled efforts, did not
arrive at a labour theory of value and thought that value and price
were determined by demand and supply in the sphere of exchange.
Fundamental to his theory of price was the concept of money of
account, 'Money, which I call of account is no more than *an arbitrary
scale of equal parts, invented for measuring the respective value of things
vendible*' (Steuart, 1767, vol. II, p. 270, emphasis in original).[4] Money
of account establishes a system of prices by measuring the value of
'things vendible'. On the other hand, money is also metal, which
Steuart (ibid., p. 279), never one for accurate classifications, called
'artificial or material money'. Material money is a practical approximation of the money of account. Since the value of material money
(determined by demand and supply) is variable, such money cannot
satisfactorily realise the system of prices established by the money of
account. Material money is necessarily a poor approximation of the
ideal money of account.

Steuart's claim that the accounting system of prices has an abstract
existence was an important advance for economic theory. There is
no denying that commodity values can indeed be expressed in
many different types of money, and this money need not be corpor-
eally present in order to render values into prices.[5] Marx (1867,
pp. 189–98) also stressed the difference between abstract money,
which renders value into price, and real money, which renders price
into a concrete equivalent. The actual translation of abstract into real
money in the process of capitalist exchange is never an easy process.
The problem with Steuart's analysis, however, is that he treated
metal coin as a practical approximation of an abstract numeraire.
While it is undoubtedly true that coin is a social convention,

Smith was on more solid ground than Steuart when he treated coin as simply a socially conventional division of monetary metal and not as an approximation of some abstract measure of value. Smith's labour theory of value allowed him to posit money and commodities as commensurate prior to their coming into contact in exchange on the grounds of production of both money and commodities entailing human toil. Steuart, who lacked a labour theory of value, was instead led to argue that the abstract system of accounting prices arises from the arbitrary approximation of the ideal value measure.

1.1.2   The Quantity Theory of Money

Money, however, does not only establish prices but also functions as means of circulation. A monetary economy with a developed division of labour and autonomous producers, such as the capitalist one, relies on several well-functioning markets to provide producers with their inputs, and workers and others with their means of consumption. A regular, but not consciously organised, exchange of goods with money has to take place to sustain such an economy. At any moment in time, flows of commodities both enter and exit the sphere of exchange, respectively seeking sale or having been sold for money. The aggregate quantities of commodities and money in the sphere of exchange during any given period of time are clearly important economic magnitudes in this connection, as is also the velocity of money. Values and quantities of commodities and money, moreover, certainly have a connection with aggregate prices. Fully to appreciate the classical arguments on these issues, however, we must first examine Hume's quantity theory of money and Steuart's critique of it.

David Hume devoted very little effort to political economy, but managed in a few short essays to capture for posterity the gist of an entire monetary tradition. There was a complex background to Hume's mid-eighteenth-century theory: the collapse of John Law's 'System' in the 1720's, which is further discussed below; the struggle against mercantilism, including the latter's treatment of money as the substance of national wealth; and the steady European price inflation of the sixteenth and seventeenth centuries, associated with the Spanish discovery of precious metals in the New World. The core of Hume's theory was not original (others, including Cantillon and Montesquieu, had made similar points earlier), but he gave to the quantity theory of money coherence and conciseness.

For Hume (1752, p. 48), money only has 'fictitious value', and is a 'representation of labour and commodities' in the sphere of exchange (ibid., p. 37). The 'fictitious value' of money is essentially the rate of exchange of the aggregate quantity of commodities for the aggregate quantity of money (the inverse of the price level). Money, moreover, is a pure means of exchange, 'only the instrument which men have agreed upon to facilitate the exchange of one commodity for another' (ibid., p. 33). Hume's theory possesses an inextricable international aspect: money flows between nations in the manner of water between vessels, and seeks the same 'level' in all countries (ibid., pp. 64–5). If the domestic quantity of money is increased by, say, silver discoveries in the New World, money's rate of exchange with the quantity of commodities is disturbed. The value of money naturally falls (commodity prices rise). The international 'level' of money having remained the same, however, the monetary metal flows out of the country and there is a balance of payments deficit. The disturbance stops when money has again attained its correct 'level' internationally. Opposite results follow a sudden reduction of the domestic quantity of money. Hume also incorporated a 'transmission mechanism' into his basic price-level-specie-flow theory. In the short run merchants, finding themselves in possession of larger than usual quantities of money, increase their effective demand, putting more artisans to work and giving a boost to production. With the passage of time, however, the temporary boost to real activity fizzles out, leaving output the same as before but prices higher. In the long run money is a 'veil' on real activity, and economically neutral. However this analytical detour, despite the high esteem in which it is held in contemporary literature, was not essential to the thrust of Hume's argument. Ricardo, who mostly concerned himself with the configuration of the long run, never dallied with such ideas.[6]

Hume's formulation of the quantity theory had a powerful, but entirely deceptive, simplicity. At a stroke it explained European price inflation and rejected the mercantilist view that money was the only true wealth. It should be stressed, however, that the quantity theory of money was not necessary to achieve either of these aims. Smith, despite his familiarity with Hume and his willingness to adopt other people's views, meticulously avoided Hume's quantity theory in his critique of the mercantile system.[7] As for European price inflation, the decline in the value of the precious metals, attendant to the discovery of rich mines in the New World and exploited through the enslavement of the native population, could also explain price rises and without recourse to the quantity theory.

Hume's theoretical argument soon came under attack by Steuart. For Steuart (1767, bk II, ch. 27) the circulation of money is the successive passage of commodities and money from hand to hand, a process representing the fundamental exchanges among the great classes of society. If the proper exchange of equivalents among the classes does not take place, consumption is limited and 'industrious-ness' suffers. Consequently the 'statesman', the reference point for Steuart's political economy, who has to oversee economic activity and ensure that all are provided with food and necessaries, *'ought at all times to maintain a just proportion between the produce of industry, and the quantity of circulating equivalent, in the hands of his subjects, for the purchase of it'* (ibid., p. 53, emphasis in original). The 'statesman' has to know the propensity of the rich to consume, the disposition of the poor to industriousness, and the proportion of circulating money with respect to both propensity and disposition. Metallic money is problem-atic in this respect because people are inclined to hoard it as soon as they have no desire to consume, and so render it lost to circulation. Metallic money, in other words, gives rise to an insufficiency of domestic money, a fact that inhibits the growth of industry. To stimu-late 'industriousness' the 'statesman' has to draw metallic money out of its hoards. Even better, however, the 'statesman' can rely on the creation of paper money by the banks. Steuart called this process 'the melting down of solid property', which amounts to the acquisition of illiquid assets by banks through the issuing of liquid liabilities, as is further explained below. The landowner class could thereby increase its consumption and spur industry.

Steuart was prolix and, compared with Smith, not a great system builder. For instance, though he relied on paper credit money in order to analyse the process of circulation, he discussed the properties of such money only much later in his work. His analysis of circulation suffers from the misconception that greater durability of commodities stands for more value, but nevertheless it has a dynamic and 'modern' feel compared with Hume's. His summary rejection of Hume's quantity theory of money is remarkably penetrating, and worth quoting at length:

The circulation of every country ... must ever be *in proportion to the industry of the inhabitants, producing the commodities which come to market* ... if the coin of a country, therefore, fall below the propor-tion of the produce of industry *offered to sale*, industry itself will come to a stop; or inventions, such as symbolical money, will be fallen upon to provide an equivalent for it. But if the specie be found above the proportion of the industry, it will have no effect in raising prices, nor will it enter into circulation: it will be hoarded up in treasures, where it must wait not only the call of desire in the proprietors to consume, but of the industrious to satisfy this call (ibid., p. 95, emphasis in original).

This is an uncompromising rejection of the quantity theory of money based on the hoarding of metallic money, the endogenous creation of credit money to meet the needs of circulation, and the non-neutrality of money. In reply to Hume's statement that the only result of a drastic reduction in the quantity of circulating money would be lower prices, Steuart (ibid., p. 98) observed that if paper money was proscribed, industry and employment would collapse and direct exchange would rapidly substitute itself for the destroyed monetary exchange. Prices would indeed fall, but they would not maintain their initial proportion to the quantity of money. More broadly, money is not a 'representation of commodities' in a freely functioning market. This would be an appropriate idea only if a 'statesman' were directly to 'perform all the operations of circulation' by regulating all commodities and all money and ascertaining the proportion among them. Finally, according to Steuart, no conclusions can be drawn about prices from the assumption of arbitrary changes in the quantity of money. An increase in the latter might not be translated into an expansion of consumer demand, and a decrease would certainly lead to a decline in industry and a rise in unemployment.

Some of Steuart's other important insights into monetary circulation ought to be mentioned here since they reappear in the work of later critics of the quantity theory of money, including the banking school and Marx. As well as money hoarding, Steuart (ibid., bk IV, pp. 255–6, emphasis in original) stressed that money pays debts, a fact that gives rise to a type of money circulation that is very different from plain commodity exchange:

We have distinguished between *necessary* and *voluntary* circulation: the *necessary* has the *payment of debts*; the *voluntary* has *buying* for its object. We have said that he who owes is either a bankrupt, or *must pay*, as long as there is a shilling in the country...By withholding money for the uses of circulation, which banks may do for some time, buying *may* be stopped; paying *never can*.

The forced, obligatory character of debt repayment, later also emphasised by Marx (1867, pp. 232–40), makes it doubly important for a

country to have access to flexible and manageable bank paper money.
This opinion accorded well with Steuart's overall view of monetary
circulation: where Hume had posited an undifferentiated mass of
commodities confronting an equally undifferentiated mass of money,
Steuart (1767, bk IV, ch. 19) distinguished among (1) the domestic
circulation of coin, (2) the domestic circulation of paper money issued
by banks, and (3) the payment of balances abroad, that is, the international circulation of money. Steuart (ibid., p. 285) remarked that
'These three objects are absolutely different in their nature, and they
are influenced by different principles.' Coin and credit money, in
other words, circulate according to different principles, and money
does not move among the nations of the world in the manner of water
seeking the same level among vessels. Compared with Hume, who put
inordinate stress on the function of means of circulation alone,
Steuart offered a considerably richer analysis, discussing money as
unit of account, means of debt repayment, means of hoarding and
means of payment in international transactions. Marx's analysis of the
functions of money owes much to Steuart's work.

1.1.3 The 'Channel of Circulation'

It is a characteristic view of the classical economists that a certain
quantity of money must necessarily exist in the sphere of commodity
exchange during any given period of time.[8] The necessary quantity of
money depends on commodity values, money value and money velocity. Smith (1776, bk I, p. 210), whose favourite metaphor in this
respect was 'the channel of circulation', argued that when a country
becomes wealthier the quantity of circulating coin increases 'from
necessity'. Were more than the 'necessary amount' of metallic
money to find itself in the 'channel of circulation', the latter would
'overflow', a notion that Smith put to good use in the analysis of credit
money. Furthermore, for Smith the metallic money that comprises
'the great wheel of circulation' is clearly not a part of the net revenue
of society, but merely facilitates the accrual of the net revenue as
wages, profits and rent. Yet extracting metal from the bowels of the
earth costs labour, and thus represens a net subtraction from the net
revenue of society. Smith (ibid., bk II, pp. 313–14), unlike Hume, was
sympathetic to paper money issued by banks as it provides a cheaper
means of circulation, 'a sort of waggon-way through the air'.

David Ricardo, the most powerful model builder among economists, analysed the principles of the 'necessary' quantity of money in

the same spirit as Smith but with greater accuracy. Ricardo (1817, pp.
18–20) identified the ambiguity in Smith between value as labour
commanded and value as labour embodied. He rejected the former
and put forth the finished classical position of value as labour embodied.[9] The value of money, as that of all other commodities from which
it is indistinguishable, is determined by the labour embodied in its
production (Ricardo, 1810, p. 52). If only metallic money circulates in
the world, in equilibrium each country possesses a quantity of money
determined by the number and frequency of the payments that have
to be completed domestically. This 'necessary' quantity varies directly
with the total value of commodities circulated (or the value of
payments to be made), inversely with the value of the money metal,
and inversely with 'the degree of economy practised in effecting these
payments' (the velocity of money) (Ricardo, 1816, pp. 55–8). The
question that emerges at this point is what happens when the actual
quantity of money in circulation diverges from the 'necessary'? Here
Ricardo followed an entirely different path from Smith, and adopted
Hume's quantity theory of money.

The background to Ricardo's quantity theory of money was very
different from that of Hume's, and included the restriction of convertibility of Bank of England banknotes into gold after 1797 and the
subsequent bullion controversy. Nevertheless the gist of Ricardo's
theory is very similar to Hume's, but with the important exception
that money (and commodities) has intrinsic value determined by
labour content. In Ricardo's schema, the intrinsic value of money
has to be made compatible with Hume's 'fictitious value' of money,
that is, with the rate of exchange of the aggregate quantity of commodities for the aggregate quantity of money (the inverse of the price
level). Ricardo reconciled these two values of money in a complex and
elegant manner.[10] If money were exclusively metallic across the world,
at equilibrium each country would possess the quantity of money
'necessary' to its sphere of exchange. Since for Ricardo the 'necessary'
quantity of money is determined by the value of money, the value of
commodities and velocity, it follows that at equilibrium no disparity
exists between the intrinsic value of money and money's aggregate
rate of exchange with commodities. Moreover, given that equilibrium
is global, the intrinsic value of money as commodity prevails across
the world. Thus there is no economic motive to transfer money
between countries, and international transactions involve only commodity flows. International equilibrium is balance of trade equilibrium, trade being, in effect, barter. A shock to equilibrium, such as

the discovery of a new gold mine or the printing of more money by the banks, *ceteris paribus*, sets off a complex train of events. As Hume had assumed, the rise in the domestic quantity of money initially lowers the value of money relative to commodities (raises prices). Since the intrinsic value of the monetary metal has remained the same across the world, however, bullion can be exported at a profit. The holders of coin can melt it into bullion and send it abroad, in the process creating a balance of trade deficit and depressing the exchange rate of domestic to foreign currency. However this reduces the domestic quantity of money and eventually re-stablishes equilibrium: the value of money relative to commodities is once again in accord with money's intrinsic value. The opposite process takes place if the circulating quantity of money falls short of the 'necessary'.

Paper money (Ricardo did not discriminate between bank-issued and state-issued notes) does not disturb this automatic mechanism, as long as it is fully convertible into gold. If the original shock originates in extra issues of paper money by banks, the holders of the notes simply convert them into coin, which is then melted down and exported. Inconvertible paper money, however, is a different thing altogether. An increase in its quantity drives coin out of circulation and results in an aggregate rate of exchange of money for commodities that is permanently below the intrinsic value of the money metal. The exchange rate of domestic to foreign currency falls commensurately. Ricardo, unlike Hume, was not against paper money, provided that such money is convertible. Indeed he argued that paper money is superior to metallic precisely because its quantity can be consciously manipulated to produce a stable aggregate rate of exchange of money with commodities (Ricardo, 1816, p. 57).

Since Ricardo's theory relies on the continuous and free conversion of coin into bullion and *vice versa*, it cannot allow for non-circulating, hoarded money, held by traders for no reason other than that it is money. By the same token his theory cannot envisage commodity owners specifically demanding money in exchange for their goods, rather than any another commodity. If traders find it necessary, rather than profitable, to use and to hoard money in the course of commercial operations, it follows that money is a special commodity. Yet Ricardo's reconciliation of the labour theory of value with the quantity theory of money is premised on the assumption that money is an ordinary commodity among the many.

Nevertheless, in practice money is regularly hoarded and exported among nations for reasons evidently unrelated to the arbitrage gains of traders; for instance money is specifically used to effect urgent purchases of foodstuffs abroad when crops fail, or to settle international debts. This is precisely the aspect of money's operations that Steuart stressed in his critique of Hume. Ricardo, however, could not incorporate such phenomena into his theory, and attacked other theorists who had done so. He asked Thornton to explain why foreigners should refuse to accept English goods and instead demand money (Ricardo, 1810, p. 61); he dismissed Bosanquet's suggestion that England was 'compelled' to import corn when the harvest was bad (Ricardo, 1811, p. 208); he befuddled Malthus who sensed, rather than knew, that something was amiss (Ricardo, 1951, p. 26). For Ricardo's quantity theory of money to possess coherence, money has to be a means of exchange pure and simple.

1.2 MONEY AND THE PROCESSES OF CREDIT

1.2.1 Historical and Institutional Background

The advance of mercantile capitalism throughout the eighteenth century, and its eventual replacement by industrial capitalism, were accompanied by a proliferation of new, non-metallic money forms that more often than not were associated with credit relations. Political economists were much exercised by these forms of money. In order fully to appreciate the classical debates on credit money, the rise and fall of John Law's 'System' in the first quarter of the eighteenth century must be considered, and a broad outline sketched of the English credit system during the high period of classical political economy.

Toward the end of Louis XIV's reign, wars, extravagance and the lack of regular tax income had severely dented the creditworthiness of the French state. In 1715 John Law, a remarkable financier, theorist and adventurer from the early days of capitalism, was allowed to establish a bank in France, capitalised mostly by deeply discounted government debt instruments.[11] From such modest beginnings Law rapidly erected his 'System'. The intention was to use the power of credit to create a great national economic venture and so galvanise the productive forces of France. By 1719 the Compagnie des Indes, with Law as director-general, had taken over the tobacco monopoly, Colbert's East India and China Companies, the mints, the slaving companies of West Africa and the general farms. These enormous acquisitions were financed by issuing banknotes (the bank having soon become nationalised and its notes made legal tender) and stock. In 1720 the bank and the Compagnie des Indes merged. Increasing reliance on fresh equity issue, and Law's dextrous cultivation of rumours and expectations of lucrative future returns, encouraged a tremendous stock exchange bubble across Europe. In 1720 the speculative bubble inevitably burst and panic spread in the European stock exchanges. The burst of the bubble, and the lack of a guarantee of regular interest payments on the French state debts, caused the crash of Law's 'System' amidst a deluge of worthless banknotes.

Law's major work in English (1705) makes it clear that he was a mercantilist,[12] and like Steuart he believed that a shortage of metallic money leads to insufficiency of output and employment. To deal with such shortages, the supply of money has to be supplemented through credit processes, which implies that banks must be created to advance loans backed by their reserves. Law's real innovation, however, was to argue further that the banks should be allowed to issue inconvertible banknotes secured by land. This would at a stroke demonetise silver, and transform land fully into an alienable commodity. Absent from Law's work, and ultimately contributing to the collapse of his 'System', is an analysis of how banknote quantity is to be limited, thus preserving the value of banknotes relative to metallic money and commodities. Property in land is not a principle of limitation of banknote issue. Steuart (1767, bk IV, p. 141), who admired Law and rescued the pioneering elements of his thought, was forced to seek a 'real' and not an 'imaginary' foundation for credit. Steuart nevertheless (and Smith soon after him) had the advantage of observing the early workings of the first national credit system.

By the fourth quarter of the eighteenth century the English credit system had developed to a form that it maintained until at least the middle of the next century. The semipublic Bank of England, formed in 1694, loomed large over the English credit system: banker to the state, zealous guardian of its monopoly of issue in London, holder of the reserves of other banks and holder of the largest gold reserve in the country. Its notes were the means of settlement at the London Clearing House, the means of payment among large merchants and traders in the London markets, the indisputable money of commerce. Until well into the nineteenth century only the so-called London banks could withstand the competition of the Bank of England in the London area. These, however, were non-issuing private banks, specialising in personal loans to the rich. In the provinces a great number of so-called country banks did energetic business. Those based in the agricultural areas, such as Norfolk, typically had a surplus of loanable funds but few local investment outlets. Those based in the new industrial areas, such as Lancashire, faced a scarcity of funds but had plenty of investment opportunities. Country banks were allowed to issue banknotes, which they did mostly in the discount of bills of exchange, the banknotes circulating primarily in each bank's local area. Country banks in the industrial areas received large numbers of bills of exchange and sought to rediscount them in order to give to their assets a still more liquid form. Agriculturally based banks, which were especially awash with funds in the months after the harvest, sought to purchase such bills. The flow of bills was centred in the London bill market, the efficient running of which was guaranteed by bill brokers. Since the brokers operated mostly with borrowed capital they were absolutely dependent on fast turnover, hence they were the first to be alerted to impending financial crises. The Bank of England played an important role in the bill market, both by discounting bills and by lending outright. The Bank's discount rate was a benchmark for other rates, though the Usury Laws kept rates below 5 per cent until 1832.

1.2.2   The Reflux and the Balance of Payments

In his polemic against Hume, Steuart employed the term 'symbolical' money, which really referred to credit money: 'Bank notes, credit in bank, bills, bonds, and merchants' books (where credit is given and taken) are some of the many species of credit included under the term *symbolical money*' (Steuart, 1767, bk II, p. 39, emphasis in original). The term 'symbolical' is unfortunate because it is more appropriate for fiat money issued by the state rather than credit money issued by banks. The issuing of fiat money, resting exclusively on the authority of the state, was common throughout the late eighteenth century in Prussia, Russia and, above all, the revolutionary France of the Assignats. Opponents of the quantity theory, unlike its partisans, generally differentiated between fiat money and credit money, and sought the principles of the behaviour of the latter in the operations of the credit system.

For Steuart, the creation of 'symbolical' money (credit money) is the easiest and most flexible way of regulating exchanges among the classes, and hence stimulating employment and wealth creation. The difference between 'real' (metallic) and 'symbolical' money is that the former definitively settles transactions, while the latter, since it is essentially a promise to pay, does not (ibid., bk III, p. 268). Moreover, while metallic money tends to be locked up in hoards, 'symbolical' money follows a different regulating principle,

> [when] it happens that the money already in the country is not sufficient for carrying on these purposes [trade, industry, consumption], a part of the solid property, equal to the deficiency, may be melted down (as we have called it) and made to circulate in paper: that as soon again as this paper augments beyond this proportion, a part of what was before in circulation, must return upon the debtor in the paper, and be realised anew (ibid., bk IV, p. 147: terms in [] introduced by the authors).

The superfluous amount of credit money that returns to its issuer, Steuart called 'regorging' money. 'Regorged' money does not remain idle but is either turned into metals and exported, or the government intervenes and borrows it (ibid., p. 149). In short, unlike metallic coin, the excess of which stagnates in hoards, the excess of credit money flows back to its issuers to be converted into metallic money and subsequently exported as metal, or is lent to the state (see also ibid., p. 228). Three quarters of a century later this characteristic movement of credit money was called the law of the reflux, by which name it is still generally recognised in monetary theory.

The significance of 'regorging' for Steuart's critique of Hume is evident in his analysis of international transactions. From the context it is fairly clear that Steuart (ibid., pp. 217–19) treated disequilibria in the balance of payments, including the payment of international debt and the making of fresh loans, as short-term phenomena. A surplus leads to a rise in the exchange rate and the inflow of coin into the country. Several possibilities arise at that point, the most likely of which is the redundancy of a part of the domestically circulating quantity of money. This leads to the 'regorging' of some of the circulating paper money towards the banks, hence to lower interest rates and a reduction in the securities held by banks (ibid., p. 228). This is a reversal of the 'melting down of solid property'. A deficit, in contrast, could mean the loss of part of the country's coin to foreigners. In this case the banks have to supply the deficiency by 'melting down solid property' and acquiring more assets. If the deficit proves long-lasting, the banks have to borrow abroad to make good the flow of coin to the foreigners. Finally, in cases of panic the quantity of circulating coin declines rapidly, and, Steuart thought, the banks should not refuse to replenish circulation in order to protect their bullion reserves. The source of the drain of metallic money is the external deficit, and the pressure abates as soon as the payments abroad are completed. The banks would only compound the trouble, and harm domestic circulation, if they refused to issue their own money.

There are several obvious loose ends in this analysis (the ultimate cause of disequilibria being one) but the difference with Hume is striking. For Steuart, no automatic equilibrating mechanism exists, operating through international flows of commodities and money. Rather, foreign deficits have several implications for the balance sheets of banks: on the asset side, banks probably lose some bullion reserves and acquire some securities; on the liability side, banks have more banknotes outstanding. These financial changes do not by themselves restore equilibrium in the balance of payments.

Steuart's clear exposition of the reflux and his original examination of balance of payments disequilibria were considerable achievements. Nevertheless he had no clear theory to offer on how the reflux of credit money is related to the lending policy of the banks. He urged complete security of collateral, but that did not link the reflux to the regular operations of banks and industrial capitalists. Smith's more powerful synthetic mind was necessary to provide a theoretical (though fallacious) foundation for the reflux, what later became known as the real bills doctrine.

1.2.3   The Real Bills Doctrine

Smith's analysis of credit money reveals close familiarity with Steuart's work: banknotes replace metal coin, leaving 'the channel of circulation' 'precisely the same as before'. For Smith (1776, bk II, p. 318), 'The whole paper money of every kind which can easily circulate in any country never can exceed the value of gold and silver, of which it supplies the place, or which (the commerce being supposed the same) would circulate there, if there was no paper money.' Banknotes that in practice prove 'superfluous' to the 'channel of circulation' are converted into gold and exported abroad (ibid., pp. 311, 319). To sustain his claim that the 'overflow' of banknotes returns to the banks rather than raises prices, Smith had to consider more closely the operations of banks.

In his analysis of banking Smith adopted a very different attitude to that of Law and Steuart, the intention of whom was to strengthen the productive mechanism of a country through the advance of credit. For Smith, the size of the annual revenue of a country is determined by 'real' factors: the division of labour, saving and the accumulation of capital. The advance of credit does not increase the capital of a country; it merely enables capitalists to avoid holding idle stocks of money, and speeds up the turnover of the country's capital (ibid., pp. 340–1). By this token, the proper operation of banks is to advance to capitalists precisely that part of the latter's capital that would have been kept as idle, precautionary hoards in the normal run of business:

> What a bank can with propriety advance to a merchant or under-taker of any kind, is not either the whole capital with which he trades, or even any considerable part of that capital, but that part of it only, which he would otherwise be obliged to keep by him unemployed, and in ready money for answering occasional demands (ibid., pp. 322–3).

If an individual bank issues quantities of banknotes larger than can be used in the 'channel of circulation', the bank will find that its notes return to it much faster than usual. Were it to attempt to maintain the abnormal amount of notes in circulation, the bank would have to keep an unusually high level of reserves to be able to continue converting the returning banknotes into metallic money. Therefore the bank's profitability would decline accordingly. Smith thought that banks operating in this manner were not rare, and that their lending was typically associated with 'The over-trading of some bold projectors in both parts of the United Kingdom' (ibid., p. 322). Thus Smith put across the following rule in order to guide the lending of banks:

> When a bank discounts to a merchant a real bill of exchange drawn by a real creditor upon a real debtor, and which, as soon as it becomes due, is really paid by that debtor; it only advances to him a part of the value which he would otherwise be obliged to keep by him unemployed and in ready money for answering occasional demands (ibid., p. 323).

This argument has become known as the real bills doctrine. Banks that solely discount real bills, as opposed to fictitious bills not backed by the sale of goods, can be certain that their reserves will never run low since fresh advances of bank money are regularly counterbalanced by the repayment of old advances. Real bills are discounted with banks because the traders aim at procuring the funds they would have kept idle to facilitate the turnover of their capital. More by association than reasoning, Smith then implied that if banks were to discount only real bills the channel of circulation would never overflow. For Smith, if banks follow the best banking practice, as he defined it, the quantity of credit money will adjust itself to the precise requirements of circulation. Harmony will reign between the quantity of commodities and the quantity of credit money created by the spontaneous processes of capitalist production and exchange. This is a theoretical *tour de force* compared with Steuart's plain statement of the law of the reflux; nevertheless it is a fallacy for reasons discussed immediately below.

1.2.4 The Bullion Controversy

Smith exercised a strong influence on English monetary theory until the emergence of Ricardo. Ricardo's quantity theory of money was considered earlier in this chapter, but fully to appreciate its rise to prominence a brief look at the backdrop of political and institutional events is necessary. In 1793 England went to war against revolutionary France. Lack of military success and domestic social unrest inspired by the French Revolution raised the spectre of a bank run to convert banknotes into gold. To forestall disruption of the credit system the convertibility of banknotes into gold was suspended in 1797. The supposedly temporary restriction lasted until 1821 and gave rise to a classic monetary debate, the bullion controversy.[13] Despite the initial worries, nothing dramatic happened until 1802. Then the exchange rate of the pound against the franc and the mark fell sharply, there was a severe gold drain out of the country, and the market price of gold rose significantly above its mint price of £3 17s 10 1/2d. A flood of mostly mediocre pamphlets contested the explanation of these phenomena. On the one hand the bullionists argued that the monetary unrest was due to the restriction, and advocated a return to gold convertibility. On the other hand the anti-bullionists believed that banknotes were not the source of the trouble, and that the effects of the war should not be overlooked.

The exception to the general mediocrity was the work of Henry Thornton (1802), a banker and the brains behind the famous Bullion Report of 1810.[14] Thornton took an intermediate position between the two sides, though by the time the Bullion Report was written he had sided with the bullionists. The vicissitudes of Henry Thornton's book are evidence that for intellectuals life after death could be better than the real thing. After a brief career of modest influence Thornton's work was consigned to oblivion, to be rescued more than a century later by that inveterate bookworm, Jacob Viner (1924). Thornton's intellectual stock has since risen sky-high, helped more than a little by Hayek's (1939) glowing introduction to the re-edited book and by Hicks' (1967) masterly recapitulation of its arguments.

It is a measure of Smith's influence and of Steuart's eclipse, that throughout his book Thornton conducted a polemic against Smith and did not even mention Steuart. Thornton's aim was to produce a theoretical treatise on monetary questions, but even his most ardent admirers admitted that his book 'lacked system' (Hayek, 1939, p. 46). Despite Smith's ground-breaking work on value and price, Thornton (1802, ch. 8) argued that commodity prices are determined by demand and supply in the sphere of exchange, and he made little use of the notion that money has value as a produced commodity. This premise actually weakened Thornton's critique of Smith's analysis of the 'channel of circulation'.[15] Smith had claimed that paper money could not exceed the value of the gold and silver that it replaces since the excess would flow back to the banks. In refutation, Thornton (ibid., ch. 3) argued that the velocity of circulation of bank-notes is higher than that of bills of exchange (another form of paper money), therefore the quantity of paper money actually in circulation depends on the mix of these two components. Thornton was clearly right to stress the variability of the velocity of money, but he also appeared to be refuting the very existence of a necessary amount of circulating money. This made his subsequent discussion of Hume's price-level-specie-flow mechanism less logically coherent, and so less persuasive, than Ricardo's was.

Thornton's attack on Smith's distinction between 'real' and 'fictitious' bills, however, had decisive results. For Thornton (ibid., chs 1,2), it is incorrect to claim that 'real' bills always represent actual property while 'fictitious' bills are imaginary. The sale of one lot of goods may give rise to several 'real' bills as the goods pass from merchant to merchant. Thornton (ibid., p. 87) recognised that 'real' bills are, on the whole, more likely to be repaid promptly than 'fictitious' bills, and that the capitalist's actual sales are a limit to the amount of 'real' bills created, but for him this was a 'very imperfect' limit. In substance there is no difference between a fictitious bill and a common promissory note, that is, a promise rather than an order to pay for the delivery of goods. Moreover the distinction between 'real' and 'fictitious' bills has little relevance to the practice of a bank. To avoid problematic lending it is much better for the bank to rely on traditional methods, that is, simply on ascertaining the creditworthiness of the debtor.

It could still be claimed, however, that some natural tendency exists for the quantity of banknotes to limit itself, contingent on the free operations of the banking system. Thornton (ibid., pp. 252-3) dismissed this argument on grounds immediately relevant to the law of the reflux. Lending on 'real' bills, insisting on collateral and taking precautions to increase 'the probability of prompt repayment' might result in some limitation on banknote issue. However if the banks were progressively to increase the volume of their outstanding banknotes, they would also be increasing the means available to capitalists to settle their existing obligations with the banks. Moreover the increase in bank lending necessary for the quantity of banknotes to rise progressively would not necessarily sate the demand for loans, and so it would not naturally limit the quantity of banknotes. For Thornton (ibid., p. 254) what matters is the rate of interest in comparison with the rate of profit. If the banks were to keep the rate of interest on loans below the rate of profit, the demand for new loans would have no limit and neither would the quantity of banknotes. As Thornton (ibid., p. 259) concluded with a nice turn of phrase, 'To suffer either the solicitations of merchants, or the wishes of government, to determine the measure of the bank issues, is unquestionably to adopt a very false principle of conduct.'

It should be noted that Thornton was sympathetic to the Bank of England and his book was a defence of the Bank. His discussion of balance of trade disequilibria is not exactly a model of clarity and coherence, nevertheless he makes important points. Short-run deficits can be caused by 'real' factors such as bad harvests, and they lead to falls in the exchange rate and the drain of gold abroad (ibid., ch. 5). Contracting the credit advances of the Bank of England, and hence the issue of banknotes, could deal with such phenomena, but not through Hume's mechanism of reducing the quantity of money and thus lowering prices. Rather the contraction of credit leads to a contraction of production and so limits imports. Since this policy involves real costs, it is better for the Bank to possess a large hoard of gold and wait for the storm to end. Long-term balance of trade deficits, on the other hand, Thornton (ibid., chs 8, 9) analysed by employing Hume's mechanism. Increases in the quantity of credit money could presumably accelerate the process of real accumulation, but they could also create higher domestic expenditure and prices, thus leading to external deficits. Thornton treated this argument as a refutation of Smith's views on the capacity of the 'channel of circulation': if prices rise, the 'channel of circulation' can take any quantity of money thrown into it.

After the first bout of unrest, relative stability returned to the financial system until 1809. By that time Britain had started to operate a naval blockade on the European continent, and Napoleon had proclaimed the Continental System forbidding the docking of British ships in French-controlled ports. In 1809 the rate of exchange once again, moved sharply against Britain, gold left the country and its market price rose precipitously. The bullion controversy flared up again and Ricardo entered the field of economic theory. Ricardo's explanation for these monetary phenomena, as discussed above, was basically a revival of Hume's quantity theory of money, with the significant difference that the labour theory of value was appended to the latter. Ricardo thus became the chief exponent of the bullionists, his rise facilitated by overwhelming intellectual power and truculent controversialism. According to him the culprit of the monetary unrest was the Bank of England, which, taking advantage of the restriction, had overissued its banknotes. The anti-bullionists, mainly the merchant directors of the Bank of England, protested, but lamely and incoherently. Ricardo (1810, p. 61) also dismissed as logically insubstantial Thornton's argument about 'real', short-run, balance of trade disequilibria: gold will go abroad only if it is cheap, hence if too much money is circulating domestically. As for the part of Thornton's work that was compatible with Hume's mechanism, Ricardo was able to make the same point from first principles, based on the labour theory of value, but with fewer words. It is not surprising that Ricardo's views eclipsed Thornton's.

The impact of Ricardo's intervention can be appreciated by casting a glance at the work of James Mill, the midwife of Ricardo's *Principles*. In an early work Mill (1808) had stoutly defended Adam Smith's treatment of the 'channel of circulation' against Thornton's critique. Mill (ibid., pp. 167–9) claimed that the difference between state-issued paper money and bank-issued paper money was common knowledge among political economists at the time. Unlike state-issued fiat notes, banknotes return to the banks to redeem bills and so withdraw from the 'channel of circulation. The most important component of Mill's argument, however, was that Thornton had failed to reconcile the presumed rise in prices caused by the overissue of banknotes with the proposition that, 'the precious metals, in all countries which are not exceedingly distant from one another, approach very nearly to an equality of price' (ibid., p. 163). Mill's famously pedagogical mind sought system in monetary theory, and he sensed that the value of the precious metals had to be an integral element of the theory of price disturbances. Thornton, despite his many strengths was no theorist of value, and of the value of the precious metals in particular. Ricardo provided precisely the theoretical foundation sought by Mill. By the time the *Elements of Political Economy* were published, Mill had entirely abandoned Smith:

> We have already seen, that the value of a metallic currency is determined by the value of the metal which it contains. That of paper currency, therefore, exchangeable at pleasure, either for coins or for bullion, is also determined by the value of the metal which can be obtained for it... The effects of an increase of the quantity, and consequent diminution of the value of the currency in any particular country, are two: first, a rise of prices; secondly a loss to all those persons who had a right to receive a certain sum of money of the old and undiminished value (Mill, 1826, pp. 292–3).

Gone is the distinction between credit money and fiat money, and no mention is made of the law of the reflux: an increase in the quantity of currency simply leads to a fall in its value. The Ricardian quantity theory of money had taken a strong hold on English monetary theory.[16]

1.2.5   The Banking/Currency Controversy

The restriction was officially over in 1821 and the British economy adjusted successfully to the end of the Napoleonic Wars, despite early fears to the contrary. The industrial revolution and the march of Napoleon through Europe had created propitious conditions for the emergence of a true world market in industrial goods, with Britain at its centre. For twenty years after the bullion controversy relative peace reigned in monetary theory. Then, towards the end of the 1830s battle was joined again, and the banking/currency controversy took shape. This time theorists were exercised by the monetary phenomena attendant to the periodic commercial and industrial crises of the emergent world market. In the classic decennial crises from the 1820s to the 1860s, merchants were unable to pay their debts, interest rates rose very high as traders desperately tried to borrow money, the balance of payments went into deficit and gold drained abroad. Merchant and industrial companies soon started to go bankrupt, workers were laid off and prices began to fall. At the peak of each crisis panic gripped the markets and there was fear that the credit system might collapse, leading to the inconvertibility of banknotes into gold. The various currents of thought contesting the explanation of these phenomena soon crystallised into the currency and banking schools.[17]

Currency school authors were the heirs and defenders of Ricardian orthodoxy. The rich and well-connected Manchester banker Samuel Lloyd Jones, later Lord Overstone, was at the time considered the great authority of the currency school. However his imprecise and meandering writings reveal no clues as to why that should have been so. The contribution to economic theory of the former marine Colonel Robert Torrens, on the other hand, has proved more substantial and durable. An incisive and determined controversialist, Torrens (1812) was originally a critic of Ricardianism but then became the theoretical pillar of the currency school. George Warde Norman, a director of the Bank of England, completed the school's leadership, though his influence was, and has remained, much less than that of Overstone and Torrens.

The currency school's main theoretical contention, the so-called currency principle, may be summarised as follows. The ideal currency of a country is a purely metallic one and currency in its ideal state behaves in a broadly Ricardian manner, that is, a change in the circulating quantity of money, all other things being equal, alters money's value and leads to the export or import of gold. However it was claimed that the actual currency of England at the time consisted of gold and convertible banknotes, and did not behave as a pure gold currency: country banks and, above all, the Bank of England tended to overissue their banknotes. Overstone (1840a, p. 189) explained the meaning of overissue in the following manner, 'This brings us to the question – what constitutes excessive issues? I understand by excessive issues, issues which render the amount of the paper circulation at any moment greater than would be the amount of metallic circulation.' The currency school, in broadly Ricardian fashion, claimed that overissued (but still convertible) banknotes depreciate relative to gold, leading to falls in the exchange rate and to the export of gold abroad. The movement of the exchange rate and the flows of gold between countries constitute *prima facie* evidence of the overissue of credit money. Torrens' (1847, pp. 10–11) 'criterion principle' stated 'that the only maintainable amount of the media of exchange, is that which is required to bring prices to the level at which exports balance imports'. Overstone (1840a, p. 190), was as forthcoming on this as on any other topic: 'I propose fluctuations of the bullion as the standard measure by which to try a paper currency'. The outflow of gold restores equilibrium, but at the cost of disturbing domestic monetary conditions. This essentially Ricardian mechanism, if one disregards the logical contradiction that it is necessary to Ricardo's theory that banknotes be inconvertible, was used to account for the monetary phenomena of the recurrent English crises. Currency school authors similarly to Thornton but unlike Ricardo, also recognised that 'real' balance of trade deficits could occur (Overstone, 1840b, p. 167; Norman, 1833, sec. II), but the thrust of their analysis was to seek monetary causes for capitalist crises.

The currency principle has a clear implication: the circulation of credit money should be made to fluctuate exactly as a purely metallic circulation would have done (Torrens, 1857, ch. 2). Harmony can then be established between credit money and commodities in exchange, but in achieving it the fluctuations of the gold reserve of the Bank of England play a critically important role. When the Bank's gold reserve rises it follows that an influx of gold is in process, hence the domestic quantity of money is too small; when the Bank's reserve declines it follows that the domestic quantity of money is too large. A properly managed Bank of England, therefore, ought to be increasing (decreasing) the quantity of its outstanding banknotes as its gold reserve is increasing (decreasing). It was further argued by currency school authors that such adjustments to the quantity of Bank of England notes should happen slowly and before a fully fledged crisis had actually materialised (Overstone, 1840c, ch. 2). Above all, the discretion of the Bank of England cannot be relied upon, but instead there ought to be a fixed rule binding the quantity of credit money to the gold reserve of the Bank. Not surprisingly Congdon (1980) has sought parallels here with the variant of contemporary monetarism that advocates monetary base control.

The political influence of the currency school resulted in the introduction of the Bank Act of 1844, arguably the most famous piece of economic legislation ever. The Act had been anticipated by the application of the Palmer rule in the 1830s, named after Horsley Palmer, a director of the Bank. The Palmer rule was an empirically derived principle guiding the Bank's lending policy. The securities held by the Bank were to be equivalent to two thirds of its liabilities, the gold reserve making up the balance of its assets. Since banknotes formed most of the liabilities of the Bank, Palmer's rule essentially stated that the gold reserve should be roughly one third of the Bank's outstanding notes. In a spirit similar to Palmer's rule, the Act of 1844 separated the Bank of England into the Issue and the Banking Departments. The assets of the Issue Department comprised the bulk of the gold reserve, and its liabilities comprised the bulk of the banknotes outstanding. Therefore the Act implied that banknote quantity had to change in line with changes in the reserve. The Banking Department's assets were mostly discounted bills of exchange and government securities, and the Department could carry up to £14 million in liabilities backed by government securities instead of gold. The Act gave the Bank of England banknote monopoly across the country by placing quantitative limits, which declined over time, on the issuing activities of the country banks.

The currency principle was fiercely opposed by the banking school. The main exponent of the banking school was Thomas Tooke, a wealthy merchant with a profound practical knowledge of the London markets and an avid collector of economic data. Tooke did not put pen to paper until ripe middle age, but then wrote several hefty volumes.[18] He was given vital theoretical support by John Fullarton, a retired India surgeon whose theoretical output, unfortunately for economics, was restricted to a single volume. James Wilson, the founder of the *Economist* magazine, was also a significant and original member of the banking school. Finally, John Stuart Mill, the last of the classical economists, lent considerable support to the banking school, though he also accepted parts of the Ricardian doctrine.

Thomas Tooke was not a great theorist. In his monumental *History of Prices* he examined empirically the movement of key commodity prices, such as corn, hemp and wool over three quarters of a century. His work was remarkable above all because it sought to demonstrate that changes in the quantity of money in circulation actually follow, and are caused by, changes in prices. Tooke (1844, p. 123) summarised his findings thus:

> That the prices of commodities do not depend upon the quantity of money indicated by the amount of bank notes, nor upon the amount of the whole of the circulating medium; but that, on the contrary, the amount of the circulating medium is the consequence of prices.

This is an unambiguous rejection of Ricardo and Hume, and the rediscovery after three quarters of a century (though unknowingly) of Steuart's arguments. To support the above claim, a theory of metallic circulation different from Ricardo's is necessary and thus both Tooke and Fullarton emphasised the hoarding function of money. The monetary stock of a country exists as both circulating money and stagnant coin and bullion; the latter have no influence on prices (Tooke, 1844, ch. 2; Fullarton, 1844, ch. 4). The money hoards have both a domestic and an international role. International hoards are held by major banks such as the Bank of England, the Bank of France and the public banks of Hamburg and Amsterdam, and their function is specifically to deal with imbalances of trade (Tooke, 1844, ch. 2).

Having shaken off the deadweight of Ricardianism, the authors of the banking school further explored the distinction between fiat paper money and banknotes (Wilson, 1859, article 4). The former is issued at the whim of the state and could easily overwhelm the 'channel of circulation'. The latter are issued by banks against debt and so they regularly return to the banks and withdraw from circulation. In Tooke's words, the former is *paper money* or *assignats*, the latter are *paper credit* (Tooke, 1848, pt 3, ch. 2). The substantive difference between these two forms of money lies essentially in the fact that the quantity of credit money is regulated by the law of the reflux. Steuart's original principle of regulation of credit money was rediscovered by Fullarton (1844, p. 67): '[it] is not so much by convertibility into gold, as by the regularity of the reflux, that in the ordinary course of things any redundancy of the bank-note issues is rendered impossible.'

The same idea was clearly stated by Tooke (1848, p. 185): 'This law operates in bringing back to the issuing banks the amount of their notes, whatever it may be, that is not wanted for the purposes which they are required to serve.' It was a natural step from here to declare that there is nothing special about banknotes as credit. The currency school had strenuously denied that bank deposits should be considered as money (Overstone, 1840d, p. 200; Torrens, 1857, ch. 1).[19] Fullarton's (1844, p. 38) rejection of the claims of the currency school on this score shows tremendous insight, again reminiscent of Steuart: 'There is scarcely any shape into which credit can be cast, in which it will not at times be called to perform the functions of money; and whether that shape be a banknote, or a bill of exchange, or a banker's cheque, the process is in every essential particular the same, and the result is the same.' Moreover it was the law of the reflux that the banking school authors had rediscovered and not Smith's real bills. It is true that at times they came close to asserting something akin to Smith's axiom. For instance, Fullarton (ibid., p. 64) argued that 'The banker has only to take care that they [banknotes] are lent on sufficient security, and the reflux and the issue will, in the long run, always balance each other.' However 'sufficient security' was not 'real bills', and unlike Smith the banking school authors did not attempt to base the law of the reflux on the profit and loss decisions of banks. On the one hand this was a strength because it did not openly commit the banking school to the fallacy of the real bills doctrine. On the other hand, it was a weakness because it led the banking school authors away from relating the law of the reflux to the rate of interest.

The banking school certainly did not ignore the rate of interest as an economic category. Tooke (1826, sec. 1) accepted that the rate of profit 'governed' the rate of interest. He distinguished between 'monied capital' and 'currency', called interest the price of 'monied capital', and argued that increases in banknote issue depress the rate of interest. In a slightly later work Tooke (1829, sec. 3) argued that a rash of discounts by the Bank of England failed to materialise after the end of the restriction simply because the market rate never substantially rose above the Bank's 5 per cent. Tooke also showed a keen appreciation of commodity price implications of 'overbanking', that is, of speculative transactions funded by banks. Tooke (1844, ch. 13) finally confronted the conventional view that low interest rates raise prices while high interest rates lower them. Low interest rates do not necessarily lead to speculative fever, on the contrary they represent a reduction in the costs of production, and so lead to lower prices. Fullarton (1844, ch. 8), incidentally, disagreed with his master on this score.

What is absent from the banking school's work, however, is a theory of the movement of interest rates, based on the behaviour of banks and on the cyclical pattern of economic activity already apparent by the middle of the century. Wicksell (1935, vol II, ch. 4, sec. 8) took advantage of this absence to criticise the banking school for ignoring the possibility that the banking system could lower the rate of interest and so cause price rises. In essence this was also the point Thornton had made about Smith's real bills doctrine. It was not enough to register the undoubted fact that on the approach to monetary crises the rate of interest tended to rise, and that the discount rate of the Bank of England was rarely significantly below the market rate. A theory of the rate of interest was also necessary, and the banking school did not have an adequate one. The absence of such a theory also coloured the banking school's practical proposals for dealing with foreign exchange crises and gold drains: hold a substantial reserve of gold, lend freely, and let the drain run its course (Fullarton, 1844, ch. 8).

The monetary rules put in place by the Act of 1844 certainly did not succeed in averting monetary crises. Tooke (1844, ch. 15) had claimed that dividing the Bank into an Issue and a Banking Department was a foolish and dangerous measure. According to him, if a crisis were to materialise, the Banking Department would face enormous pressure to discount bills and to lend, but it would not have sufficient reserves to do so. Meanwhile the Issue Department would be holding an enormous hoard of gold. In late 1847, a short three years after the Act was passed, a monetary crisis began to emerge. As Tooke had predicted the Banking Department was in no position to deal with the crisis, and mere knowledge of this fact was enough to create panic among the merchants of London. The government was forced to suspend the Act and the panic rapidly subsided, though the British economy went through a full-blown commercial and industrial crisis in 1848. Suspension was also the fate of the Act in the subsequent crises of 1857 and 1866.

Nevertheless the Act of 1844 was not merely problematic economic policy guided by fallacious economic theory. The Act was preceded by Palmer's rule, which favoured quantitative limitation of the liabilities of the Bank of England though in a purely empitical manner. The point is that management of its liabilities through the use of interest rates rather than quantitative restrictions was not a realistic possibility for the Bank throughout the first half of the nineteenth century. What was later known as Bank Rate policy, that is raising the Bank's lending rate in order to staunch the loss of gold mostly abroad, was not plausible during the period of the banking/currency controversy. Given the structure of the English credit system, it was highly unlikely that a rise in Bank Rate would result in capital inflows that would reverse the outflow of gold. Horsley Palmer himself seems to have realised the ineffectuality of the Bank Rate in the historical and institutional conditions of his day (Cramp, 1959).

Things changed in the second half of the nineteenth century as a different era set in for British capitalism, one not disturbed until 1914. The consolidation of the British Empire, the shift in the basis of British capitalist accumulation away from textiles and towards iron, steel and railways, and the emergence of the City of London as the centre of world finance, changed the outlook and the structure of the

British credit system. The accumulated experience of several crises, the clearing of international obligations through London, the rise of commercial banking, collecting deposits across the world, and the extensive international lending activities of British capital allowed the management of foreign exchange crises through the manipulation of the rate of interest charged by the Bank of England. In the era of Bank Rate policy the banking/currency controversy seemed irrelevant. A pronounced fatigue with the 'ancient debates' is obvious in Bagehot (1873, ch. 1), the herald of the new era. Calmer waters in the monetary sphere, however, proved dire for theory, the arid debates of bimetallism consuming the second half of the century. Only after the shocks of the First World War did theorists produce work comparable to that of the debates of the first half of the nineteenth century. By then the beacon of classical political economy had been extinguished.

Recapping key arguments of this chapter, it has to be stressed that the classical school opposed the mercantilist identification of wealth with money and the emphasis on money as a stimulant of economic activity. For classical political economy, exchange is a natural part of harmonious and self-sustaining economic reproduction, thus money is a largely passive economic category subordinate to the exchange of commodities. This view is especially characteristic of the strand of classical political economy that accepted fully the quantity theory of money, and as a result inordinately stressed money's function as means of exchange. The opposite strand, spurred by the realisation that the quantity theory of money did not satisfactorily explain the English monetary phenomena of the first half of nineteenth century, did much to restore to monetary theory the full complexity of money's functions. In this respect the anti-quantity theory tradition rediscovered the partial validity of mercantilist monetary arguments. Nevertheless even this strand of the classical school remained firmly wedded to the naturalistic view of money as a harmonious element of capitalist exchange.

Reliance on the quantity theory of money led the heirs of Ricardo in classical monetary theory to advocate the social regulation of money and credit in the form of the Act of 1844. This was so despite the classical school's liberal support for Free Trade and for the absence of direct regulation of economic affairs: in this respect classical liberalism was fundamentally inconsistent. The Act was neither based on sound theory nor was it effective in eradicating recurrent monetary and economic crises. The anti-quantity-theory current, moreover, was incapable of overcoming these weaknesses. Despite its richer analysis of the role of money and credit in a capitalist economy, the banking school advanced neither a theory of capitalist crisis nor policy proposals capable of dealing with recurrent economic fluctuations. Both currents were prisoner to the ideological emphasis on natural harmony that was characteristic of their age.

For Marxist economics, capitalism is a historically specific and narrowly based social system. As a result Marxist monetary theory, while concurring with much of the analysis of the anti-quantity-theory tradition, can clearly identify the elements of disharmony and instability imparted to economic reproduction by money and credit. The complexity of money's functions in capitalist exchange, and the social and economic power that money exerts over economic life, are inseparable from the unstable and crisis-ridden character of the capitalist economy. The elaboration and demonstration of this argument is the thread that runs through this book.

2 Value and Money in Marx's Political Economy

The labour theory of value is the cornerstone of Marx's theoretical system in economics. Marx's formulation of the theory stressed the historically specific character of the capitalist economy, while on the whole the classical school treated the market economy and capitalism as the natural order of economic life.[1] The neglect of the historical specificity of market relations and capitalism resulted in the ultimate failure of the classical school to discover the origin of the forms of value, money and capital. Section 2.1 of this chapter examines Marx's theory of value and ascertains the logical foundations for the emergence of the form of money. The relation of money to the substance of value, that is, to socially necessary labour time, is also examined. Section 2.2 turns to the several functions performed by money in a capitalist economy. Finally, Section 2.3 considers the problem of the very early historical emergence of money and its implications for the relation between money and commodity exchange.

2.1 MONEY AND THE FORMS OF VALUE

2.1.1 Marx's Theory of the Forms of Value

The classical analysis of commodity exchange essentially assumed that commodities are immediately and directly exchangeable with each other. Consequently, whatever their differences of opinion as regards the functions of money, the classical writers saw money first and foremost as a conventional means of exchange. This was a fundamental reason why the riddle of money, namely the monopolisation by money of direct exchangeability with all other commodities, was not deciphered by the classical economists. Marx offered a powerful solution for the riddle of money, based on the distinction between the forms and the substance of value. Nevertheless Marx's analysis was also considerably influenced by the classical approach to commodity exchange and money, thus introducing some theoretical tension to his work.

Marx (1867, ch. 1, sec. 1) opened the first chapter of *Capital* by assuming, in the manner of the classical economists, the direct exchange of commodities; he then deduced the substance of value as abstract human labour crystallised in commodities.[2] In the second chapter of *Capital*, and still in the classical manner, Marx posited money as the solution to the well-known problems of direct exchange. These problems, as Marx had already argued in an earlier work (1859, pp. 37–52), are rooted in the opposition between use value and value, inherent in the nature of the commodity. Put simply, use value is particular but value is general; as values, commodities are qualitatively the same, perfectly divisible, homogeneous; as use values they are qualitatively different, imperfectly divisible, heterogeneous. Direct exchange inevitably breaks down as each commodity tries to be both use value and value at the same time. The breakdown could be avoided if one commodity represented value generally for all commodities: commodities would then be use values as themselves and values as the single commodity. The spontaneous interaction of all other commodities isolates the money commodity, which emerges as the representative of value.[3] In this respect, and despite clearly differentiating between abstract human labour, which forms value, and concrete human labour, which creates use values (1867, ch.1, sec. 2), Marx's analysis of commodities and money displays the heavy influence of classical political economy.

In section three of the first chapter of *Capital*, however, Marx also offered a highly original theory of the form of value, which more persuasively explains the logical origin of money.[4] The riddle of money, that is, the monopolisation by money of direct exchangeability, was deciphered in successive steps by Marx, starting with the 'simple, isolated, or accidental' form of value (ibid., p. 139). When twenty yards of linen request exchange with one coat (20 yards of linen = 1 coat), linen (the active commodity) represents the relative form of value. The coat (the passive commodity), on the other hand, serves as the material (the use value) in which the value of the linen is expressed; the coat represents the equivalent form of value and is accorded direct exchangeability with twenty yards of linen. Since the request of exchange by the linen owner can guarantee neither the reverse request nor the assent of the coat owner, the relation between the relative and the equivalent form of value is not generally reversible. Actual exchange materialises only when the coat owner accepts the request of the linen owner. This is the basic dialectic of the anarchical process through which commodity exchange emerges among people unfamiliar with each other, and as diverse communities came into contact at the very beginning of historical time.

The direct exchange of linen and coat is a particular transaction that may never materialise. The owner of the linen, its value still represented in the relative form, may similarly request exchange with several other commodities, such as tea, coffee, corn and gold, each of which acts as a particular equivalent. This gives rise to the 'total or expanded' form of value (ibid., pp. 154–5):

20 yards of linen = 1 coat
10 yards of linen = 5 lbs of tea
5 yards of linen = 10 lbs of coffee
40 yards of linen = 2 qts of corn
10 yards of linen = 1 oz of gold, etc.

The expanded form of value already indicates the non-accidental character of commodity exchange. Nevertheless the relative expression of the value of the linen is incomplete as the equivalent side has no terminus, turning the relative form of value into 'a motley mosaic of disparate and unconnected expressions of value', (ibid., p.156). Correspondingly, each equivalent remains particular and cannot act as a uniform means of account of the relative form of value.

The defects of the expanded form can be overcome in the 'general' form of value, (ibid., p. 157). The general form of value appears gradually and slowly as a certain commodity, say tea, is frequently chosen to act as the equivalent of other commodities. Thus tea acquires an additional use value, namely it is directly exchangeable with many other commodities.[5] As a result commodity owners begin more generally to request the exchange of their own commodities with tea. Tea begins to emerge as the universal equivalent form of value, at the same time completing and generalising the relative form of value, since value is now expressed generally in a uniform means of account. Consequently, tea, placed in the position of the universal equivalent through the requests for exchange by other commodities, begins to monopolise direct exchangeability.[6]

20 yards of linen = 10 lbs of tea
1 coat   = 10 lbs of tea
10 lbs of coffee = 2.5 lbs of tea
0.5 qts of corn   = 5 lbs of tea
2 oz of gold   = 10 lbs of tea, etc.

In principle any commodity can be the universal equivalent. However the complete relative form of value achieves fixity and social validity only when a specific commodity is singled out as the universal equivalent. Historically, precious metals, especially gold, were socially chosen for the role of the universal equivalent because of their physical properties: durability, divisibility, homogeneity, portability and so on. When gold is fixed as the universal equivalent, the money form of value, or the price form of commodities, is established (Marx, ibid., p.162). In the money form of value, money as the universal equivalent becomes the socially acceptable independent form of value.

> 1 yard of linen = 0.1 oz of gold
> 1 coat   = 2 oz of gold
> 1 lb of coffee   = 0.05 oz of gold
> 1 qt of corn   = 2 oz of gold
> 1 lb of tea   = 0.2 oz of gold, etc.

The state normally determines the conventional subdivision of physical quantities of the money commodity (usually on the basis of weight and fineness of the metal), as for instance in the historic British division of a troy ounce of gold into £3 17s 10 1/2d (where £1 = 20s = 240d). The state provides a conventional standard of price in this regard but creates neither money nor the money form of value.

Marx's theory of the form of value posits money as the spontaneously emerging nexus of the anarchical exchange process. Marx's theory also provides a foundation for analysis of the several economic and social functions of money that are not confined to simple means of exchange. In the course of development of the capitalist economy, credit money also emerges spontaneously and substitutes itself for commodity money in certain functions of exchange. Even when the state suspends the intervention of commodity money in economic activity, as has happened in contemporary capitalism, the spontaneous emergence of credit money can neither be negated nor easily controlled. In all its forms, money remains the independent form of value in the position of the universal equivalent. However the ability of different forms of money adequately to represent value cannot be taken for granted and must be demonstrated in theory and practice.

2.1.2 The Labour Theory of Value and Commodity Exchange

Marx's theory of the forms of value, and the clarification of the logical relations between commodities and money, can be presented without explicit reference to the substance of value as abstract labour embodied in commodities.[7] Far from weakening the labour theory of value, this approach demonstrates both its logical coherence and social inevitability in a capitalist economy. Marxist political economy, in contrast to both the classical school and neoclassicism, is concerned with identifying the historical specificity of the relations of production. In the first three chapters of *Capital*, Marx attempts logically to derive the substance of value (the crystallisation of abstract human labour) purely by examining the exchange relations among commodities. Marx's attempt has inevitably resulted in confusion within the Marxist tradition regarding the social relations within which labour is undertaken and becomes value. Marx appears to have assumed the existence of a fully fledged capitalist mode of production, since he seems to have taken for granted the elastic reallocation of labour across society according to the fluctuations of commodity demand and supply. Yet Marx actually undertook a theoretical examination of the capitalist process of production in the subsequent chapters of *Capital*, after the analysis of commodities, money and the transformation of money into capital.

Engels (1894) argued that the first three chapters of *Capital* reflected the early historical existence of societies of petty commodity producers. However Engels' argument is quite misleading since it implies the existence of classless egalitarian societies in pre-capitalist history.[8] In defence of Marx's procedure, it could also be argued that Marx wrote the first three chapters of *Capital* under the working hypothesis of pure commodity exchange based on equal quantities of labour in order to facilitate the derivation of the labour theory of value and the analysis of capitalism. However that would not provide a very strong defence of the foundation of Marx's labour theory of value: assumptions in social science must have historical foundations and should not be ideally abstract. Another serious problem for analysis of the fundamental principles of the theory of value can also be identified at this point. Marx argued that:

Things are in themselves external to man, and therefore alienable. In order that this alienation [*Verausserung*] may be reciprocal, it is only necessary for men to agree tacitly to treat each other as the private owners of those alienable things, and, precisely for that reason, as persons who are independent of each other. But this relationship of reciprocal isolation and foreignness does not exist for the members of a primitive community of natural origins, whether it takes the form of a patriarchal family, an ancient Indian commune or an Inca state. The exchange of commodities begins where communities have their boundaries, at their points of contact with other communities, or with members of the latter (Marx, 1867, p. 182; see also 1939, p. 103).

This is a powerful insight into commodity exchange stating that the origins of the latter lie in the relations between communities. However the labour theory of value is primarily concerned with the social relations implicit in the exchange of the annual product of labour within a society (or a national economy). If the ancient origin of commodity exchange lies in intercommunal economic interaction, as Marx is suggesting above, it is problematic to locate the logical foundations of the money form in intrasocial relations of labour summed by the labour theory of value.

The position taken in this book is that it is impossible to base the logical derivation of the forms of value and the explanation of the spontaneous emergence of money on the substance of value as crystallised labour. The forms of value arise out of the common property of commodities to request exchange, and can be understood independently of the substance of value. All forms of value imply the existence of quantitative relations (exchange ratios) among commodities; these relations give rise to relative prices once the money form of value has been established. It is clear in the examples discussed above, however, that the request of twenty yards of linen for exchange with one coat, two ounces of gold, or £7 15s 9d, always contains an element of subjective expectation that must be socially tested and objectively validated through the real process of exchange. Subjective requests of exchange, and the prices that derive from them, are not based on fully established values. Commodity prices formed in this manner tend to be socially corrected and standardised through the process of repeated market exchange.

All societies exercise some economy of the time devoted to the repeated production of goods. Marx (1939, p. 173) argued that 'Economy of time, to this all economy ultimately reduces itself. Society likewise has to distribute its time in a purposeful way, in order to achieve a production adequate to its overall needs.' Society cannot afford entirely to ignore the proportion of its time devoted to producing goods that are frequently and repeatedly exchanged. Equally, however, so long as the core of social reproduction is characterised by non-market communal social relations, no pressing social necessity exists to ensure the full replacement of labour-time costs through commodity prices. Put differently, though commodity prices are standardised through repeated exchange, no social mechanism exists to guarantee either the systematic transformation of labour time into value or the economy of labour time effected through commodity prices.

Capitalist conditions of production, as Marx explained at length in the first volume of *Capital*, are predicated upon the production of surplus value through the exploitation of wage labour in the process of production. Under such conditions, the forms of value become related to the substance of value, that is, capitalist commodity prices inevitably become related to the socially necessary labour embodied in commodities. The specific character of capitalist commodity prices arises from a fundamental social requirement of capitalism: prices must secure both the replacement of labour time costs and the proportionate distribution of unpaid labour time (surplus value) among competing capitals. This fundamental social requirement results from the functioning of the capitalist economy. The value of a capitalistically produced commodity i comprises past labour transferred from the means of production that have been used in the process of production (c_i), plus living labour newly created in production ($v_i + s_i$, where v_i is the necessary part of living labour replacing the value of labour power already paid to workers as a cost by the capitalist, and s_i is the surplus part). For capitalist production to continue (or for a capitalist enterprise not to collapse), the capitalist must recoup at least the cost of means of production and labour power ($c_i + v_i$) through the sale of output. It is a social requirement that capitalist commodity prices guarantee at least the replacement of the labour-time costs of commodity production. This, however, is still a rather inexact requirement upon capitalist prices. The relation of capitalist prices to the substance of value acquires more precision when the tendency of the equalisation of the rate of profit among individual capitals is considered, a point that is briefly dealt with below.

The process of profit equalisation among capitals is essentially a redistribution of the total produced surplus value among individual capitals on a *pro rata* basis. Given capital mobility, all competing capitals that have participated in the production and circulation of the periodic output earn the same proportionate share out of the total available surplus value. For profit equalisation to take place, commodities must acquire prices of production. These comprise the cost price (which enables the replenishment of $c_i + v_i$ and is also the individual capital advanced to start production), plus average profit (to acquire a portion of the total surplus value, equal to the individual capital advanced multiplied by the average rate of profit). Prices of production subsequently act as centres of gravity for the perennially fluctuating commodity market prices. Thus capitalist commodity prices, though they are closely related to the labour embodied in commodities, are not proportionate to the substance of commodity values. Economy of time in the production of goods is indeed effected through commodity prices, but in a specifically capitalist manner that precludes direct proportionality between prices and the substance of values. That is the manner in which the law of value achieves its fullest development under capitalist conditions.

2.2 THE FUNCTIONS AND FORMS OF MONEY

Marx's derivation of money made it possible to present money's functions in all their rich complexity. The key methodological point in this respect is that the independent representative of value has to perform certain functions in the capitalist economy. That is, what money does follows from what money is. For neoclassical economics, in contrast, the opposite holds: money is what money does and anything that can fulfil certain abstractly determined functions is treated as money. For Marxist analysis there is a strict ordering of the functions of money, which derives from what money is and provides logical foundations for the evolution of the form of money. To understand the path of development from commodity money to state-issued fiat money to credit money, it is necessary to examine the correspondence between the particular forms of money and the functions which money has to perform in capitalist exchange.

2.2.1 Measure of Value

The first function of the independent form of value is to serve as the material in which commodity values are expressed, and thereby measured. Value measurement is undertaken directly in the body of the money commodity: a quantity of gold is posited as the equivalent of the value of a commodity through the process already analysed above. Since the expression of commodity values in terms of money always involves a more or less subjective dimension, the repeated transformation of commodities into money (or the failure to do so) is necessary in order constantly to validate and rectify the individual expression of values into money. In this manner, money's function as measure of value acquires concrete social content.

The determination of the standard of price, on the other hand, must not be confused with the operation of the measure of value. The standard of price typically emerges through the action of the state; the latter formalises the conventional division of the material of the money commodity, as did the British state in the classic division of the troy ounce of gold mentioned earlier. Given a standard unit of the money commodity, commodity values divided by the value of the money commodity give rise to the accounting system of prices. Steuart, as explained in Chapter 1, argued that the standard of prices was a socially conventional approximation of an hypothesised ideal unit of value. Marx (1859, pp. 79–80; 1939, pp. 791–802), on the other hand, treated the standard of price as the name of a conventional division of the body of the money commodity. The important implication of Marx's argument is that the accounting system of prices, though clearly abstract, has a real social foundation in the system of commodity values; a foundation, moreover, that is independent of the determination of the standard of price itself. It also follows that the actual transformation of abstract prices into concrete quantities of the standardised money unit can never be taken for granted; indeed it is a process fraught with uncertainty.

One complex issue that emerges at this point is whether Marx's analysis implies that money must itself have value in order to measure commodity values and set prices. Put differently, is commodity money the only adequate form of money for the construction of the accounting system of prices?[9] An answer to this question is provided by the performance of commodity money itself under explicitly capitalist conditions. As mentioned earlier, capitalist commodity producers have to earn the average rate of profit; hence their goods exchange with each other and with money on the basis of prices of production, not proportionate to the labour embodied in commodities. The implication is that a redistribution of surplus value takes place in the process of capitalist exchange: capitals in industries with higher than average organic composition (that is, c_i/v_i) appropriate more surplus value than they have produced. The same result holds for capitals in industries with typically

slower turnover than elsewhere. This is a zero sum game for all competing capitals, since it merely involves the redistribution of the existing
surplus value. Now, whether money is itself a commodity, and thus
possesses value, does not have a direct bearing on the redistribution
of surplus value among capitals. The accounting prices that enable the
process to take place depend on the prevailing average rate of profit, on
the organic composition of the competing capitals and on the length of
turnover. There is no reason why these accounting prices could not be
set in units of a valueless money.

To pursue the issue a little further, assume that the money commodity is capitalistically produced, therefore it must itself have a price
of production. Properly speaking, the accounting system of prices also
incorporates money's price of production. Since the money commodity itself has a price of production, however, there cannot be direct
proportionality between its value and its quantity, conventionally
defined as the unit of account. For instance, when the money commodity is gold produced with a below-average organic composition of
capital, commodity prices are generally higher than when gold has an
above-average organic composition; higher prices reduce the purchasing power of gold relative to other commodities. On this score, too, it
is clear that although at a simple analytical level the formation of
accounting prices appears as the division of commodity values by the
value of the unit of money, under capitalist conditions the expression
of value in accounting prices bears a highly mediated relation to the
value of money. There is room here for valueless money to facilitate
the formation of accounting prices.

The upshot is that commodity money, under capitalist conditions
of production and exchange, renders value into price through a
series of mediations. Prices of production are the outcome of the
movement of capital in search of higher profit; they allow the redistribution of total surplus value among the components of the total
social capital. Whether the unit of account does or does not possess
value is irrelevant to the formation of relative prices of production. A
valueless unit of account, such as a contemporary inconvertible banknote, could also set capitalistically formed prices of production. However determining the price level of commodity output as a whole is a
different thing altogether. In this respect a valueless money faces
fundamental difficulties, both logical and practical, which are particularly severe if there is a complete absence of commodity money. An
examination of these difficulties comprises a significant part of the
discussion below.

2.2.2 Means of Exchange (or Means of Purchase)

The second function of money is to mediate the exchange of commodities. This is the only function of money purely specific to simple market processes, and the one typically recognised by all traditions in economics. For Marx (1867, p. 200), the characteristic formula of simple commodity circulation in the sphere of exchange is commodity (C_1) – money (M) – commodity (C_2), or sale–purchase.[10] In this connection the characteristic form of money is currency, often in the form of coin. Though the possibility of privately minted coin cannot be denied, the minting of coin is traditionally an activity of the state, since the latter can confer on coin the widest social acceptability. In Marx's words, 'The business of coining, like the establishment of a standard measure of prices, is an attribute proper to the state' (ibid., pp. 221–2).

In the sphere of exchange (or circulation) coined money is characterised by constant movement, while commodities simply enter and leave.[11] For an individual coin the path followed in the sphere of circulation comprises a series of moves from transaction to transaction; the path has no determinate shape. The concept of velocity consequently has natural applicability to the means of exchange. For Marx (1939, pp. 186–7), money velocity is an average of transactions per unit of money per period, determined by institutional, geographical and customary factors.

Money in the sphere of circulation is also characterised by quantity. Much in the manner of Ricardo, Marx (1867, p. 237) argued that the necessary quantity of money varies directly with commodity values and indirectly with money's value and velocity.[12] Marx, however, decisively parted from Ricardo on the issue of how the actual quantity of circulating commodity money relates to the necessary. Where Ricardo had posited the exogenous supply of metallic money, Marx argued that meeting the monetary requirements of the sphere of exchange depends on the output of the money commodity but also on the existing hoards of money. For Marx (ibid., pp. 231–2), metallic circulation is premised on the presence of substantial money hoards held outside the sphere of exchange (as well as money metal that could easily be coined). The hoards act as regulators of the quantity of circulating money, absorbing excess amounts and meeting shortfalls. Hoard formation is a mechanism external to circulation but endogenous to economic reproduction as a whole; hoards make possible the matching of the actual and the necessary quantities of circulating metallic money. For Marx this point is fundamental for the rejection of the quantity theory of money: through hoarding, the quantity of circulating money is determined by commodity prices.

Marx also accepted the Ricardian view of money as a 'veil', but in a partial and limited sense. If one claims that prices determine the quantity of money, one is also necessarily implying that the primary economic phenomenon in the sphere of exchange is the circulation of commodities and not of money. The movement of commodities is a *sine qua non* for capitalist reproduction, while the perpetual movement of money is a secondary process elicited and determined by the movement of commodities (ibid., pp. 210–12). However, as is further discussed below, for Marx money also functions outside circulation, and in this capacity it is not at all a 'veil' on economic activity.

The adequacy of commodity money for the performance of the exchange function cannot be taken for granted. Circulation inevitably entails loss of substance through abrasion, and might also encourage the sweating, clipping and rubbing of coins. Circulating coin possesses less weight, and hence less value, than it purports to do. Despite this, so long as its deterioration is not too severe the coin continues to facilitate the exchange of commodities. For Marx (1859, pp. 108–14), this is possible because in simple circulation, C_1–M–C_2, money appears fleetingly between two commodities, hence its material substance becomes unimportant. Degraded coin can function as full-weight coin, the former in effect symbolising the latter. The practice of exchange itself creates room for the emergence of symbolic money. Proper symbols of commodity money (base metal coin or valueless paper) are typically issued by the state; they are state fiat money with compulsory circulation, such as the French Assignats or First World War British Treasury Notes. Similar to commodity money, symbolic fiat money moves constantly along a path of articulated transactions that has no definite shape. However, while the actual circulating quantity of commodity money in circulation is regulated by hoards held alongside circulation, that of symbolic fiat money is determined by the state. If the state issues large quantities of fiat money systematically and rapidly, the quantity of such money in circulation simply expands.

There are two fundamental reasons why fiat money is deficient for hoarding and thus cannot abandon the sphere of circulation: first, fiat money does not possess value in its own body; and second, fiat money has no organic connection with the credit system and real capital accumulation. In sharp contrast, valueless, bank-issued credit money does possess organic connections with both the credit system and real accumulation. Even when the state actively regulates its creation, credit money retains its organic connections with the credit system, a fact that allows it to have an economic role outside the sphere of circulation. Fiat money, on the other hand, receives its social validity from the mere word of the state; while the state's imprimatur allows fiat money to circulate, it cannot provide such money with a role outside the sphere of circulation, except in the narrow sense of requiring that payments to the state (above all taxes) are made in fiat money.

Arbitrariness in the determination of its quantity, however, severely affects fiat money's functioning as the unit of account. Fiat money is a symbol of commodity money, its quantity 'standing in' for the necessary quantity of gold, the latter determined by commodity values, velocity and the value of the money commodity. Commodity values are measured in quantities of gold, but they are expressed as prices in sums of fiat money symbolising gold coin. If the symbolisation rate is one to one, that is, the standard piece of fiat money symbolises a standard unit of gold (say, one pound sterling, or roughly one quarter of a troy ounce of gold), the accounting system of prices is not disturbed. If, however, the state arbitrarily augments the quantity of fiat money, while the necessary quantity of gold remains the same, the symbolisation rate declines. Consequently, although commodity values might remain the same, prices expressed in units of fiat money rise. This is pure price inflation, which could potentially lead to hyperinflation if the state continuously increased the issue of fiat money. Inflation is a characteristic inadequacy of fiat money in performing the function of measure of value and standard of price. A simple form of the quantity theory of money could provide some analytical insight into pure price inflation.

2.2.3 Money as Money

Money as the independent form of value also undertakes functions not purely determined with reference to the process of exchange. In performing these functions money reveals the complexity of its social role which goes far beyond the mere facilitation of commodity exchange. Marx summarised them as hoarding, means of payment, and world money, and included them in the envelop term 'money as money'.

Hoarding

Money is always to be found in a state of rest as well as movement: it is always hoarded as well as circulating. For Marx (1885, pp. 158–9, 162–5, 572–4, 410–12), there are several structural reasons why the hoarding of money must take place in the course of the reproduction of total social capital. Precautionary money hoards enable commodity owners successfully to confront unforeseen price fluctuations; the 'lumpiness' of fixed capital investment, and of the accrual of surplus value, also entail the formation of temporarily idle sums of money; the need to maintain the continuity of capitalist production during the time it takes to sell the output necessitates the holding of a money hoard on the part of the capitalist.[13]

The hoarding of money is a precondition for money's circulation since hoards release sums to and absorb sums from circulation. Thus the total money stock of a country comprises a part in movement and a part at rest, the dividing line shifting incessantly in line with the requirements of commodity circulation. Apart from this technical monetary role, however, hoards also have a broader economic function. Hoarding concentrates the ability to buy and to pay in an independent form, unrelated to the use value of ordinary commodities. In a capitalist society characterised by the commodification of all aspects of human relationships, hoarded money affords its owner enormous social power; money can buy social standing, education, political power. The broader social power of hoarded money is most evident in the relations among capitalist states; money can secure national alliances and provide the 'sinews of war'. The mercantilists, whose thinking was preoccupied with determining national power in a world of competing states, understood this aspect of money more fully than classical political economy.

Hoarded precious metals are accumulations of value, hence wealth, in a durable form. In societies that do not possess a systematic social mechanism for the expansion of value, hoarding metal is the primary form of wealth accumulation. As Marx (1859, pp. 128–30) pointed out, in such societies a contradiction exists between the qualitatively infinite desire to accumulate value in money and the quantitatively limited size of money hoards. Capitalist society, on the other hand, possesses a social mechanism for the expansion of value, namely exploitation sustained by the investment of capital in the process of production. Capitalist hoarded money is, on the one hand, a durable accumulation of value, and, on the other, money that could become capital, that is, it could be ploughed back into production and expand itself. The twin aspect of capitalist hoards is an important factor in the development of the capitalist credit system.

With the development of capitalism and the emergence of an advanced credit system, money hoards are socialised and their form changes. At an immediate level, the hoarder of money no longer holds accumulations of the money commodity, but rather bank deposits, company certificates of indebtedness, state bonds and other financial instruments. Hoards held by individuals become claims on future output and value, and they are held against credit institutions in the first instance. At the same time, however, capitalist credit institutions themselves begin to undertake some of the social hoarding function; the reserves of banks are a vitally important form of purely capitalist hoards. The money hoards of banks, however, also tend to lose their metallic substance in the course of development of the credit system, and become a graduated structure of claims on others. The bulk of the enormous metal hoards of a capitalist society gradually retreats into the vaults of the central bank, the bank of banks. Historically, even the hoards of national central banks have tended to lose much of their metallic character and to contain the valueless credit money of a few dominant capitalist countries.

Means of Payment

Given the existence of money, the act of selling, *C–M*, can be split in two: the advance of the commodity against a promise to pay later, and the subsequent intervention of money in settlement of the promise to pay. In a capitalist economy this possibility allows for the spontaneous advance of commercial credit among capitalists.[14] Commercial debt is subject to clearing, that is, to the cancelling of one debt against another. With the development of capitalism, this practice acquires historical and institutional specificity. How much of the means of payment is necessary in a given period of time depends on the efficiency of the clearing process, on geographical distance and on the patterns of trade within a country. Money as means of payment completes several preceding transactions at once, and so economises on the use of means of purchase. However a certain quantity of means of payment is always necessary for the settlement of commercial debt, since clearing and fresh credit are very unlikely completely to settle all past obligations in a given period.

The movement of the means of payment as it settles past obligations is neither smooth nor continuous.[15] The main reason for this is that the circulation of the means of payment has an obligatory character, distinct from the apparently voluntary character of the narrow means of exchange. While reproduction decisions can be postponed, debt settlement cannot. The necessity to possess a certain quantity of means of payment on the part of debtor capitalists is absolute. Failure to settle commercial obligations when these are due implies bankruptcy and the forced sale of the debtor's assets.

The form of money that emerges in relation to money's payment function is credit money (Marx, 1867, p. 238). At its most elementary, credit money is rooted in the promises to pay generated by commercial credit. The bill of exchange, that is, a draft by the creditor ordering the debtor to pay at a future date the equivalent value of commodities delivered now, is a typical early form of credit money, as is more fully explained in Chapter 4 below. Endorsed by its holder, the bill of exchange can circulate among capitalists, allowing the further exchange of commodities. This rudimentary form of credit money provides a foundation for more advanced banking credit practices. The discounting of bills of exchange, that is, money advanced to the bill holder in exchange for the bill, enables banks systematically to issue their own promises to pay in the form of banknotes. Bank credit money is originally created as bank liabilities in exchange for assets, in the first instance by the issuing of banknotes in the purchase of bills of exchange. The deposit liabilities of banks can also perform the paying function of money through the use of cheques or direct transfers, provided that a system of clearing the obligations among banks is in place. The actual process of transformation of credit money (that is, bills, banknotes and bank deposits) matters less here than the intrinsic fluidity of form of credit-based money. With the development of capitalism credit money takes different forms as the liabilities of financial institutions change. These forms depend on the historically specific institutional structure of the credit system, and of capitalist accumulation in general, but credit money remains a claim on financial institutions backed by their assets.

This conclusion has important implications for the movement and quantity of credit money, most clearly seen for banknote credit money. When banknotes are issued by private banks in the purchase of commercial debt, the assets of banks comprise largely commercial bills. When these bills mature, banknotes are returned to banks when capitalists use them (among other means of payment) to pay the banks. Analogously, bank deposit liabilities are cancelled (they are lost to the banks) when capitalists use deposit funds to settle their maturing obligations with banks. In short, credit money is regularly created by financial institutions as these make advances to capitalists, and is regularly destroyed as the debts of capitalists held by the financial institutions mature. The path of credit money in capitalist circulation has a cyclical shape, which distinguishes it from the shapeless path of both commodity money and fiat money. This is the theoretical foundation of Steuart's 'regorging' and of the banking school's law of the reflux, discussed in Chapter 1. The cyclical movement of credit money matters greatly for the determination of credit money's quantity in circulation. This quantity depends on the advance and repayment of loans by capitalists to each other, and by financial institutions to capitalists. The determinants of both types of loan advance, as well as of the regularity of debt settlement, are rooted in the process of real accumulation. At the same time, however, credit possesses significant power to 'stretch' accumulation, that is, to finance the generation of additional value and surplus value, creating the conditions for its own repayment.

Credit money is not 'neutral' as far as capitalist accumulation is concerned. Credit money appears in capitalist circulation from the outside as capitalists and financial institutions advance credit to other capitalists, and spurs the creation of value and surplus value. It follows that the relation of credit money's actual quantity in circulation to the necessary quantity of money is determined by factors considerably broader than those relevant to narrow commodity circulation. Particularly important in this respect is the success of loan advances in generating surplus value, and consequently in creating the wherewithal for the settlement of debt. There can be no guarantee at the outset that the 'channel of circulation' is always filled precisely and harmoniously to capacity with credit money.

Certain conclusions follow regarding the ability of credit money to function as measure of value, particularly in relation to the aggregate price level. The preceding analysis of fiat money claimed that the exchange value of fiat money is determined primarily by the quantity of symbol in circulation, but always bears a relation to the value of the money commodity since fiat money symbolises the latter. For Ricardo, (who did not differentiate between fiat money and credit money) the exchange value of bank credit money was also regulated by the value of the money commodity, provided there was convertibility between the two. However determination of the exchange value of credit money is a theoretical problem of quite a different order of difficulty than that implied by Ricardo, some aspects of which are as follows.[16]

When credit money circulates concurrently with commodity money, and the latter also plays an active role as a reserve on the balance sheets of banks, the value of commodity money does indeed exercise a regulating influence on the exchange value of credit money, but not in the manner suggested by Ricardo. The proper theoretical framework for the analysis of this issue is the capitalist business cycle (see Chapter 6 below). In the representative pattern of the business cycle, the exchange value of credit money (and that of the money commodity) falls (the price level rises) in the course of a capitalist upswing, the value of the money commodity having remained the same. The fall of the exchange value of credit money, however, comes to an end as industrial, commercial and monetary crises follow the boom. In the course of the monetary crisis, money as means of payment is strongly demanded, much credit is destroyed and commodities are often forcibly sold. The banking system meanwhile finds itself obliged to defend its reserves of the money commodity, and so to limit its advance of fresh credit. Precisely because of this complex set of influences, elaborated in Chapter 6 below, the exchange value of credit money (and that of the money commodity) once again rises (prices fall), and the pivotal role of the money commodity in the determination of the price level is reasserted. The rise in the exchange value of credit money during the crisis and the slump, meanwhile, goes beyond simply redressing the fall that occurred during the upswing. Be that as it may, it is clear that the analysis of the exchange value of credit money requires a theory of capitalist accumulation in addition to the monetary analysis of commodity circulation.

When commodity money has no active role in capitalist accumulation, as has happened through state intervention in the last quarter of the twentieth century, the exchange value of credit money completely loses its anchor in the value of the money commodity. Under such conditions, determination of the quantity of credit money is still not totally arbitrary and exogenous to the process of accumulation. Instead the quantity of credit money continues to depend on the operations of the credit system relative to real accumulation, and still exhibits elements of self-regulation, though the latter is far from harmonious. Under such conditions the quantity theory of money acquires a certain degree of validity, and the exchange value of credit money (the price level) tends to reflect the ratio between commodity values in circulation and the quantity of credit money. There is thus an ever-present possibility of a rapid decline in the exchange value of credit money (price inflation), particularly if state intervention in the processes of the credit system is widespread and capital accumulation faces difficulties in expanding the supply of output.

World Money

Marx (1867, pp. 240–4) further claimed that money in the world market functions as an internationally acceptable means of payment that has no national peculiarities. It follows that world money is purely metallic. Gold had to be paid by one country to another to settle balance of payments obligations, to purchase necessary food supplies, to fight wars. Marx's stress on the international paying function of gold is in complete and evident contrast to Ricardo's treatment of gold as a pure means of exchange.[17] For Marx, world money is primarily a means of payment, and as a consequence countries are often compelled to seek resort to world money in order to meet their international obligations. It also follows that countries that want to participate in the world market have to possess a gold hoard, the size of which indicates their ability to confront the fluctuations of the world market and to protect their political power.

Marx's argument that gold is the most appropriate form of world money has not stood the test of time particularly well. With hindsight, the form of world money has varied according to the development of the global credit system, with its own centres of activity, and to political relations among the capitalist states. The emergence of a global credit system has allowed credit money to function as a means of payment across frontiers, though gold has not ceased to be used. What is also paramount in this respect is the historical emergence of dominant powers among the capitalist nations, first Britain and then the United States. The emergence of a global credit system, centred on the economy and territory of the dominant powers, has enabled credit money of a particular nationality to function as world money. Equally, however, this development has made the maintenance of stable relations of equivalence among the several national monies of the world a considerably harder proposition.

In conclusion, it is clear that Marx's analysis of the functions and forms of money makes full use of the complexity of money's operations in a capitalist economy. The Ricardian tradition of classical political

economy had narrowed the functions of money down to simple means
of exchange. Though the banking school had rediscovered much of
Steuart's analysis of the functions of money, it had done so without
providing an account of the logical thread running through money's
functions. Marx filled this lacuna by basing his analysis of the functions
and forms of money on an examination of the forms and substance of
value. Moreover Marx's approach indicates the path of development of
the form of money itself, and shows that commodity money provides a
firm foundation for analysis of state-issued fiat money and credit
money. In contrast, neoclassical economic analysis, though it recognises
the complexity of money's functions and has produced a considerable
volume of work on the generation of credit money, has demonstrated
neither the internal coherence of money's functions nor the logical link
between commodity money and credit money.

2.3   MONEY, THE *NEXUS RERUM* OF CAPITALISM

Economic theory, whatever the fundamental differences between its
several currents, has tackled the genesis of money in terms of the
interaction among commodities. There is an influential counterview,
however, which has drawn its strength mostly from anthropological
work and argues that money does not arise in the processes of
exchange.[18] Polanyi and his colleagues (1957, pp. 250–6), have distinguished between three forms of social integration: reciprocity, indicating the mutual swapping of products among symmetrically located
groups of individuals; redistribution, denoting the concentration of
products by a social centre and their subsequent dispersal throughout
the social hierarchy; and exchange, referring to the equivalent and
opposite movement of products among market traders. For Polanyi,
trade, understood as the movement of products across long or short
distances in order to effect their consumption by persons other than
their producers, is considerably broader than market trading, which
incorporates haggling, results in market prices and is based on the
private gain of participants. The vast expanse of human history, with
the exception of the last few centuries, is characterised by the absence
of market trading.

   In Polanyi's view, money is a considerably broader phenomenon
than the narrow means of exchange. The latter was improperly
stressed by classical political economy in the course of treating market
trading as a natural component of human economic activity. Polanyi

(ibid., p. 264) proposed a 'catallactic' definition of money, that is, money is a means of indirect product exchange that also functions as means of payment and standard of commensuration of products. The earliest forms of money were particular (not general) objects, used to effect the necessary acts of reciprocity and redistribution in ancient societies rather than the market exchange of commodities. For Polanyi (1944, ch. 5), nineteenth-century European liberalism turned the market into the foundation of society and in the process threatened the very viability of society itself. A critical aspect of this development was the complete absorption of money by the market process, and the transformation of money into a commodity. The gold standard was a pillar of liberal Europe, but its blindly automatic functioning also undermined nineteenth-century capitalism. Polanyi treated the rise of managed non-commodity money in the interwar years, as well as protectionism and state economic intervention, as the natural defensive action of society in the face of market processes driven by private gain.

Polanyi's approach is attractive in that it goes beyond a narrow, exchange-related view of money. It also seems well-suited to the analysis of modern credit money, which overwhelmingly tends to be used by capitalists to pay, rather than to purchase. Moreover its stress on the role of money outside exchange, makes Polanyi's work suitable for the analysis of precapitalist societies, which contained the money form but did not possess developed exchange. The attractiveness of Polanyi's approach, however, is severely limited by the fact that he consciously sought to detach the logical derivation of money from the process of commodity exchange. The approach of classical political economy to money was indeed narrow, but that does not mean that it is logically possible to derive money in abstraction from the essential properties of commodity interaction.

Grierson (1977) has also advanced a complex argument that seeks to show that the origin of money was not in commodity exchange. According to Grierson (ibid., pp. 15–19), primitive 'limited purpose' (not general) money functioned mostly as a standard of measurement rather than a means of exchange, setting prices and establishing equivalencies among disparate things. The measure of value was the foundation of the means of exchange. Therefore Grierson argues that it is unlikely that money originated in commodity exchange as:

> Units of value, unlike units of area, volume, and weight, could only be arrived at with great difficulty, in part because natural units are absent, in part because of the much greater diversity of commodities

that had to be measured and the consequent difficulty in finding
common standards in terms of which they could reasonably be
compared (ibid., p. 18).

Grierson consequently sought the origin of money in the practice of
wergeld, that is, compensation paid for wrongs inflicted on others,
including murder. Plentiful evidence exists of elaborate ancient laws
among the Anglo-Saxon, Celtic, and Russian peoples that indemnified
wronged parties for injuries such as loss of limb, blows to the body,
loss of a moustache, rape and murder. The principles underpinning
indemnification was assuagement of anger and making good the loss
of public reputation. According to Grierson (ibid., pp. 19–24), value
measurement by money originated in such practices, then spread to
bridewealth and slavery, and from there to commodity exchange.

However, Grierson's argument loses much of its persuasiveness
when a logical basis is sought for the commensuration of injuries
inflicted on people of different social status, wealth, age and sex.
Commensuration of disparate commodities might be difficult,
but commensuration of injuries as diverse as the ones listed above is
not much easier. It is pure assertion for Grierson to claim that:

> The tariffs for damages were established in public assemblies, and
> the common standards were based on objects of some value which a
> householder might be expected to possess or which he could obtain
> from his kinsfolk. Since what is laid down consists of evaluations of
> injuries, not evaluations of commodities, the conceptual difficulty of
> devising a common measure for appraising unrelated objects is
> avoided (ibid., pp. 20–1).

The 'conceptual difficulty' of commensuration, if anything, becomes
even greater when it is injuries that one has to compare. On what
logical grounds can losing one's moustache be made equivalent to,
say, 'a blow to the head such that the brain is visible and the
bone projects'? Undoubtedly customs, religious practices, hierarchical relations and so on helped ascertain such equivalencies in
practice. However that is not a logical elucidation of the genesis of
money; the practice itself may have relied on the prior existence of
money to possess an objective and thing-like basis for the commensuration of injuries, bridewealth and slavery. Economic theory is right to
attempt to establish the logical grounds for the emergence of money
in the interaction of commodities. The point, however, is to

do so without losing sight of the broad historical functioning of money.

The Marxist analysis of money can meet the above requirements, provided that the forms of value are properly analysed. For Marx (1939, p. 223; 1894, pp. 447–8), trade and the pure trading peoples of antiquity – the Phoenicians and the Carthaginians – were present in the 'intermundia' of ancient societies, like the gods of Epicurus. The simile is important: the gods of Epicurus were in a sublime state, detached from the human world and indifferent to the affairs of men. Analogously, trade was largely indifferent to the reproduction of human societies until the rise of capitalism; precapitalist societies organised their affairs mostly on the basis of custom, hierarchy and command. Money and trade arose chiefly where communities and societies came into contact with each other. Money, however, possessed a corrosive power in precapitalist societies since it allowed acquisition of goods and projection of social power that were unrelated to hierarchical and customary privilege.

Money's corrosive power allowed it to penetrate society and to maintain a presence in society's margins, but it also ensured money's disruptive and antagonistic influence on the hierarchical and custom-ridden core of such societies. Under capitalist conditions of production the process of exchange becomes intrinsic to social reproduction and money abandons its marginal role. Capitalism is characterised by the undermining of social hierarchies and custom, and their partial replacement by social links articulated through the market. Money as the independent form of value is the *nexus rerum* of capitalist society. It is an economic form intrinsic to capitalist society, the supreme encapsulation of that society's social relations, which revolve around value. The centrality of money's role in capitalist reproduction is reflected in the multiplicity of the functions of money.

This view is compatible with Polanyi's analysis, with the critical proviso that for Marx the capitalist character of production is paramount. Marx's analysis is, however, incompatible with the anthropological claim that money was originally an ideal unit of account without a corporeal means of exchange. Insofar as past societies sought a unit of account to express the equivalence of disparate use values, they were forced to do so by their external relations. It is highly unlikely that economic relations among precapitalist societies rested on trust, mutual obligation or reciprocity, requiring money only as an abstract numeraire. A corporeal money was also necessary to effect the exchange of commodities. That is not to say that the corporeal money in use was necessarily the same as the money of account: clearly the two could have been different. It is to say, however, that all monies of account were real means of exchange at some point in their past. Historical research bears out this claim without exception, even for the early modern era (Braudel, 1981, p. 465).

In precapitalist historical societies, money was naturally intertwined with customary, religious, ritual and even magical practices. Money appeared in Sumerian and Babylonian texts mostly as measure of value, but there is no reason to assume that the various measures of value were entirely ideal. Money also made frequent appearances in the world described by Homer, who reflected the self-perception of the landed Greek aristocracy of the early first millennium BC. In the *Iliad* money was famously a measure of the value of armour, but also functioned in ways reminiscent of *wergeld*, particularly in securing a bride, indemnifying blood wrongs or making formal gifts (von Reden, 1994). Thus, in Homeric society money played an important role in a social practice that was characteristic of the elite, namely to create reciprocal obligations among its members. Yet money's role was largely secondary to the material reproduction of archaic Greek society, a society not predicated upon the exchange of commodities.

The first regular use of coin took place in western Asia Minor in the middle of the sixth century BC. By the beginning of the classical fifth century, coin was found in all the major Greek *poleis*. The gift of the Greeks for generalisation predisposed them quickly to recognise silver and gold as adequate general forms of wealth and social power. The most important factor in the spread of coinage was the rise of the *polis* regime itself, and of the networks of trade among the communities of the eastern Mediterranean. The payment of money subsidies by the state, for instance to attend the theatre, the imposition of monetary fines and the collection of voluntary contributions for war and emergencies (*eranos*) popularised the use of money within the *polis*. Nevertheless monetary relations remained subsidiary to customary or hierarchical relations in the economic life of the *polis*. Finley's (1973, ch. 1) thesis that the ancient Graeco-Roman economy was not based on impersonal market relations, and therefore hardly admitted of analysis based on modern economic analogues and concepts, has retained its persuasiveness. The rhythms of Athenian social reproduction were dictated by the expenditure of agricultural labour by small free producers, and by the labour of slaves in the mines and elsewhere.[19] The extent to which the monetisation of the classical Athenian peasant democracy contributed to the corrosion of its foundations is a matter of interest and relevance to the analysis of money.

About fifty years after the first documented use of coinage in Asia Minor, rough coins were cut in Thrace, a tribal 'barbarian' country to the north of Greece. Soon after that Alexander I of Macedon, the distant grandfather of the legendary king with the same name, cut coins in his own backward and tribal kingdom bordering Thrace (Borza, 1990, pp. 126–30). Most of Macedon's trade was in exporting its abundant timber to meet the shipbuilding needs of the southern Greeks. Alexander I minted elaborate and very large silver octa-drachms, which could not possibly have been of use internally in his weak kingdom. Possession of silver mines, external relations and the projection of royal prestige domestically and abroad were probably more significant factors in encouraging the Macedonian kings to mint coin.

The Persian Achaemenids, on the other hand, might not all have been Great Kings but they all were certainly great hoarders. Persepolis, Sardis and Ecbatana were fabled for their accumulations of gold, amassed through centuries of tribute. The Persian kings held the gold as bullion and cut their famous darics mostly to bribe Greeks or to hire them as mercenaries. Alexander the Great took possession of the Achaemenid hoards by right of conquest and spent with abandon (St Croix, 1981, pp. 118–19). The release of Persian gold stimulated the monetary economy of the eastern Mediterranean during the apogee of the Hellenistic era of the third century BC (Green, 1990, ch. 21). However, even during that more materially wealthy, trade-oriented and culturally introspective historical period, money did not play remotely the same social role that it plays in a capitalist society. To indulge their Alexandrian fripperies the Ptolemies ran the whole of Egypt as a private estate, but the gold they craved had little impact on the lives of the exploited and despised *fellaheen* of the Nile.

The evidence from history certainly does not contradict the view that the form of money emerges necessarily out of the interaction of commodities. It also supports the argument that in precapitalist societies money tended to be a social phenomenon that was largely marginal to the essential processes of social reproduction. Under capitalism, exchange relations have become an integral part of the economic order of society, and production has been organised on the basis of the exploitation of wage labour. Historically, capitalism is the most developed and broadest form of the market economy; unlike precapitalist societies, money is an integral part of the reproduction of

capitalism. Marxist economic analysis is aware of the historical specificity of capitalism and tends to be monetary from the outset. Neither
classical political economy nor neoclassicism, both of which consider
commodity exchange as the natural order of society and typically
identify it with barter, have successfully developed a money-based
economic analysis of capitalism.

3 Interest-Bearing Capital: The Distinctive Marxist Approach

3.1 PRELIMINARY ANALYTICAL CONSIDERATIONS

The concept of commercial credit, that is, the sale of commodities against promises to pay that are subsequently settled by the payment of money, was introduced in Chapter 2. Commercial credit emerges spontaneously and continuously across the surface of capitalist exchange. Equivalently, capitalist sellers and buyers typically become creditors and debtors in the normal course of capitalist accumulation. Commercial credit relations form the necessary background for the emergence of the capitalist credit system, as Chapter 4 explains in detail. In analytical and practical terms, moreover, commercial credit serves as the foundation for banking (or monetary) credit, the other major and distinct form of credit. Banking credit refers to the lending of money itself on condition of repayment plus interest, and is considerably more complex than commercial credit (though the two also overlap). Banking credit relations give a clear content to the capitalist categories of interest and interest-bearing capital, the latter being a special type of capital remunerated through the payment of interest.

The source and nature of interest as a form of revenue have been extensively disputed, and remain relatively obscure in economic theory. Classical political economy identified three major sources of revenue and linked them to the three great classes of capitalism: profit (capitalists), wages (workers) and ground rent (landlords). Interest was not on a par with these. However, the classical economists also identified a fourth social group, the 'monied interest' (Smith, 1776, bk II, ch. 4, p. 374), a section of the capitalist class that 'could not be at the trouble of employing' its capital itself, and so lent it out at interest. Consequently it was typically held by the classical economists that revenue accruing in the form of interest differentiated 'monied' capitalists from industrial and commercial capitalists. In this vein, interest tended to be treated as a portion of the profits on capital, and the rate of profit as the 'regulator' of the rate of interest, though the precise nature of 'regulation' was ambiguous (Ricardo, 1817, pp. 363–4).

3.1.1 Marx's Two Approaches to Interest-Bearing Capital

In certain parts of his work, Marx (1894, chs 21, 22, 23, 24) adopted an analytical approach to the concept of interest that is very similar to that of the classical school. In this connection, he accounted for the character of interest-bearing capital by partly relying on the assumption that lending capitalists (who simply own money) advance loans to borrowing capitalists (who simply possess investment projects). Interest, is therefore a fraction of the profits generated by the investment projects of the borrowing capitalists. This approach is problematic for several reasons (Itoh, 1988, pp. 257–60). First, the assumption of a pure 'functioning capitalist', who possesses an investment project but no money, is ideally abstract. In practice borrowing capitalists typically possess some of their own capital in addition to that which they borrow. Second, revenue in the form of interest tends also to accrue to industrial and commercial capitalists, and cannot be the exclusive foundation of a social group. The separate and often opposite interests of lending and borrowing capitalists cannot be fully analysed in terms of the 'functioning' section of the capitalist class confronting the 'monied' section. In order to analyse the conflicts of interest that arise in the realm of the lending of money, one should first examine the creation, advance and repayment of interest-bearing capital as an integral part of the process of industrial capitalist accumulation. Third, and as Marx (1894, ch. 36) himself pointed out, interest-bearing capital is an 'antediluvian' form of capital that was present in ancient precapitalist societies. If the character of interest-bearing capital is sought in the relationship between a lending 'monied' capitalist and a borrowing 'functioning' capitalist, it is very difficult satisfactorily to show the difference between the modern and the ancient character of interest-bearing capital.

In other parts of his work, however, most notably throughout the second volume of *Capital*, Marx attempted to show that concentrations of stagnant (or idle) money are systematically generated in the course of the reproduction of total social capital. Temporarily idle profits, the depreciation funds of fixed capital, precautionary reserves and reserves that allow the continuity of the turnover of capital as production and circulation alternate, are all purely capitalist forms of money hoarding. The regular creation of stagnant money in the course of capitalist reproduction provides an objective basis for both commercial and banking credit, and serves as a foundation for the capitalist credit system. Put in the broadest possible terms, the credit system mobilises the stagnant money generated in the course of capitalist reproduction, transforms it into interest-bearing (loanable) capital and redirects it toward accumulation. In the first instance the credit system is a mechanism for the internal reallocation of spare funds among industrial and commercial capitalists. By this token, interest payments are a redistribution of surplus value among capitals, based on the prior generation of idle money by these capitals. The motion of the rate of interest reflects the demand for and supply of interest-bearing capital in the normal course of accumulation. Interest can thus accrue to all industrial and commercial capitals, and does not provide the foundation for a distinct social group.

Posing the issue in this manner allows for the possibility that interest-bearing capital might also be created out of the temporarily idle parts of the money revenue of workers and other social groups.[1] Precisely because the credit system is a social mechanism specialising in the concentration of stagnant money, and possesses an objective social basis in the reproduction of the total social capital, it can spread its activities across the surface of society and begin to concentrate all spare sums of money. Analogously, the further advance of interest-bearing capital by the credit system need not be directed exclusively towards real capitalist accumulation but also towards other activities not productive of surplus value. Seen broadly, interest is not only a portion of the surplus value generated in accumulation, but also part of the money income accruing to borrowers across society. In a country that contains an extensive small-holding peasantry as well as a developed capitalist mode of production, for instance, the practices of the credit system might provide a mechanism for the systematic extraction of monetary surpluses from the peasantry.

The analysis of banking credit and interest is best undertaken on the basis of Marx's second approach, namely that stagnant money is systematically generated in the course of industrial accumulation, transformed into interest-bearing capital by the credit system and returned to accumulation to receive a share of surplus value. This process provides an objective social foundation for the credit system. It also places interest-bearing capital at one remove from capitalist accumulation. Temporarily idle money becomes interest-bearing capital essentially outside the process of accumulation, despite deriving from and returning to the latter. On this basis it can further be shown that the operations of the credit system possess a degree of relative autonomy from real accumulation. This is manifested as much in the ability of credit institutions to collect spare money from all sections of society, as in their ability to continue making profits when real accumulation has met with difficulties. The relative autonomy of the credit system is an important factor in explaining financial instability in mature capitalism, as Part III of this book makes clear. However, despite its relative autonomy, the fact that the objective foundation of the credit system is provided by the idle money generated by capitalist firms means that, ultimately, its operations broadly comply with the essential motion of capitalist accumulation.

3.2 THE FORMATION OF INTEREST-BEARING CAPITAL AND THE CIRCUIT OF INDUSTRIAL CAPITAL

3.2.1 'Monied' Capitalist and 'Functioning' Capitalist

The characteristic movement of industrial capital represents the unity of production and circulation. It is usually summarised as the circuit of money capital:

$$M - C(lp, mp) \cdots P \cdots C' - M'(M + \Delta M)$$

At stage $M - C$, money capital M purchases labour power, lp, and means of production, mp. At stage P these inputs are transformed into finished output, C', which contains surplus value generated through the exploitation of labour. At stage $C' - M'$, finished output is sold, resulting in the return of the original money capital plus profit ΔM. Stages $M - C$ and $C' - M'$ together represent the sphere of circulation, and stage P represents the sphere of production. Surplus value gives the circuit its capitalist character and constitutes the qualitative difference from the simple circulation of money and commodities, $C - M - C$. The circuit can be thought of as a summation of the characteristic movement either of an individual industrial capital, or of the total social capital of an industrial capitalist economy.[2] Value takes three forms in the circuit: money, commodities and factors of production (workers and means of production). Money in the circuit is found exclusively in the sphere of circulation, and in this narrow sense money retains a precapitalist aspect that is common to all market processes. Nevertheless the circuit also organically links money to production; the extraction of surplus value provides a mechanism for the continuous expansion of value in the money form. Under capitalist conditions, therefore, the plain money of commercial transactions becomes money capital, a starting point for the fundamental movement of industrial capital. The transformation of plain money into money capital has profound implications. Since money is the independent representative of value and can always buy, money is a more general starting point for the circuit than either commodity or productive capital. As long as the circular movement of capital is the characteristic form of society's economic reproduction, money buys means of production, hires workers and results in the production of profit.

In the abovementioned four chapters of the third volume of *Capital*, and in the spirit of the classical analysis of interest, Marx (1894, p. 459) claimed that under capitalist conditions money acquires the peculiar use value of functioning as capital. This is a purely capitalist use value, namely to be able either to initiate the circuit of capital *ab ovo*, or to expand existing circuits and produce profits. Possession of this peculiar use value allows the trading of money as interest- bearing capital. As a peculiar commodity, interest-bearing capital also has a peculiar price.[3] To posit the price of interest-bearing capital theoretically a little more precision is necessary, namely money can in general produce the average profit for its user. Interest-bearing capital is formed as the average profit-generating capacity of money is bought and sold. Ownership of money capital as the bearer of the capacity potentially to generate average profit remains with the seller; interest-bearing capital is borrowed and lent. The owner's reward for parting with money capital for a specific period of time is a share of the average profits generated, that is, interest. The formula of interest-bearing capital is thus predicated upon the money form of the formula of industrial capital (i, the rate of interest):

$$M \cdots\cdots\cdots\cdots\cdots\cdots\cdots\cdots\cdots M''(M + iM)$$
$$\downarrow \qquad\qquad\qquad\qquad\qquad \uparrow$$
$$M - C(lp, mp) \cdots P \cdots C' - M'(M + \Delta M)$$

To recap, according to the above strand in Marx's analysis, money under capitalist conditions possesses the peculiar use value of being able to generate average profits, hence its owner can temporarily part with it for a share of the potential profit. As for classical economics, the lender advances capital but does not take the trouble to employ it directly in the production of profit. In Marx's words:

> The owner of money who wants to valorize this as interest-bearing capital parts with it to someone else, puts it into circulation, makes it into a commodity *as capital*; as capital not only for himself but also for others. It is not simply capital for the person who alienates it, but it is made over to the other person as capital right from the start, as value that possesses the use-value of creating surplus-value or profit (Marx, 1895, pp. 464–5, emphasis in original).

Thus the 'monied' capitalist advances interest-bearing capital to the 'functioning' capitalist and is rewarded with interest, which is a share of the profits. The remainder accrues to the functioning capitalist and is the 'profit of enterprise', (ibid., p. 497). Consequently there is opposition between interest and profit of enterprise, which starts as a purely quantitative division of total profit but becomes a qualitative distinction. While interest is treated as revenue gained purely by possessing capital, profit of enterprise is treated as revenue gained purely for functioning as a capitalist and organising production. Thus profit of enterprise might even be conceived of as the wages of capitalist management and supervision, though in all instances it incorporates surplus value from the exploitation of labour power. In the spirit of classical analysis, Marx treated interest and profit of enterprise as sources of revenue that give rise to two distinct and antagonistic sections of the capitalist class: 'monied' capitalists and functioning capitalists. The more surplus-value that is appropriated by one, the less that remains for the other.[4]

As already indicated above, the problem with this approach, despite its many insights, is that it attempts to posit the nature of interest-bearing capital in an ideally abstract fashion, and tends to identify interest with one social stratum. At the level of the transaction between two individuals, even when one is a 'monied' and the other a 'functioning' capitalist, the character of interest-bearing capital appears as a matter of the intentions of the lender and the understanding of the borrower. Even if it is claimed that a social background of capitalist accumulation was assumed by Marx, the analysis smacks of assertion since the borrowing capitalist might employ the money unproductively but still return it plus interest. Moreover if money generally possesses the use value of being able to generate the average rate of profit, it is hardly credible that the owner of money does not realise this use value but remains satisfied with interest. Marx's conjecture that interest-bearing capital is alienated from its owner on condition that it returns when it has 'realized its use-value of producing surplus-value' (ibid., p. 465) is quite impossible to demonstrate logically in the relations between the 'monied' and the 'functioning' capitalist.

The position taken in this book is that in the lending of money among capitalists the owner of money does not sell the potential to generate surplus value since the latter already exists in the business plans of the borrower. At the individual level, what is originally advanced when money is lent is simply money. Moreover the money lent has lain idle in the lender's hands: if realistic opportunities for average-profit-making had existed they would have been exploited. Interest in this connection is a reward received by the owner of money for parting with his or her property, and simply reflects the general possibility of augmenting a sum of money through lending. This possibility is not specific to capitalism but can be found in many different social systems (a point that also holds for the possibility of making money through the operations of merchant capital).

3.2.2 Stagnant Money and the Circuit of Capital

A more fruitful analytical path for the analysis of interest-bearing capital is to postulate that money systematically becomes interest-bearing capital after a social mechanism (the credit system) has been constructed that collects stagnant money generated in the course of the circuit of capital, that is in the turnover of capital. The credit system transforms stagnant money into a homogeneous commodity, gives to it the character of interest-bearing capital, and systematically channels it back to accumulation. The intentions of lender and borrower, and the actual use to which the money is put, are entirely irrelevant in this respect. Insofar as a credit system exists, comprising institutions such as banks and open markets, the money lent through the system's mechanisms has already become interest-bearing capital and commands the payment of interest. Given the existence of the process of real accumulation, which typically absorbs the bulk of the advanced interest-bearing capital, interest acquires an objective social foundation as a share of the regularly produced profit. In this light the processes of banking credit represent the reallocation of spare funds and the redistribution of surplus value among different functioning capitals, rather than the advance and remuneration of the capital of the 'monied' section of the capitalist class.

The approach proposed here allows for a structured analysis of the credit system as the social mechanism that forms interest-bearing capital in a capitalist society. It provides a better theoretical foundation for the analysis of lending for non-productive purposes to workers, capitalists and other social classes. It coheres with the observation that capitalist firms often earn substantial sums of interest by lending their spare funds. It also allows for the analysis of lending for investment purposes that might fail to generate the expected returns. Regardless of the use to which the money is put, the lender can still command the payment of interest since the credit system has transformed the borrowed money into interest-bearing capital. Moreover, despite acquiring an objective social foundation in the generation of profit, interest remains simply a general form of the augmentation of money by lending. Thus interest can be extracted from all money revenues across society regardless of whether these can be ultimately reduced to surplus value.

There are several structural reasons why value systematically abandons the circuit of capital in the normal course of its traverse and becomes stagnant in the money form. Put another way, the circuit constantly 'leaks' value, the 'leaks' appearing as sums of money held alongside the value traversing the circuit. 'Leaked', or disengaged, value is characterised by rest and approximates the character of a hoard. Indeed if it is assumed for the sake of analysis that money is purely gold and no credit system exists, value disengaged from the circuit can only be a hoard. It should be stressed that this approach to money hoarding differs substantially from Keynesian liquidity preference. The latter ultimately relies on unexplained personal and psychological motivations for the hoarding of money (De Brunhoff, 1976, p. 41). There are no such motivations here: hoarding takes place as capital traverses the circuit for objective reasons pertaining to the circuit itself. Furthermore 'leaks' from the circuit do not immediately and necessarily imply a shrinking of the flow of value. Value is disengaged from the circuit in the money form and for limited periods of time, frequently in order to enable the circular flow as a whole to maintain a certain size. Capital can continue to reproduce itself at the same level while regularly forming and dissolving hoards. The sources of such hoards are as follows.

First, there are hoards associated purely with circulation. At stage $M - C$ the capitalists have to form precautionary hoards to meet unforeseen payments and purchases, as well as confront the inevitable price fluctuations of capitalist exchange. These are 'reserve funds', 'part of the functioning money capital', and the capitalist must hold such reserves at the very beginning of the circuit (Marx, 1885, p. 165). Moreover, at stages $M - C$ and $C' - M'$ the gradual purchase of means of production and labour power and the gradual sale of the finished product also result in money hoards. The proper elucidation of these is undertaken below when the circuit is viewed as a whole. Second, there are hoards associated with production. Fixed capital (machinery, plant and equipment) releases its value gradually and over several repetitions of turnover. Until a minimum size sufficient for reinvestment has been reached, for instance to replace used-up machinery, the disengaged value forms a hoard, a depreciation fund. For Marx (ibid., pp. 248–61), the most obvious use of these depreciation funds for the individual capitalist was as a temporary fund from which to effect various repairs on the operating fixed capital. Third, and still related to production, money hoards are also formed as profits accrue and become available for reinvestment. Until such profits reach a minimum size consistent with the material characteristics of reproduction they accumulate as money funds held by the capitalist. Both depreciation funds and accumulated profits are typical capitalist hoards since they have their roots in capitalist production.

Finally, fourth, there are hoards associated with the unity of production and circulation, or with the turnover of capital as a whole. Marx (ibid., ch. 15) called this type of hoard formation 'the mechanism of the turnover', and devoted a lot of effort to ascertaining its technical characteristics. The traverse by capital of stages $M - C$ and $C' - M'$ taken together requires a definite period of time: the circulation period. The traverse of stage P analogously gives rise to the production period. The part of capital that is traversing circulation (commodity output being sold and money seeking inputs and paying wages) has temporarily left production. However the capitalist is under competitive pressure continuously to use fixed capital in order to ensure continuous production. It follows that, at the inception of the turnover of capital, the capitalist must hold money capital sufficient to purchase inputs and pay wages in excess of the requirements of one production period. Indeed the capitalist must possess sufficient money capital to continue production until the revenues from output sales become regular.

In addition to this indisputable conclusion, however, Marx (ibid., pp. 353–9) attempted to show that, as part of the mechanism of turnover, some of the returning sales revenue becomes temporarily redundant to the financial requirements of production, hence it accumulates as money hoard. Marx's argument relies on an analysis of the overlapping pattern of the production period and the circulation period for 'fluid' capital, that is, labour power and raw materials. Marx's technical substantiation of this argument is incorrect, as is briefly shown below, nevertheless the thrust of his argument is both correct and important for our purposes.[5]

To demonstrate the 'mechanism of the turnover', Marx (ibid., p. 203) assumed that the sale of final output takes place 'at one stroke', while inputs are purchased gradually. The generality of these assumptions is problematic since the sale of final output could very well take place gradually across a broad range of industries. Indeed it seems to be the exception that sales revenues will accrue in one lump sum 'at a stroke'. Be that as it may, Marx subsequently argued that in all instances in which the circulation period is not an exact multiple of the production period, temporarily idle money is formed as sales revenues accrued (ibid., p. 355). The reason is that, under the assumed conditions, the sudden accrual of sales revenues at the end of each circulation period necessarily takes place after a production period has already partly elapsed. Hence it seemed to Marx that part of the sales revenues becomes temporarily unnecessary for the continuity of production.

This conclusion is not generally correct, even within the framework of Marx's assumptions. The value of the sold output accruing 'at a stroke' is, by construction, equal to the value of the capital necessary to run one production period. Nevertheless the accruing money capital is fluid and can be spread over the present and the next period of production. If continuity of production is to be maintained, and given strict regularity of the circulation period (assumed by Marx), the lump sums of sales revenues accruing at the end of each successive circulation period in the future are wholly necessary in order to maintain continuous production. Whether the circulation period is an exact multiple of the production period, and indeed the relative lengths of the production period and the circulation period, matter not at all in this respect. Only if the circulation period is irregular and uncertain, forcing the capitalist to keep extra spare funds at all times in order to maintain the continuity of production, could parts of the sales revenue become temporarily redundant for the rest of the production period during which they accrue. This result, however, arises from the uncertainty of returns and not from the interplay of production and circulation time, which was what Marx intended.

The final point above indicates the manner in which it is possible to rescue Marx's argument that idle money is formed as a result of maintaining the continuity of the turnover of capital. Capitalists are inevitably confronted with variable and unpredictable flows of sales proceeds, the timing of which is necessarily different from the scarcely less variable and unpredictable outlays to purchase productive capital (including the payment of wages). Given the competitive pressure to maintain the continuity of production, capitalists need to hold a precautionary reserve of means of payment. This 'turnover' reserve allows the capitalists to iron out problems with the timing of flows of receipts and expenditures, temporary disparities of both flows, sudden changes and other irregularities. The 'turnover' reserve is not money 'released' in the course of turnover, but rather a reserve that must be present at the outset to ensure the continuity of the turnover of capital.

The regular disengagement of value from the circuit – in the form of various precautionary reserves, temporarily unutilised profits and a depreciation fund – provides the social foundation for the credit system under capitalist conditions. The credit system collects 'leaked' value, transforms it into interest-bearing capital, and channels it back into real accumulation. It follows that interest-bearing capital does not permanently remain within the circuit of total social capital; rather it is systematically formed outside the circuit, and continually enters and exits the latter. The full significance of this point for the remuneration of interest-bearing capital is discussed below, after a brief and necessary digression on Marx's analysis of merchants' capital.

3.2.3 The Rate of Interest and the Rate of Profit

Merchants' capital, comprising commercial and money-dealing capital, is an ancient form of capital, that has always had extensive connections with interest-bearing capital (Marx, 1894, ch. 20). In a capitalist economy, commercial capital buys and sells commodities, and remains entirely within the sphere of exchange. Commercial profit accrues through the resale of the commodities originally bought by merchants, and not through the employment and exploitation of labour power. The social function of commercial capital is to minimise the costs of conducting the circulation of commodities for capital as a whole.[6] Consequently there are objective grounds for the remuneration of commercial capital out of the total surplus value on the same *pro rata* basis as industrial capital. By the same token, money-dealing capital specialises in managing the money that is necessarily present in the sphere of exchange, also remaining entirely within the sphere of exchange. Given extensive capitalist exchange, accounts have to be kept, deposits have to be safeguarded, sums transferred and, above all, money of one nationality has to be changed into money of another. Money-dealing capital reduces the costs of undertaking these activities on a social scale, and is consequently remunerated on the same basis as commercial and industrial capital. As the capitalist credit system grows and develops, banks tend to appropriate the functions of money-dealing capital, leading to the disappearance of the latter as an independent form of capital.

For Marx, both commercial and money-dealing capital (or banking capital as the advanced capitalist form of the latter) are integral parts of the sphere of circulation in the circuit of total social capital. They minimise the costs of exchange and do not abandon the circuit as part of their intrinsic movement. As capitals integral to the circuit, they take part in the redistribution of total surplus value on the same footing as industrial capital. In short, they participate in the formation of the average rate of profit. Interest-bearing capital, on the other hand, is continually formed outside the circuit, and enters and exits the latter. By so doing, interest-bearing capital mobilises the spare money funds present in the course of accumulation, and reallocates them among the capitals integral to the circuit (thus also accelerating the turnover of these capitals, as Chapter 4 below explains in more detail).[7] Consequently interest-bearing capital also earns a share of the total surplus value, but not on the same basis as industrial, commercial and money-dealing (or banking) capital. Interest-bearing capital does not take part in the determination of the average rate of profit, but earns interest instead.

Approaching the nature of interest-bearing capital in this manner, rather than in terms of the relation between 'monied' and 'functioning' capitalists, makes it easier to assess Marx's claim that the average rate of profit is normally higher than the average rate of interest, and usually forms its upper limit (though in certain phases of the capitalist business cycle this might not hold) (ibid., p. 482). This characteristic position of Marxist economics is in complete contrast to neoclassicism (and Keynesianism), which essentially postulates the tendency of the rate of profit and the rate of interest to move towards equality. For Marxist economics, the inequality of the two rates reflects the structural difference between a capital integral to the circuit and a capital that appears from the outside and subsequently exits the circuit. It also reflects the ultimate reliance of interest-bearing capital on the spare funds generated by industrial capitals.

For capitals integral to the circuit, the principle of the mobility of capital underpins the equalisation of the rate of profit. The social capacity to produce surplus value is constantly reallocated among the different branches of production (including exchange specialisations) ensuring the *pro rata* remuneration of all capitals participating in the operations of the circuit. Even at this high level of abstraction it is clear that the principle of capital mobility cannot operate in the same manner between interest-bearing capital and capitals integral to the circuit. To join interest-bearing capital, for instance, industrial capital has to abandon the circuit altogether, thereby removing itself from the social capacity to generate surplus value, instead of merely reallocating this capacity among different tasks. On the other hand, by permanently transforming itself into industrial capital, interest-bearing capital also establishes the conditions for its future reconstitution through augmentation of the flows of the circuit of total social capital and the resultant idle money.[8]

A full demonstration of the normal tendency of the rate of interest to lie below the rate of profit requires a considerably more complex analysis than the above general considerations. Two factors are critical in this connection. First, the inherently cyclical motion of real accumulation must be considered, during which the rate of interest and the rate of profit tend to move in opposite directions. This aspect of the capitalist business cycle will be considered in detail in Chapter 6.[9] Suffice it to state here that, although the average rate of profit in principle forms an upper limit for the average rate of interest, there are moments in the cycle when interest payments peak and consume not just the profits but also the very capital of functioning capitalists. These are precisely the moments at which the average rate of profit does not form an upper limit for the average rate of interest. Despite its socially beneficial function of mobilising and reallocating spare funds, interest-bearing capital can also eat into the capital of industrial capitalists. This potentially destructive role is fully in line with interest-bearing capital's relatively autonomous, partly external position with respect to total social capital. Second, the structure of the credit system, its institutional ability systematically to mobilise funds across society, also matters greatly for determination of the rate of interest relative to the rate of profit. Evidently, several significant institutional and historical differences exist among the various credit systems that have appeared in the history of capitalism. It is claimed in the next chapter that a certain institutional structure, namely that possessed by Britain in the heyday of liberal capitalism, can be considered as the general reference point for the developed capitalist credit system.

A further important point with regard to the relationship between the rate of interest and the rate of profit is that no objective material aspect of social reproduction is reflected in the formation of the rate of interest. Put differently, there is no objective material basis for the division of total profit into interest and profit of enterprise. The rate of profit captures in a capitalistic way the fundamental process of generating spare resources for reinvestment, and the sharing of these among competing capitals. There is a material foundation for the rate of profit, found in the organic composition of the participating capitals, the length of the turnover of capital, and the length and the division of the working day. No profound relationship of capitalist reproduction is expressed in the rate of interest. That is the deeper meaning of Marx's well-known rejection of the notion of a 'natural' rate of interest (ibid., p. 487).[10] The rate of interest simply expresses a division of total profit, based entirely on the balance of demand for and supply of interest-bearing capital. Regularities can certainly be identified in the motion of the rate of interest in the course of the business cycle, but there is no more profound foundation for these than alterations in the market conjuncture. The rate of interest is a pure price without a necessary relationship to the law of value. Precisely because of this, however, the rate of interest achieves a sharp clarity in the markets for interest-bearing capital. In contrast the rate of profit, expressed as the movement of capital among different branches of production, cannot achieve a similar numerical clarity (ibid., pp. 488–90).

Finally, the above analysis should not be interpreted as implying that banking credit is solely the concentration and reallocation of idle funds generated in the turnover of capital. Credit is an inherently flexible and pliable social relationship. In a developed credit system, to acquire credit is to possess the liabilities of financial institutions. It is certainly possible that such liabilities can be created within the credit system without stagnant funds having first accrued from real accumulation. The social role of the credit system is, at one remove, to concentrate money value disengaged from the circuit, but, at another remove, it is also to take a view on the prospects of real accumulation in order to allocate interest-bearing capital. Financial institution liabilities can be created purely on the expectation of future returns, and in the hope that these will validate the liabilities. The credit system is necessarily a repository of elements of rational foresight within the unplanned order of the capitalist system. By the same token, the formation of the rate of interest also appears to depend on expectations and assessments of the future. In this regard, individual capitalists will not normally borrow funds if the rate of interest exceeds the expected rate of profit on projected activities. That is yet another aspect of Marx's fundamental proposition that the rate of interest normally lies within zero and the average rate of profit.

3.3 PRECAPITALIST MONEY LENDING

3.3.1 Usury and Interest-Bearing Capital

Marx (1894, pp. 728–9) claimed that interest-bearing capital (more properly usurer's capital) is an ancient form of capital; in precapitalist societies usurer's capital was mainly lent to 'extravagant magnates' (usually landowners) and small producers (usually peasants and artisans). Usurer's capital had an essentially external position relative to the core of social reproduction in precapitalist societies. Moreover its disposition was predatory, often destroying the conditions of existence of both landowners and small peasants through the extraction of interest. The fundamental reason for the external position and the predatory disposition of usurer's capital was that no mechanism for the self-expansion of value in society could be found prior to the establishment of industrial capitalism. Similarly to trade, usury was present in the 'intermundia' of the precapitalist world (ibid., p. 733). Interest-bearing capital, on the other hand, is quite distinct from usury in that the credit system, through which interest-bearing capital is continually constituted, is fully integrated into the capitalist mode of production. Banking credit is a condition of capitalist production, while the latter regularly generates the wherewithal of banking credit. Nevertheless, despite its integral position in capitalist reproduction, interest-bearing capital possesses a relative autonomy, which at times translates into the ability to destroy the conditions of existence of industrial capitalists. Interest-bearing capital retains some of the predatory character of primitive usury.

3.3.2   Money Lending and Social Reproduction

The relation of credit to the reproduction of precapitalist societies is a more complex issue than the relationship of money to their reproduction. In Chapter 2 it was argued that money arose in the course of the impersonal and anarchical contact between commodity owners who belonged to different societies or communities. Money penetrated precapitalist societies and acquired a host of complex functions, but it remained external to the core of their reproduction until the rise of capitalism. In marked contrast, credit in general could not arise at the point of contact of different societies. Credit is essentially trust and it is very unlikely that such trust existed among people not bound by customary, religious, familial and hierarchical ties. The origins of credit probably lie in the reciprocal gift-giving characteristic of precapitalist peasant communities, as Mauss (1954) argued.[11] The creation of reciprocal obligations through the giving of gifts or the offer of help in times of need, is an ineluctable part of the existence of small peasant communities even in modern times.

In archaic and classical Greek the words to give, *didomi*, and to lend, *daneizein*, are inextricably linked, and a process of transformation of the former into the latter can be identified (Millett, 1991, pp. 28–30). Credit in the archaic Greek context is still hard to separate from the reciprocal, obligation-creating exchange of products and labour typical of Hesiod's seventh-century Boeotia. However the classical Greek word for lending money at interest is *tokizein*, an entirely separate concept that probably refers to money's apparent ability to give birth (*tokos*) to more money. Here we have a different form of credit, one that relies on the existence of money to confer to it a thing-like objectivity, but also one that begins to shed the customary and communal garb of reciprocal gift giving. Inasmuch as money entered precapitalist societies from the outside, money-lending easily acquired the character of an alien and potentially malevolent practice.

Classical literature provides ample testimony of the existence of money lending in classical Greece. In the Athenian world of the fourth century BC, about which evidence is plentiful though fragmentary, the lending of money was undertaken on a non-professional basis by rich landowners and by temples, and on a professional basis by 'bankers' (*trapezites*). Money lending in classical Athens, despite some lending of money by bankers and others to finance long-distance shipping, typically had non-productive purposes: to pay prisoners' ransom, to sustain prestige expenditure, to confront exceptional circumstances, (ibid., ch. 3). Borrowing was almost never undertaken in order to invest and expand wealth. Consequently the repayment of loans was rarely easy, and often entailed the misuse of state power by the elite. Frequently the money lender's purpose was to appropriate other people's land, or to lead the borrower into debt bondage, a state akin to slavery (Finley, 1981, chs 4, 9).

Despite the weight of evidence and argument, some historians are still attempting to prove that classical Greek money lending was akin to modern capitalist banking credit. Their efforts often involve incredible assertions, and the unthinking acceptance of the spurious timelessness of neoclassical economics, as for instance in the work of Cohen (1992) and Thompson (1978, 1982). However there is no evidence that the classical bankers operated in the modern manner, that is, by systematically collecting deposits and other spare funds and advancing these as loans in order to promote economic activity. No evidence has been found of a system of banking credit, with clearing, book transfers, cheques or any kind of credit money at all (Finley, 1973, p. 141). Moreover the bankers' social status was low as they were often manumitted slaves. The lending of money in ancient Greece was an activity peripheral to the core of society's economic reproduction. Lending money as a regular economic activity has meaning only if it regularly results in more money. For money lending to become intrinsic to any mode of production the latter must possess a systematic social mechanism for expanding value in the money form. This was conspicuously absent in the classical Greek world, which notoriously lacked both the practice and the notion of wealth expansion through the reinvestment of surpluses. For the Greeks, wealth accrued through direct exploitation of the labour of others (mostly slaves), through war or through sheer chance. Moreover the contempt of the landowning ruling class for the lowly (*banausic*) activities of craftsmen and artisans, further contributed to blocking the introduction of technical advances in production. This attitude was hardened in the chaos of the wars of the Hellenistic and early Roman period, which brought a tremendous growth in the number of slaves.

Precisely because it was external to economic reproduction, money lending had a deeply corrosive character in classical Greece. The accumulation of debt by peasants and the subsequent loss of their land were commonly observed phenomena. The Solonic reforms in

Athens in the sixth century BC had two major aims – debt forgiveness and land redistribution – and were probably a response to a very serious social crisis. The same two demands were made of the landowning rich by the free poor with determined regularity across the Greek world in the subsequent centuries (though not in fourth-century Athens). The rise of Rome worsened the lot of the poor in the Greek world as the Romans invariably sided with the rich landowners. Money lending, often connected with tax farming, was a quick way to fabulous fortunes in the early Roman era. Rapacious Italian tax farmers and bankers (*publicani* and *negotiatores*) pitilessly bled Asia Minor white,[12] and with an equal lack of pity they were massacred in the Mithridatic revolt of the first century BC, the last frantic striving by the Greeks for national independence with social justice. The Romans craved gold, a point brutally underscored by Mithridates when he ordered that molten gold be poured down the throat of Manius Aquillius, the captured Roman governor of Asia Minor.

In general the economic role of money lending in precapitalist societies was consistent with their imperfect monetisation. A sum of money could possibly be augmented through tax, war or the sale of property or produce, but there was no systematic social mechanism to effect such an augmentation. While interest could arise as a form of remuneration consistent with the general possibility of money's augmentation, it lacked a systematic social foundation. Therefore money lending could neither finance production nor give rise to a market-based, economy-wide rate of interest. Precisely because it lacked a firm social foundation, precapitalist money lending assumed a predatory rapaciousness that profoundly disturbed the core of economic reproduction. Conditions permitting, interest could absorb the bulk of surplus labour, and even eat into the assets of small producers and the wealth of landowners. In stark contrast to usurious money lending, the character of modern interest-bearing capital emerges clearly when the latter's advance is considered in connection with the circuit of industrial capital. The regular augmentation of money value and the financing of production by means of credit, both of which are natural aspects of industrial capitalism, provide objective foundations for the advance of interest-bearing capital and the payment of interest. Still, interest-bearing capital maintains an arms-length relationship with the underlying material reproduction of capitalist society. Some aspects of the ancient predatory and destructive character of money lending are still manifested in the course of capitalist crises.

3.4 NEOCLASSICAL THEORY OF INTEREST AND OPTIMAL CONTRACT DESIGN

It is instructive to juxtapose the above discussion with the recent neoclassical literature on the analytical foundations of lending and banking. This work incorporates the economics of information, and attempts to provide theoretical foundations for the influence exercised by credit institutions and markets on growth and output fluctuations. Its underpinnings are profoundly neoclassical insofar as it adopts methodological individualism. It has no fundamental quarrel with the Arrow–Debreu general equilibrium analysis of exchange. General equilibrium, since it assumes that perfect information is available to all market participants, does not significantly differentiate between own capital and borrowed capital, and leaves no room for intermediary financial institutions such as banks. The recent literature's aim is to establish analytical room for credit within a general equilibrium framework, given that information is asymmetrically held by exchange participants.

The original insight in this field goes back to Akerlof's (1970) 'lemons' paper, in which he argued that sellers know more about their used cars than prospective buyers. Consequently the market price reflects the buyers' perception of average quality, and the sellers of poor cars ('lemons') receive a premium at the expense of high-quality cars; this could lead to the collapse of the used car market. Along similar lines Jaffee and Russell (1976) argued that lenders cannot distinguish between 'good' and 'bad' borrowers prior to lending. Thus the interest charged must contain a premium to cover bad risks. Moreover, since the probability of default varies with the size of the loan, adverse selection sets in: 'good' borrowers prefer small loans whereas 'bad' borrowers prefer large loans. In a slightly different vein, Leland and Pyle (1977), argued that entrepreneurs know more about their projects than the lenders. The borrowing entrepreneur signals the true value of the project to the market by dedicating an amount of own capital to the project, varying directly with the project's risk. Gathering information about project riskiness cannot be done commercially because the information becomes public and loses its value soon after it starts being traded. Consequently financial intermediaries emerge to collect such information, incorporate it directly in their own assets, reduce their risk by diversifying their assets, and hence need not hold large amounts of their own capital.

Townsend (1979) made a significant breakthrough in this debate. In an Arrow–Debreu world of perfect information there is no room for a typical debt contract, that is, for an agreement to return to the lender a certain sum of money (principal plus interest) that is not conditional on the actual returns to the borrower's project. In this world, on average it is more beneficial for the owner of money to enter into a partnership-type agreement with the project owner, dividing the actual project proceeds when these materialise, rather than enter into a standard debt contract.[13] Townsend's explanation of the existence of money lending was premised on the assumption that the owner of a project knows more about the latter than the owner of money. An agreement to divide the actual proceeds gives to the project owner an incentive to lie and defraud the money owner by concealing some or all of the returns. To avoid this moral hazard, the money owner must monitor the project owner. Since monitoring is a costly process, the optimal contractual arrangement between money owner and project owner is not immediately apparent and must be investigated.

Townsend offered a resolution for this theoretical problem, which was subsequently refined by several others, including Diamond (1984), Gale and Hellwig (1985) and Williamson (1986), and achieved elegant mathematical simplicity in the work of Morgan (1994). Given the methodological individualism of neoclassicism, the optimal monitoring arrangement is the one that maximises the money owner's expected returns (and so the expected utility) from the putative agreement. Monitoring, however, is costly and this entails a dichotomous solution. A fixed return is specified for the money owner. If it is received there is no monitoring of the project owner, thus avoiding the monitoring costs; if it is not received the project owner declares default (bankruptcy), the actual returns are monitored and as much as possible of the original advance is recouped. Therefore, in a world of informational asymmetry, the optimal contract between a money owner and a project owner is debt with the possibility of costly default.

This fundamental analysis of the nature of debt has been extensively used to derive conclusions about the nature and practice of financial intermediation. If there are many lenders for the same borrower the deadweight costs of monitoring are multiplied in a socially wasteful way. For Diamond (1984), financial intermediaries are an endogenously arising, socially superior solution to the monitoring problem. Banks are 'delegated monitors': they write, monitor and enforce contracts with ultimate borrowers; they hold well-diversified portfolios; they give a smoother pattern to the returns on lender assets. Diversification is key since it makes the probability of bank bankruptcy very small. Consequently, while the monitoring costs are not duplicated by the various lenders, the banks need not be monitored themselves. Subsequent extensions of this approach have aimed at establishing reasons why the banks might ration the volume of their lending to below the market clearing levels, a practice that might contribute to business fluctuations if these had already been set off by some external shock (see for example Bernanke and Gertler, 1989; Morgan, 1994).[14]

Marxist political economy has argued for more than a century that interest results from a conventional division of total profit; a division, moreover, that reflects nothing other than a balance between demand and supply of interest-bearing capital. In this regard the modern literature has rediscovered the wheel, adding some entirely unselfconscious insight into the noxious nature of trust among capitalists. The 'proof' of the optimality of the debt contract, on the other hand, bears all the methodological hallmarks of neoclassicism. What matters is not how the world is, but why it diverges from the ideal model of market interaction among individuals. The institutional and historical background within which such interaction is possible is entirely omitted from the equations. The 'proof' is only a game in logic, equally applicable to all other instances in which a person with a material resource meets a person with some specialist knowledge, exchange being the only social nexus between the two. That there is nothing specific to debt in the conclusions of this type of analysis is evident from the fact that similar results arise from application of the analysis to the labour market.

Analysis based on political economy need not prove that a dichotomous debt contract is somehow optimal: it is a social and historical fact that the lending of money, aimed at interest generation, differs generically from direct investment in production, aimed at profit. The point is to specify the precise social content of this difference, as well as the social relations involved in the interaction of profit and interest. With this in mind, the recent theory's assumption of a pure 'money owner' confronting a pure 'project owner' is weaker than Marx's analogous (and problematic) distinction between a 'monied' and a 'functioning' capitalist. At least Marx ascribed a definite social content to this distinction in terms of fractions of the capitalist class sharing out the available surplus value. However, as argued above, it is still misleading to assume pure 'money owners' and 'project owners'. The capitalist lending of money is best analysed in terms of the mobilisation of stagnant money generated in the essential motion of accumulation. Industrial, 'functioning', capitalists also partake of the advance of 'monied' capital. In a capitalist economy, moreover, interest is a pure price that acquires society-wide applicability when a credit system is in place to concentrate and direct spare money capital towards the social mechanism for the expansion of value. The return of interest-bearing capital to its owner expresses that capital's relative autonomy with respect to real accumulation, its arms-length relationship with the latter, and hence its potentially predatory and essentially indifferent attitude to the process of production.

The asymmetry of information between lender and borrower is a poor substitute for the distinction between idle money becoming interesting-bearing capital alongside accumulation, and capital functioning in the production of surplus value. In neoclassical theory, the richness of social determinations implicit to the distinction between interest-bearing capital and industrial capital, and the primacy of the production of surplus value in the course of social reproduction, collapse into the banal observation that the lender usually knows little about the business of the borrower.

Part II

Principles of Credit and Finance

The most fundamental meaning of credit is trust. Credit denotes the belief and expectation that payment will be effected at some later point in time for goods supplied now, or that lent money will be returned. In a capitalist economy, highly sophisticated mechanisms of credit (a credit system) are invariably put in place. Money, particularly in its functions of means of hoarding and means of payment, serves as one of the foundations of the credit system. The principal forms and functions of the capitalist credit system emerge spontaneously in the process of facilitating commodity transactions among capitals. These forms and functions of the credit system involve the utilisation of idle money capital (hoards) generated in the turnover of capital. As the credit system grows, credit money (such as commercial bills and banknotes) becomes an important means of circulation.

Finance denotes the several ways of providing either money capital or simply money funds to a person or firm. Credit naturally constitutes an essential component of finance. However finance is broader than credit; it also relates to the mobilisation of idle money in the form of joint-stock capital rather than simply lending and borrowing. Chapters 4 and 5 analyse, respectively, the credit system and joint-stock capital as the principal constituents of finance in a capitalist economy. Chapter 6 turns to the monetary and credit aspects of the capitalist business cycle, especially its crisis phase. Chapter 7 completes Part II by examining the nature and functions of central banks.

4 The Credit System

4.1. PRELIMINARY REMARKS

4.1.1 The Early Historical Development of Credit

The emergence of elementary forms of credit long preceded industrial capitalism. Forms of money lending and interest payment generally appeared in various precapitalist societies in the practice of usury. Centuries before capitalism became the dominant mode of production, rudimentary bills of exchange functioned as convenient means of economising on the costs (and reducing the risks) of sending money to distant places. After the sixteenth century, as mercantile capitalism reached maturity, bills of exchange (or commercial bills), which were the chief form of payment in the operations of foreign trade, were increasingly employed as an important means of facilitating commodity transactions among merchants in the domestic economy. Modern banks appeared in Western Europe as institutions of finance that gave credit by employing their own liabilities, such as customers' deposits, in the discount of commercial bills. Unlike the money-lenders of old, the banks' ability to extend credit was not limited by their own capital. The capitalist market economy penetrated the core of Western European society in the course of the protracted primitive accumulation of capital that took place during the mercantilist era, and it firmly established itself as the main arena of social reproduction during the English industrial revolution. Against this background the forms of credit further developed their organic connections with each other and with real accumulation, emerging finally as a credit system, an integral mechanism of the domestic economy. The representative paradigm of a capitalist credit system appeared in the age of liberal nineteenth-century capitalism in England.

The leading role of cotton manufacturing in early nineteenth-century English capitalism shaped the main features of what can be seen as the representative, spontaneously emerging, capitalist credit system. The latter engaged mainly in the advance of mostly short-term commercial and banking credit to enhance the fluidity of motion of industrial circulating capital. In this manner the various forms of commercial credit that were originally employed in international trade became firmly entrenched in intrasocial transactions among industrial capitals. Long-term investment in fixed capital, on the other hand, tended to be undertaken by individual capitalists, financed by profits. The relatively modest fixed capital investment required by the cotton industry could be, and was, provided by the numerous, competing, self-financing capitalists. In addition the fact that giant monopolistic corporations (industrial and banking) were neither numerous nor crucial to capitalist accumulation also contributed to the shaping of the representative credit system. It became habitual to think of the dominant banking practice of advancing short-term credit, typically by discounting commercial bills, as 'sound banking' in the Anglo-Saxon tradition. However the sound banking principle neither guaranteed the stability of the credit system nor prevented the emergence of periodic credit crises, an unavoidable aspect of the capitalist business cycle.

4.1.2 The Representative Form of the Capitalist Credit System

Three important principles for the theoretical analysis of the capitalist credit system have already been established in Part I of this volume. First, the several functions of money, particularly as means of hoarding and payment, are indispensable building blocks for credit theory. Marx's theory of money is superior to classical Ricardian theory in this respect as the latter tends to narrow down the functions of money to means of circulation alone. Second, money hoarding in a capitalist economy acquires an objective foundation in the turnover of capital. In the course of the latter, stagnant money necessarily emerges in the form of depreciation funds for fixed capital, reserves for the expansion of accumulation, reserves guarding against price fluctuations, and reserves that help maintain the continuity of production in the face of the constant alternation of production and circulation. The modern credit system is constructed as a set of specifically capitalist social mechanisms that utilise stagnant money and promote the further generation of surplus value. Third, it is problematic to attempt an analysis of the credit system on the premise of 'monied' capitalists, who possess money capital available for lending (loanable capital), and 'functioning' capitalists, who possess industrial and other projects. This approach tends to treat stagnant money capital as the result of the hoarding and saving decisions of monied capitalists, largely extrinsic to the turnover of total social capital. Yet under normal circumstances, only capitalists who already possess some capital are allowed access to loans for investment. Purely 'functioning' capitalists are an ideally abstract assumption. Given capitalist social relations, it is very unlikely that the owner of the money capital with which it is proposed that a project be entirely realised would simply become a lender. Rather the money owner would probably become the owner and supervisor of the proposed project.[1] Thus unlike other forms of revenue, interest is not the exclusive economic foundation of a social class, but also accrues to industrial and merchant capitalists. It accords better with even casual observation to treat interest as a form of internal redistribution of surplus value among all capitals participating in the process of accumulation.

The approach adopted in this work is that the core foundation of the credit system is provided by the generation of idle money capital in the course of the turnover of total social capital. Idle funds become interest-bearing (loanable) capital through the mediation of the credit system, and are subsequently utilised by all the capitals that participate in the generation and realisation of surplus value. This is also the approach suggested by Marx in several places in the second volume of *Capital*. Idle money generated out of the savings of social groups unrelated to the circuit of total social capital also becomes internal to the motion of total social capital; such savings are absorbed by the credit system, directed to real accumulation through lending, and recreated as loanable capital when loans are repaid. Moreover, the motion of the rate of interest, which reflects the fluctuations of demand and supply of loanable capital in the course of the business cycle, can be adequately theorised when the credit system is treated as a social mechanism constructed by all the capitals participating in accumulation.

The structured separate interests between capitalists who mediate the motion of loanable capital, capitalists who receive significant interest revenues and capitalists who directly participate in real accumulation, can be systematically analysed based on the above analytical premises. The array of social groups that receive significant money revenues in the form of interest is complex and changes with the development of capitalism. In late capitalism, income in the form of interest is received by industrial and commercial firms, individual savers among the middle and even the working class, and substantial numbers of relatively modest money owners who derive most of their income from money savings ('rentiers'). To derive the social functions of interest and the credit system from the putative transactions between 'monied' and 'functioning' capitalists is to miss much of the complexity of the above relations. The fundamental theory of interest is best expounded on the premise that the credit system is a mechanism for the concentration and allocation of loanable capital among industrial and commercial capitals.

The following three conditions are necessary for the initial theorisation of the capitalist credit system; first, commercial credit is regularly advanced among several competing capitalist firms; second, short-term loans for circulating capital are regularly advanced by competing banks; and third, there is regular use, both domestically and internationally, of commodity money (gold). This framework broadly corresponds to the empirical reality of the English credit system during the age of liberal capitalism, and allows us to construct the representative paradigm of a capitalist credit system. The theoretical structure developed below serves to clarify the essential functions of interfirm commercial credit and basic banking credit in a manner that has broad applicability to contemporary capitalism.

Modern banks also advance loans for long-term investment in fixed capital. Typical countries for such banking practices are Germany and Japan, where capitalism developed later than in England.[2] The specific character of this aspect of modern banking can be naturally incorporated into the analytical framework developed here, a task undertaken in Chapter 5. As long as the capitalist credit system remains a spontaneously emerging social mechanism that mobilises stagnant money capital, the analysis of the representative capitalist credit system proposed here continues to offer many valid insights into the apparently altered credit practices of contemporary capitalism.[3]

4.2   COMMERCIAL CREDIT

Marx (1894, p. 610) defined commercial credit as the 'credit that capitalists involved in the reproduction process give one another. This forms the basis of the credit system. Its representative is the bill of exchange, a promissory note with a fixed date of payment, i.e. "a document of deferred payment".' Commercial credit facilitates commodity transactions among industrial and commercial capitals by deferring payment. In its representative state, commercial credit gives rise to financial instruments such as promissory notes and bills of exchange. In the later stages of capitalism, commercial credit is still widely employed among firms, but frequently takes the form of book credits. The basis of commercial credit is provided by the function of money as means of payment, as the latter is found in simple precapitalist commodity circulation (as is the corresponding relationship of creditor and debtor). Historically, bills of exchange were used for the transmission of money to distant places (Kindleberger, 1984, pp. 39–41). Money transmission combined with deferral of payments provided the broad basis for the proliferation of credit relations in the capitalist economy. As industrial capitalism took root, commercial credit progressed from a form of economic intercourse found primarily among merchants engaging in foreign trade to a set of economic relations integral to the domestic economy. By utilising the idle money capitals generated in the turnover of industrial capital, commercial credit allowed more efficient commodity selling and buying among capitals.

To illustrate the character of commercial credit, a chain of four related capitalists directly or indirectly involved in successive production processes, is assumed in Figure 4.1 below: a cotton weaver (A), a spinner (B), a trader of raw cotton (C) and a raw cotton grower (D). This example accords with the historical basis of our analytical abstractions. The main theoretical conclusions of the analysis are applicable to contemporary forms of interfirm commercial credit, though the specific differences made by institutional and historical developments should not be ignored. Commercial credit in its representative form gives rise to commercial bills in the form of promissory notes or bills of exchange discussed immediately below.

4.2.1 Promissory Notes and Bills of Exchange

The most elementary form of commercial credit emerges in transactions typified by the purchase of cotton thread by a cotton weaver (A) from a spinner (B) through the drawing of a promissory note with a fixed date of payment (on the assumption that B can wait for the deferred payment). To be able to accept A's promissory note it is necessary that B should possess idle money capital sufficient to allow production to continue during the period of the deferral of payment, say three months.[4] In effect B is sustaining the sale of his or her commodity output (cotton thread) by mobilising his or her idle money capital. For A, this simple form of commercial credit is an effective technique with which to continue or expand production.

A promissory note is a promise to make a return payment of a certain amount of money after a specified period of time; it is not a promise to return the commodity transacted (cotton thread). Though it is issued and received in relation to a commodity transaction, a promissory note represents debt of a certain monetary value with a specified maturity time. Assuming that no further credit is forthcoming, A has to accrue a definite sum of money as means of payment in order to settle with B when the note falls due. It is, however, open to B to endorse A's promissory note and hand it over to trader C when purchasing raw cotton. Having added a further endorsement, C may use the note to purchase raw cotton from cotton grower D. The endorsement of B and C signifies the existence of joint liability as far as the person who gives commercial credit is concerned. If A is insolvent at the due date, either B or C has to pay the promised amount of money to D, the final owner of the note.

Joint liability enhances the acceptability of the endorsed promissory note, especially when the endorsers are known to the likely receiver of the note. In this manner a promissory note functions as credit money and enables the purchase and sale of commodities among a series of capitalists, in the above instance the chain A–B–C–D. Such transactions lead to the spontaneous emergence of credit money, requiring neither the existence of sophisticated financial institutions nor the intervention of the state. The promissory note is different from cash in that a return payment must be made on the due date, a payment for which there is joint liability. Consequently the promissory note's acceptability as credit money critically depends on the creditworthiness of the capitalists who have drawn or endorsed it.

Bills of exchange represent a more general form of commercial credit. Under the external pressure of competition, spinner B seeks to match the commercial credit he or she has given when selling output (thread) to A by commercial credit received in purchasing inputs (raw cotton) from C. To achieve this, B can draw a bill of exchange that commands A to pay C a certain amount of money, the equivalent of thread sold, on a due date after a certain period. The bill is accepted by A and is then passed to C in exchange for the raw cotton sold to B; C expects final payment from A. This basic process is illustrated in Figure 4.1. If A cannot pay on the due date, C, or the eventual owner of the bill, can immediately demand payment from B who is necessarily a surety, jointly liable for the bill. Since a bill of exchange bears at least two names jointly responsible for payment, it is more acceptable in exchange for commodities than a promissory note bearing a single name, other things equal.

Figure 4.1 A chain of commercial credit

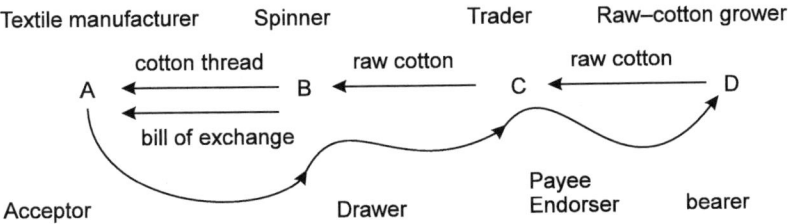

Trader C can subsequently endorse the bill to signify further joint liability, and pass it on to cotton grower D in exchange for raw cotton. A's debt to C is thus further changed into a debt to D. Their inherently greater acceptability implies that bills of exchange can acquire broader circulation than promissory notes as elementary capitalist credit money among industrial and commercial capitalists. Since bills of exchange are private promises to pay, issued and received among industrial and commercial capitalists according to their own will and necessity, they introduce elasticity in the expansion of transactions among capitalists, relatively independently of the existing amount of money or loanable money capital.[5]

4.2.2 The Functions and Limitations of Commercial Credit

The main function of commercial credit is to enable capitalists cooperatively (and individually) to economise on capital in circulation. Commercial credit thereby facilitates the increase of capital directly engaged in production and the further generation of surplus value. In the example above, commodity capitals in circulation (cotton thread and raw cotton) enter the production processes of capitalists A and B faster than if payments had been undertaken solely by cash. By receiving commercial credit, capitalists A and B can spare a part of their money capital and increase the efficiency of their capital as a whole in producing surplus value. In principle, capitalists who advance commercial credit also benefit since they economise on the costs of circulation (such as storage of finished output) and on the money reserve needed to guard against price fluctuations. Moreover they may be able to use the issued bill to purchase necessary commodity inputs from other capitalists, as C did above. By this token, when transactions are repeatedly completed through the use of commercial credit, capitalists such as A and B above can spare a part of the idle money capital they have to hold in order to ensure continuity in the process of production. The economised money capital can be converted into capital directly engaged in production.

A chain of commercial credit contains a terminal capitalist, D, who acts as the final holder of the bill of exchange until maturity, and has to wait for the deferred payment. Put differently, there are two polar positions in the chain of commercial credit: the terminal capitalist, D, who only gives credit, and the initial capitalist, A, who only receives credit. To maintain the continuity of his or her own production process until the bill matures, the terminal capitalist must be able to mobilise sufficient idle money capital, probably hoarded through the turnover of his or her own capital. This ability on the part of the terminal capitalist is a precondition for a chain of transactions mediated by commercial credit to be sustained. In this regard, the mobilisation of idle money capital by D not only serves the purposes of this particular capitalist but also accommodates the acceleration of transactions and the extension of production of the other participants in the chain of commercial credit.

Commercial credit can foster the expansion of capitalist production as a whole. By economising on the amount of idle capital held overall, and by speeding the turnover of capital, commercial credit can raise the general rate of profit. Moreover commercial credit is a vital element in equalising the rate of profit. Consider, for instance, branches of industry that are earning above-average profits due to raised output prices caused by a relative shortage of supply. By relying more heavily on commercial credit these branches of industry can increase their purchases of means of production faster than others. This contributes to the faster relative growth of their output, leading to a lowering of their rates of profit towards the average. Branches of industry in the opposite position reduce their credit-financed purchases of means of production, and increase the sale of their output through the advance of their own commercial credit. In this complex manner, commercial credit usually helps to readjust the imbalance between industrial spheres and serves to equalise the rate of profit. However the beneficial effect of commercial credit cannot always be assumed: under certain conditions, considered in detail in Chapter 6, commercial credit can become a destructive influence on capitalist accumulation.

There are severe limitations to the role commercial credit can play relative to real accumulation. First, commercial credit is largely confined to the exchange relations of capitalists whose production processes are intrinsically linked, despite the fact that commercial capitalists, such as C above, could potentially join the industrial capitalists and broaden the network of commercial relations. It is not likely that commercial credit could result in the emergence of credit relations among capitalists engaging in unrelated production processes, for instance between car-making and cloth weaving. Second, beyond a certain point in a chain of commercial credit the sum of money due and the terms of payment of a bill are likely to become unsuitable for further transactions. For instance the money that the raw cotton grower, D, has to pay in order to purchase fertiliser from a trader E may be smaller than the amount due on the bill received from C. Alternatively E may not be able to defer payment for the remaining period to maturity. Third, even with the joint liability of several endorsers, the bill's acceptability might still not be widespread enough: some capitalists might not have sufficient trust to accept the endorsed bill in exchange for their commodities. Consequently the chain of commercial credit formed through a bill of exchange cannot extend without limit, and always has a plain debtor and a plain creditor at, respectively, the beginning and the end. A corollary of these limitations is that the ability of commercial credit to economise on capital in circulation, and to contribute to the raising and equalisation of the rate of profit, is also restricted. Banking credit is a more advanced component of the capitalist credit system, which places credit on a more general social foundation and overcomes the limitations of commercial credit.

4.2.3 Interest in Credit Prices

In commercial credit, interest is generally claimed and accrues as the excess of the credit price over the cash price of commodities. For the purchasing capitalist, rational grounds for the payment of interest can clearly be found in the additional profit obtained through the expansion of accumulation based on commercial credit. The rational grounds on which selling capitalists can claim interest on commercial credit are less clear. Forgone opportunities for profit making cannot provide an answer here. As argued above, capitalists who sell their output by advancing commercial credit are able to do so by mobilising money capital that would have lain idle in the normal course of accumulation. Given the assumed absence of other forms of credit, such mobilised capital does not afford its owners any opportunities for further gain. Rather, the grounds on which interest can be claimed for commercial credit given lie simply in the historical existence of the form of interest in commodity economies. The form of interest has an ancient pedigree and was inherited by capitalism from the historical past; all advances of monetary value, even as the mere price of commodities sold on credit, can thus command interest. By this token it is possible to claim usurious rates of interest in a certain phase of the business cycle in which the opportunity for profit-making generally declines. At such times interest becomes destructive, loses its capitalist rationale for the debtors, and is no longer paid out of additional profit generated through debt.

Interest in commercial credit transactions is not independent of either commodity (credit) prices or of the sale and purchase of commodities. The rate of interest is still buried in credit prices; it cannot be generalised and is individual and particular. For a commodity whose demand increases more rapidly than its supply, the difference between credit price and cash price tends to rise above average, reflecting the anticipated increase in the commodity's market price in the near future. In the opposite case, the difference between cash price and credit price becomes less than the average. Furthermore the individual creditworthiness of debtors in the eyes of creditors inversely affects the rate of interest charged for commercial credit. The absence of a general rate of interest, in this context, originates in the nature of commercial credit: a private credit relation formed between individual capitalists in the process of commodity exchange.

4.3 BANKING CREDIT

4.3.1 The Discounting of Bills of Exchange

Banking credit typically emerges upon a foundation of commercial credit. Banking credit is a capitalist social mechanism that mediates the utilisation of idle money capital among capitalists on a broader scale than that of commercial credit. Bank activities give rise to relations of credit and debit between the banks on the one side, and several industrial and commercial capitals on the other. Within the analytical framework specified earlier, bank liabilities are typically formed through the receipt of money deposits or the issuing of private banknotes. At first sight the issuing of banknotes appears more actively to sustain the supply of bank credit, compared with the passive receipt of deposits. However both forms of bank liability operate in a fundamentally similar manner. A bank can advance credit to a customer (and so acquire assets on its own balance sheet) either by creating a deposit in the customer's favour or by directly issuing banknotes to the customer. Within our analytical framework, and as Figure 4.2 shows, a bank typically advances credit by discounting bills of exchange or promissory notes generated in commercial credit. On the asset side of the bank's balance sheet appear commercial bills, and on the liability side banknotes and deposits.[6]

In their representative form, banknotes are a bank's promissory notes: they are written promises to pay on sight a quantity of commodity money. Banknotes are a higher grade of credit money, and have a broader circulation than private credit money based on commercial credit. The limitations of fixed nominal value and set maturity date, which characterise commercial bills, do not exist when credit money takes the form of banknotes. If capitalist D in the chain of commercial credit described above is unable to purchase inputs using a received bill of exchange, he or she could complete the transaction by obtaining banknotes at a bank in exchange for the bill. The bank does not pay D the full nominal value of the bill but discounts the latter by a certain amount, the discount being a form of interest. If the annual rate of interest is 6 per cent for example, a £10 000 bill with three months to maturity bears a discount of roughly £150; £9850 in banknotes are advanced by the bank in exchange for the bill. The bank thereby holds a financial asset (a bill upon a debtor A), and simultaneously creates a monetary liability in the form of banknotes issued. When A pays £10 000 in settlement of the bill on the due date, the bank recoups the principal of £9850 plus interest of £150.

Figure 4.2 A simplified bank balance sheet

ASSETS	LIABILITIES
Reserves	Own capital
Loans	Banknotes
Commercial bills	Deposits

Capitalists who obtain banknotes by discounting bills can usually accelerate the turnover of their capital, thereby increasing their profits, all other things being equal. Consequently rational grounds exist for the payment of interest as a share of the additional profits. The burden of interest on a discounted bill of exchange is shared among the various capitalists who have employed the bill on its way to the bank, such as A, B, C and D above. The distribution of this burden depends on the rate of interest contained in the credit price of the commodities sold in each individual transaction, as well as on the length of time the bill has remained in the hands of each capitalist. Moreover the interest obtained by banks as discount is no longer buried in the credit prices of commodities but appears overtly as interest on a loan of money. The obvious presence of interest as a distinct form of remuneration inevitably sharpens the capitalists' awareness of interest contained in the credit prices of commodities exchanged on the basis of commercial credit.

4.3.2   The Liabilities of Banks, Bank Capital and Bank Profit

In the course of bill discounting, banks simultaneously acquire assets in the form of bills and create liabilities in the form of issued banknotes. Capitalists who sell bills to banks might spend less than the full amount of the proceeds in the first instance, placing the balance as deposits with the banks. From the standpoint of the banks, however, banknotes issued to the public and deposits received are similar liabilities. To support both types of liability, especially to be able to meet demands for the immediate payment of liabilities, a bank must possess certain reserves of cash. When commodity money circulates together with credit money, such reserves typically consist of gold coins. However reserves can also be banknotes of a circulation broader than that of the bank's own notes.[7]

   In the early days of a bank's business the bank's own capital contributes a significant part of the reserves. As a bank matures, however, its reserves increasingly consist of funds accruing from deposits received and payments in settlement of discounted commercial bills. When a bank's own banknotes are returned to it in settlement of bills, the bank's liabilities and assets are correspondingly reduced; the ratio of the bank's reserves to its liabilities rises as a result, making it easier for the bank to advance fresh credit. The effect is similar to that of either the pure inflow of deposits or the simple settlement of bills, both of which directly increase the bank's cash reserves. Since the acquisition of reserves through the inflow of deposits enables a bank more easily to extend credit, banks actively seek to absorb the idle money capitals of industrial and commercial capitalists in the form of deposits. Banks often require industrial and commercial capitalists to place the temporarily redundant part of their bill discounts with the banks as deposits. Industrial and commercial capitalists, on the other hand, benefit by holding bank deposits, as they can economise on the costs of storing, paying and receiving money, as well as on the costs of settling credit transactions.

If a bank can reliably expect to receive plentiful deposits, it need not issue banknotes to pursue its operations. However in order to increase the elasticity of its business, the bank might occasionally issue banker's cheques or bank drafts, that is, the bank's own promissory notes. Since, *ceteris paribus*, a larger inflow of deposits implies a greater facility for lending and more interest earned, banks may themselves pay interest to depositors to encourage the inflow. Insofar as they pay interest on deposits, banks behave as a type of commercial capital whose business is to purchase cheaply the use of money as a commodity in order to sell it at a higher price. This is also the way in which financial intermediation emerges. In this connection, interest appears as a price for a particular commodity, namely the use of money for a certain period of time as a fund.

In a capitalist economy, in principle, banks are profit-making enterprises similar to private industrial and commercial capitals. Thus it is important to examine more fully the uses to which a bank's own capital is put. As mentioned above, in the early days of a bank's business its capital constitutes a significant proportion of its reserves; as the bank matures, however, this source of reserves becomes less important than others. A significant part of bank capital is further advanced to meet the costs of circulation related to monetary processes. These include the costs of money storage and transmission, organising and running financial intermediation, and settling credit transactions. More concretely, bank capital covers the costs of office buildings, business equipment, dealing with credit inquiries, collecting payments on matured bills, storing money, bills and other certificates, and meeting the salaries and wages of bank personnel. These costs are pure costs of circulation (Marx, 1885, pp. 207–14); from the point of view of society as a whole, they are the *faux frais* of social reproduction. As such, these costs are replenished out of the total surplus value produced in a given period.[8]

There are rational grounds for the deduction of bank costs from surplus value because the activities of bank capital result in economies in the amount of capital in circulation, and in the costs of circulation, for industrial and commercial capitals. Bank capital increases the efficiency of production of surplus value as a whole, creating room for the replenishment of its own costs out of surplus value. Without a beneficial effect on their profit rate, it is unlikely that industrial and commercial capitalists would systematically employ the services of banks. A part of the additional profits industrial and commercial capitals obtain by employing the services of banks accrues to the banks themselves as interest. The interest obtained by banks per period is distributed in three ways: one part is paid out to depositors as deposit interest; the second replenishes the bank capital invested and consumed during the period; the third represents the profit on the total bank capital invested.

Theoretically there can be no definite standard (no necessary magnitude) for the amount of bank capital employed in a specialised area of bank activities, nor in the banking business as a whole. With a given amount of bank capital invested in reserves and covering the costs of banking, the amount of money capital that can be collected and lent can vary greatly. It is incorrect to seek to establish a theoretical relationship between the amount of bank capital and the volume of credit handled by the bank, determined by the narrow technical realities of bank credit advance. In this respect there is no analogy at all with the relation between the level of productive activity and the amount of capital in an industrial sphere.[9] Excessive investment in bank capital manifests itself gradually (and as the capitalist business cycle is repeated) in the form of a rate of banking profit that is generally lower than the average rate of profit. As a result the growth of bank capital through the reinvestment of bank profits becomes slower than the social average; a part of bank capital converts into industrial or commercial capital, contributing to the elevation of bank profit towards the average. In the opposite case, the growth of bank capital is accelerated, and parts of industrial and commercial capital move into the banking business. Under generally competitive conditions, the rate of bank profit is subject to the law of the equalisation of the rate of profit, pivoting on the general rate determined by the technical conditions of reproduction of industrial capital.

4.3.3   The Money Market

Banking is a sphere of private business that is open to capital investment in a manner similar to manufacturing and commerce. Individual banks in possession of limited capital tend to concentrate on servicing the needs of particular branches of commerce and industry within given geographical areas.[10] As a result, individual banks' mediation of the movement of the demand and supply of loanable capital has a particular character deriving from the nature of the business activities in the territory served by each bank. In the classic example of English banking of the liberal era, banks in the agricultural areas had a surplus of loanable capital, particularly after the crops had been sold, while banks in areas with rapidly growing industries were generally short of loanable capital.

As far as an individual bank is concerned, fluctuations in the demand and supply of loanable capital are reflected in the ratio of its reserves to its total liabilities, that is, in the bank's reserve ratio. For reasons similar to those applying to determination of the size of bank capital, no clear technical conditions exist that allow for the theoretical determination of the reserve ratio of banks. The reserve ratio naturally exhibits considerable elasticity. Nevertheless, in order to be able to meet demands for cash and make payments, banks are obliged empirically to ascertain a necessary minimum reserve ratio. Banks with relatively plentiful loanable capital, reflected in the plentifulness of their reserves, can more easily assent to loan requests than other banks. If on the other hand their reserves are insufficient, banks find it difficult to expand their lending business.

Banks that cannot satisfy the demand of their customers for loans due to the insufficiency of their reserves, tend to request loans from other banks. The latter can rediscount bills of exchange endorsed by banks, or simply discount other bankers' bills. This is the typical form of credit among banks, the operations of which are concentrated in the money market. The money market is basically a rediscount market for banks, which also functions as an efficient mechanism for the daily settlement of matured commercial and bankers' bills. Money markets tend to have a clearly defined geographical location, usually part of an urban commercial centre.

In the money market the peculiarities of individual banks in discounting bills of exchange, reflecting the territorial specialisation of each bank and the degree of creditworthiness of each bill, tend to disappear. Through trading in the money market, the creditworthiness of bills – both endorsed and issued by banks – becomes homogeneous. Individual banks with access to the money market are able to expand and run their credit business more elastically. At the same time the balance between demand and supply of loanable capital is concentrated in a single market, and rid of local particularities. In the money market, loanable money capital becomes a homogeneous commodity transacted at the same price, that is, the market rate of interest, according to the law of one price. A general rate of interest emerges clearly. The money market rate of interest serves as a general standard for the pricing of individual and local credit advances by banks:

> As far as the permanently fluctuating market rate of interest is concerned, this is a fixed magnitude at any given moment, just like the market price of commodities, because on the money market all capital for loan confronts the functioning capital as an overall mass; i.e. the relationship between the supply of loan capital on the one hand, and the demand for it on the other, is what determines the market level of interest at any given time. This is all the more true, the more the development and associated concentration of the credit system gives loan capital a general social character, and puts it on the money market all at once, simultaneously (Marx, 1894, p. 488).

Despite representing a degree of social centralisation of the processes of credit, the money market remains a mechanism for partial accommodation of the credit requirements of banks. The relatively independent advance of individual banking credit to capitalist businesses continues to exist and flourish alongside the money market. Elementary commercial credit, and the credit relations represented by the spontaneous emergence of commercial bills, also continue to emerge unceasingly across capitalist exchange. Seen as a whole the capitalist credit system forms a pyramid-like structure comprising (from the top downwards) the money market, individual banking credit and spontaneously emerging interfirm commercial credit. The pyramid itself rests upon the process of capitalist accumulation undertaken by industrial and commercial capitals. Within the pyramid-like structure of the credit system, commercial credit and individual banking credit fluctuate relatively independently of the demand and supply of loanable capital in the money market. The money market rate of interest, though it serves as a standard for the rates of interest in commercial and banking credit, is broadly regulated by the conditions of advance of these two forms of credit.

4.3.4 The Central Bank

The character and functions of the central bank are fully discussed in Chapter 7 below. Here they are examined only with respect to the essential features of the representative capitalist credit system. Considered in its fundamental role – above all, independently of the role of the state in the capitalist economy – the central bank is a bank of banks that operates especially in the money market. Generally speaking, banks with regular and easy access to the money market need not issue their own banknotes in order to extend their business flexibly; instead such banks can rely on the receipt of deposits and regular debt repayment by capitalists whose trade is concentrated in the commercial centre. Money market banks are also well placed to receive money funds from more remote banks in order to facilitate debt settlement; furthermore they can easily seek to borrow funds in the money market in order to supplement their cash reserves. Money market banks can increase their efficiency and flexibility in both handling credit transactions and settling payments among themselves, by depositing a part of their reserves with a single bank and then using its banknotes for payments. The economies and elasticities arising from this practice are analogous to those that emerge when individual industrial and commercial capitals hold their reserves with a local bank. A central bank emerges as a private bank with a definite and limited capital size; it fulfils the function of holding the central reserve of the banking system; it can also fail or be replaced by another bank. The pyramid of the capitalist credit system is complete when the central bank emerges at its apex.

The banknotes issued by the central bank are typically used as a means of settlement among the banks in the money market but also in the commercial transactions of the commercial centre; they are 'the coin of wholesale trade' (Marx, 1894, p. 529). Naturally the circulation of central bank notes gradually spreads to commercial and credit transactions between and within local areas closely related to the commercial centre in which the central bank is based. Nevertheless, as long as the central bank remains a private bank with limited capital and circumscribed business activities, central bank notes cannot become a country's generally circulating money. For the bank of banks, issuing and handling banknotes of small face value is not as profitable as similar operations with large notes undertaken among banks.

A spontaneously constructed representative credit system leaves considerable room for the continuing use of commodity money in the payment of wages, an operation that is not conducive to intervention by either bills of exchange or central bank notes.[11] Room is also left for the functioning of commodity money in the settlement of commercial and credit transactions between geographical areas that are relatively remote from the central bank and the money market. In these areas local banks of issue can continue to function as efficient providers of banking credit to capitalist accumulation. These limitations in the circulation of the central bank notes reflect the underlying nature of the capitalist credit mechanism: it is a social structure that originates in international commercial and credit transactions and subsequently penetrates the domestic economy. Without the conscious intervention of the state, the pivotal role of commodity money in effecting settlement in the final instance does not vanish (both domestically and internationally). Despite restrictions in their ambit, commodity money and privately issued bank money persist in domestic circulation.[12]

The persistence of commodity money in domestic circulation, and more so in international transactions, implies that the reserves of the central bank must also comprise commodity money; they become the central gold hoard of a capitalist economy. Now, the balance of demand and supply of loanable money capital is reflected partly in the movements of the rate of interest in the money market, though commercial and banking credit retain considerable autonomy. The emergence of a central bank increases the flexibility of banks in advancing banking credit, and does not eliminate the relative independence of banking credit. Nevertheless, with the emergence of a central bank, fluctuations in bill rediscount demand, debt repayment flows and deposit receipts from other banks in the money market begin to be reflected in fluctuations in the gold reserve of the central bank. The rediscount rate of the central bank in turn reflects the fluctuations in the gold reserves, and serves as a point of reference for the market rate of interest.

The gradual exclusion of commodity money from international payments among capitalist countries during the twentieth century has significantly changed the functions of the central bank and its banknotes. The First World War was an obvious threshold, past which the political decision to spare gold money in domestic and international transactions signalled the strengthening of the regulatory role of the state in the capitalist economy. Nevertheless it is impossible to derive the fundamental principles of the capitalist credit system and the role of the central bank from an analysis of the conditions of the late-twentieth-century credit system. The analysis of credit must commence with the simplest relations of commodity transactions, quite independently of the conscious intervention of the state. The analytical structure of the capitalist credit system proposed above allows for the study of the historical changes during our century, as is indicated broadly in Chapters 7 and 8 below.

4.3.5   The Social Functions of Banking Credit

The social functions of banking credit are similar to those of commercial credit, but significantly expanded. Banking credit economises on stagnant money capital held across industries, thereby promoting the expansion of production and raising the general rate of profit. At the same time, banking credit serves to equalise the rate of profit among industries in a manner analogous to commercial credit. Industries whose products sell at a higher rate of profit due to a shortage of supply, make comparatively heavier use of banking credit in order to expand their purchases of means of production; eventually the shortage of supply is reduced and profits fall towards the average. Industries with a lower than average rate of profit due to excess supply, on the other hand, tend to limit their use of banking credit with opposite results. Banking credit facilitates the reallocation of labour and other resources, making possible the readjustment of market disequilibria and tending to equalise the sectoral rates of profit. In this regard, both banking and commercial credit are mechanisms used by the competitive capitalist economy to realise the law of value, with labour time being reallocated according to social necessity.

Moreover, as far as readjustment of market disequilibria and expansion of production are concerned, the credit system allows much greater flexibility than that inherently possessed by individual industrial capitals, restricted as these are by their limited size, their limited profits, and the need to invest in fixed capital. The pyramid-like capitalist credit system is an example of socialisation of resources, allowing for their more rational utilisation, although under capitalist social relations. Consequently, since the days of John Law social reformers and others have considered the credit system as a social lever for the construction of a more stable and rational economic order. The historical evolution of the capitalist economy, furthermore, appears to point to the still greater socialisation of the credit mechanism, a point that is discussed more fully in Chapter 11.

Rational and socially-minded utilisation of resources through the credit system, however, is impossible fully to realise upon the narrow social basis of capitalism. As long as the credit system remains a capitalist social organisation, it delivers the flexible expansion of production and readjusts market disequilibria within the anarchical market order and in relative ignorance of the future plans of individual economic agents. Though information on capitalist firms is more generally and easily gathered by banks than other capitals (and by the central bank more than by other banks), a significant lack of knowledge remains among banks with respect to their customers. Similarly the central bank remains substantially in the dark about the other banks of the credit system. The relative autonomy of commercial from banking credit, and of the credit of banks from the credit of the central bank, are deeply rooted in these informational relations.[13]

The functioning of the credit system is not always beneficial to capitalist accumulation. Credit institutions constantly run the danger of making losses, or even becoming insolvent, through the unexpected failure of borrowing capitalists to make return payments. During peak periods of capitalist booms in particular, the optimistic mood in the markets conceals an enhanced danger of speculative trading. The creation of speculative booms and their collapse, leading to economic crises, show the limits of the benefits conferred by the credit system to capitalist accumulation, as well as the system's potentially destructive role. The rest of this work investigates whether stability between credit and capitalist accumulation can be achieved, and demonstrates that financial instability originates in the anarchic nature of the capitalist economy.

5 Joint-Stock Capital and the Capital Market

The credit system mobilises idle money capital and enables circulating capital to expand and acquire elasticity. Social organisations constructed on joint-stock capital, on the other hand, mobilise idle money capital and facilitate the creation of large enterprises and the construction of enormous industrial fixed capital far exceeding the limited powers of individual capitals. For Marx (1894, p. 567), formation of joint-stock companies involves a 'tremendous expansion of production, and enterprises which would be impossible for individual capitals'. Shares of joint-stock capitals are traded in the capital market.

5.1 BRIEF HISTORICAL OVERVIEW

5.1.1 The Era of Mercantilism

During the mercantilist era, joint-stock companies were frequently created as a means of effecting extensive joint investment. The basic features of the modern joint-stock company appeared in England towards the middle of the sixteenth century. They represented a fusion of, on the one hand, a form of partnership that was commonly found in capitalist businesses, and on the other, a form of corporation that was commonly found in the medieval crafts guilds. The Russia Company of Merchant Adventurers, founded in 1553, was the earliest known modern joint-stock company. In the same year a company was formed for trade with Africa, and in 1600 the East India Company was founded. The Africa-trading company used to 'raise a separate subscription to cover the cost of each voyage and repaid it when the ships returned and their cargoes were sold' (Morgan and Thomas, 1962, p. 12). From such beginnings, powerful and adventurous merchants regularly created joint-stock companies in order to take advantage of monopolies in foreign trade across the world granted by royal charter. Transactions in the shares of joint-stock companies in the capital market were in practice combined with transactions in state bonds. State bonds were simply certificates of indebtedness on the part of the state, entitling the holder to the periodic receipt of interest. Such instruments tended to proliferate during the course of the formation of the modern nation state, particularly reflecting the increase in state debt as a result of mercantilist wars. While the payment of interest on the accumulated state bonds pressed heavily on the government budget, the bonds also spurred the holding of monetary assets among the bourgeoisie, thus broadening and deepening the capital market.

In the course of the South Sea bubble in England from 1717–20, the South Sea Company issued shares in London in exchange for state bonds, and pushed up its share price by purchasing its own shares. A feverish rush to purchase shares materialised, contributing to generalised share price increases. Founding a joint-stock company by selling new shares became a very profitable business. Numerous joint-stock companies – aimed at foreign trade, manufacturing, insurance and finance – were founded by promoters in what were essentially speculative operations. The burst of the bubble in the summer of 1720 revealed how hopelessly ill-conceived most of the projected companies were, and created financial disaster for hundreds of investors and others.[1] In response to the crash, the Bubble Act, which remained in force until 1825, made illegal all joint-stock companies formed without a charter, or under a charter given for another purpose.

5.1.2   The Era of Liberalism

The influence of joint-stock capital on the course of development of British capitalism declined after the South Sea bubble. This was partly due to the nightmare memories of that episode, but also, and much more importantly, because successful capitalist accumulation gradually became possible through the investment of relatively modest sums of money in the manufacturing industry. The woollen industry had been the leading industry in Britain during the last part of the mercantilist era. After the industrial revolution, the expansion of the cotton industry ushered in the era of liberalism and turned Britain into the nineteenth-century 'workshop of the world'. The British cotton industry was characterised by competition among hundreds of relatively small capitalist firms operating in both spinning and weaving.[2]

The fundamental motive of capitalist accumulation is expansion of the value of privately owned capital; in principle capitalists are reluctant to share profit-making opportunities with unfamiliar persons.

Joint investment was not rare in cotton manufacturing, but it was typically undertaken on the basis of partnerships with family or friends. Starting and operating a cotton manufacturing business in the age of liberalism did not require extensive joint investment based on joint-stock capital and financed by many persons unknown to each other. The dominant form of capital during this stage of capitalist development was private industrial capital.[3] Nevertheless joint-stock capital did not disappear and continued to facilitate capitalist accumulation in certain areas of business activity. In banking and mining, for instance, joint-stock capital was used to create 'enterprises which would be impossible for individual capitals' (Marx, 1895, p. 567). Construction of the railways, in particular, was generally undertaken with the use of joint-stock capital. The importance of railway construction and of the related iron and steel industries increased towards the end of the age of liberalism.

5.1.3 The Era of Imperialism and After

During the Great Depression of 1873–96 joint-stock capital spread increasingly from the railways to other important industries. In its early days railway construction across the world was financed by British investment abroad. The enormous demand for steel generated by railway construction spurred the growth of the steel industry; new technologies were also introduced in steel making, using very large blast furnaces. The heavy fixed capital investment requirements of the latter were generally undertaken on the basis of joint-stock capital. Subsequently, heavy chemical industries, shipbuilding, mining (including petroleum production), machinery and the weapons industry also enlarged the size of their fixed capital investment by employing joint-stock capital. From light textile industry with modest fixed capital requirements, the leading area of capitalist accumulation became heavy industry with massive fixed capital requirements. Meanwhile, British industrial hegemony began to wane as the United States and Germany increased their strength in the newly growing heavy industries. Toward the end of Great Depression price competition among the fewer, but much larger, companies within each branch of industry became increasingly cut-throat. In response a massive merger movement materialised at the turn of the century, often resulting in powerful monopolistic organisations that mitigated competition. Company mergers were facilitated by the now widespread presence of joint-stock capital, and by rising share prices. At the same time, several new giant industrial corporations were formed, typified by US Steel. The introduction of their shares into the capital market undermined the previously dominant position of state bonds and railway shares.

A very influential theorisation of these trends within the Marxist tradition was provided in Hilferding's (1910) *Finance Capital*, which stressed the dominant role of banks in the formation of large industrial corporations. According to Hilferding, banks advanced long-term 'capital credit' that allowed industrial capitals to invest in large amounts of fixed capital; banks then promoted the conversion of industrial capitals into joint-stock companies. The banks held the dominant blocks of shares, and often promoted the merger and consolidation of industrial companies into monopolies. They could also liquidate their long-term fixed investment loans by selling the shares of the joint-stock companies. According to Hilferding (1910, p. 225), banking capital became amalgamated with industrial capital, giving rise to 'finance capital'. The latter, Hilferding thought, was to characterise capitalism in the twentieth century. Lenin's *Imperialism; The Highest Stage of Capitalism* (1917) broadly concurred with Hilferding's analysis, without concentrating on the financial aspects of joint-stock capital. For Lenin, however, 'finance capital' was only one constituent element of the broader historical trend towards 'monopoly capital'.[4] Lenin's term has been widely used by Marxists to denote the dominant form of capital in the twentieth century.

Hilferding's emphasis on the pivotal role of banks reflected the German experience at the turn of the century. Yet the general applicability of German practices is highly debatable. British banks, for instance, continued with the business of short-term banking, though the weight of their activities shifted increasingly towards the finance of foreign trade of both Britain and other countries. In Britain and the United States the issuing and sale of shares of joint-stock companies was largely undertaken by financial brokers, who exercised no control over industrial companies. Moreover the issuing of financial instruments in the capital market in these countries ensured an adequate supply of direct finance to enable the construction of massive fixed capital. In contrast the supply of indirect finance for fixed capital, mainly through long-term bank loans, remained very important in both Germany and Japan. However industrial corporations and banks in Germany and Japan came to relate to each other as equals typically without entering into vertical hierarchical relationships.

Hilferding's definition of 'finance capital' is both too specific to the German experience and too narrow to be able to capture the dominant form of capital in the twentieth century. The concept of 'monopoly capital', on the other hand, neglects an important aspect of capital in the twentieth century, namely that capital regularly assumes a financial form and is transacted as a commodity in the capital markets.[5] Furthermore, contemporary giant corporations do not necessarily adopt a monopolistic form of organisation, nor do they assume monopolistic control of the markets for their products. To be sure, both monopolistic organisation and control are present in contemporary capitalism; yet it is also common for giant corporations strongly to compete against each other especially as competition has intensified in the course of fuller internationalisation of capital in our age. In substance, the dominant form of capital since the late nineteenth century has been giant joint-stock capital rather than monopoly capital.[6] Concretely, however, joint-stock capital possesses both monopolistic features and complex relations with banks that are specific to nations and periods of time. The multinational corporations dominating the world economy since the 1960s are the contemporary form of joint-stock capital, and they have spread their factories, offices, sales and finance across the world. It is a remarkable demonstration of the social power of joint-stock capital that it has allowed the emergence of corporations whose annual sales often exceed the annual output of entire countries.

5.2 THE FORMS OF JOINT-STOCK CAPITAL

5.2.1 Joint Investment

Joint investment in potentially profitable enterprises can be undertaken in the form of a partnership among immediate (and more distant) relatives, or among personal friends. However the property rights entailed by partnerships are normally non-negotiable in an open market, and are often of unlimited liability, that is, they allow creditors to claim the owners' personal wealth in lieu of unpaid partnership debt. As a result, partnerships are difficult to establish among persons unknown to each other. Joint-stock capital, on the other hand, divides the ownership of a capitalist firm into many shares or stocks, each share representing a portion of the principal capital invested in the firm. Generally speaking, shares tend to be negotiable, and their owners' liability is limited to property in the shares. Since they represent small units of investment, moreover, shares can be sold to the general public. Joint-stock capital expands the scope of joint investment through the issue of shares with limited liability, purchased by a broad range of persons who often possess relatively small amounts of money.

Shareholders typically have the right to receive dividends out of profits, in proportion to the shares they hold. They also usually have the right to attend the annual meeting of shareholders and, again in proportion to the shares they hold, to vote on the future policy agenda of the firm. The latter typically includes the election of the top management of the company, such as the president and the directors. For small shareholders this right may amount to little as, taken individually, their vote makes a negligible difference to the final result. Indeed the larger the number of small shareholders the more concentrated the election power of a few large shareholders. In acquiring shares, small shareholders typically aim at receiving dividends, and possibly realising capital gains by selling the shares for more than the purchase price. Formal democracy among shareholders, that is, one vote for one share, significantly differentiates the power and the concerns of the large and the small shareholders. For small shareholders, the ownership of shares means little in terms of deciding how to use and manage the invested capital.[7]

The top managers of established large joint-stock companies, including the president and the directors, typically become separate from the large shareholders, and are often recruited through the labour market. There is certainly no requirement that such managers should possess a large number of the shares of the company they are running. It is a well-known characteristic of large joint-stock capital that ownership and normal management are separated. For Marx (1894, p. 567), to a certain extent this characteristic implied the 'transformation of the actual functioning capitalists into a mere manager, in charge of other people's capital, and of the capital owner into a mere owner, a mere money capitalist'. The formation of large joint-stock firms entails a complex social stratification of economic power, including small shareholders, large shareholders, and managers, thus transcending the simple division between capitalists and wage workers. Under certain historical conditions, managers can be relatively independent of shareholders and pursue their own interests. Japanese top managers, for instance, are often hired employees of companies, and tend to exhibit a bias towards retaining profits within a company rather than distributing them as dividends among shareholders.

The recent principal-agent theoretical literature has examined the ability of managers to become relatively independent. Premised on the assumption that managers ought to act as the agents of shareholders, the literature usually concludes that negative implications follow for capitalist accumulation when managers are able to act in their own interests rather those of the shareholders. Shareholders can of course voice their discontent at the annual general meeting, or exit by selling their shares. Nevertheless it has been claimed that neither of these methods effectively curbs the independence of management since the latter tend to be much better informed about both the current condition and the prospects of the company than are the shareholders (Stiglitz, 1985). An important weakness of the principal-agent analysis (quite apart from its methodological individualism) is the lack of analysis of the stratification among shareholders, and the complex social relations to which it gives rise. Shareholders are not homogeneous; the division among large and small shareholders is important in influencing the direction of a capitalist firm. As long as top managers are elected, they have to maintain the support of large shareholders and cannot become completely independent. Private property remains a decisive element in determining the behaviour of capital.[8]

5.2.2 The Facilitation of Mergers

While examining 'the general law of capitalist accumulation', Marx (1867, ch. 25, sec. 2) distinguished between the concentration and the centralisation of capital. In the process of accumulation 'the individual capitals grow, and with their growth the concentration of the means of production increases, in the proportion in which they form an aliquot part of the total social capital' (ibid., p. 776). The concentration of capital is a phenomenon effected through the growth of individual capitals; centralisation, on the other hand, occurs by 'the attraction of capital to capital', that is, by the merger of already existing capitals, or when 'capital grows to a huge mass in a single hand in one place, because it has been lost by many in another place' (ibid., p. 777), that is, by the acquisition of one capital by another.

Joint-stock capital facilitates the centralisation of capital in two ways. First, the issuing of shares extends the scope for joint investment and favours the flow of available money capitals towards a single capitalist corporation. This holds true for the issuing of shares by newly founded joint-stock firms and for the issuing of additional

shares by an existing corporation. Second, joint-stock capital promotes acquisitions and mergers among already existing capitalist
firms. Capital is not merely a stock of real assets but also the self-
expanding motion of value, which continuously and successively
adopts the form of money, commodities and factors of production.
The fact that by its own nature capital is in permanent motion implies
that individual industrial capitalists find it difficult to acquire other
independent capitals, or to merge their capitals with that of others.
Financing the outright acquisition of (or the merger with) others
without disturbing the motion of the capitals involved is a complicated
operation that is usually hard for individual capitals to undertake
successfully. If its motion stopped and capital became a stock of
assets, the components of the stock could indeed be sold as commodities. However this process is not the fusion of active and separate
capitals but the termination and cannibalisation of one of them. Firms
owned by individual capitalists cannot easily effect the centralisation
of their capitals while these capitals remain in motion.

Joint-stock capital can be employed to overcome this difficulty,
thereby facilitating the fusion of industrial capitals in motion. New
joint-stock companies, for instance, can be established through the
merger of independent individual capitalist firms by allocating shares
according to the estimated values of the individual capitals. Similarly,
an existing joint-stock company can acquire an individual capital by
simply increasing its shares according to the latter's estimated value.
Independent joint-stock companies can also merge into one company
by exchanging their shares with those of the new company in appropriate proportions. The remarkable aspect of all such transactions is
that no payment of ready money is necessary, nor is it necessary to
stop the motion of the capitals.

Marx (ibid., p. 779) further claimed that 'In any given branch of
industry centralization would reach its extreme limit if all the individual capitals invested there were fused into a single capital. In a
given society this limit would be reached only when the entire social
capital was united in the hands of either a single capital or a single
company.' It is unlikely, however, that the extreme limit of centralisation will ever be reached. Marx (ibid., p. 776) also observed that
'offshoots split off from the original capitals and start to function as
new and independent capitals'. This is particularly so in industries that
require modest investment in plant and equipment. In contemporary
capitalism several industrial spheres remain in which small and medium firms are prevalent. Even in industries dominated by large firms,

complete monopoly hardly ever arises without state intervention. The tendency of capital to centralise, promoted by joint-stock capital, should not be inordinately stressed.

There are several different motives for acquisitions and mergers.[9] Vertical mergers across related industrial spheres, for instance, could increase profitability by rationalising production technology, utilising the by-products of the merged processes of production and economising on the costs of circulation. Centralisation might also mitigate the instability of the profit rate caused by fluctuations in the price of raw materials, intermediate and finished products. At the same time centralisation reduces the number of industrial capitals in one sphere of activity, possibly resulting in cut-throat price competition and losses for all capitals. Horizontal mergers and acquisitions are a method of avoiding such an eventuality. They may also bring about economies in the costs of management and circulation. Since they tend to stabilise (or even raise) the price of output, leading to a higher profit rate, they may actually facilitate the monopolistic control of markets. The expectation of a higher rate of profit after a merger helps raise the price of shares and promotes speculation that might lead to further share price rises. Capital gains obtained by the original firm owners through share price rises, as well as by those who promote and finance mergers, also act as an important motive for mergers.

5.2.3 The Capital Market and Expected Dividend Yield

The capitalist economy is a historically specific socioeconomic formation grounded on the commodity form. Through the commodity form, capitalism systematically embraces all elements of economic life and subsumes them under the motion of capital. Commodification extends over a great number of the products of labour, but also over labour power, land and loanable money in the money market. The process of commodification finally reaches capital itself: the capital market (or stock exchange) is a market in which capital is itself transacted in the form of shares. Shares in joint-stock capital essentially represent common ownership of capital in motion. For Marx (1939, pp. 264, 275–7), joint-stock capital is the highest and most complete form of capital, which logically follows capital in general, competition and credit. Historically speaking, capitalism has not produced a form of capital that transcends joint-stock capital. Hilferding's finance capital, Lenin's monopoly capital and the contemporary multinational corporations are more concrete forms of appearance of the giant joint-stock company with its own national and transnational characteristics.

Given that transactions in the capital market can be undertaken on a daily basis, relatively cheaply and with comparatively small sums of money, idle money across society is mobilised for investment in the stock exchange. For the shareholders, the purchase of shares aims, in the first instance, at earning dividends out of company profits. In this connection the dividend yield of shares is important. In general a share's actual dividend yield at a given time is the ratio of dividends per share, D, over the share price, P_s. However, since dividends are a part of future profits, what matters for stock exchange investors are expected dividends. Thus the expected dividend yield, y^e, is given by the ratio of expected dividends per share (accruing in every period in the future indefinitely), D^e, over the actual share price, P_s:

$$y^e = D^e/P_s \tag{1}$$

Alternatively, actual share prices can be thought of as the ratio of expected dividends over the expected dividend yield. The rate of interest in the money market serves as the point of reference for the expected dividend yield for investors in the capital market. Since idle money invested in shares can also be potentially lent out at interest, the expected dividend yield of shares is regulated by the market rate of interest, i. When the expected dividend yield exceeds the rate of interest, for instance, funds tend to flow into the capital market, raising the price of shares and lowering the expected yield; the opposite tends to take place when the expected yield is below the rate of interest. Thus at the margin the expected yield per share is equal to the market rate of interest, that is, $y^e = i$. Consequently actual share prices can be thought of as the value of expected dividends capitalised by the market rate of interest, i:[10]

$$P_s = D^e/i \tag{2}$$

Thus share prices vary directly with a company's expected profits and dividends, and inversely with the market rate of interest. This simple formulation of share prices, however, must be complemented by three further factors that take into account both the fact that the future is unknown and the dynamic nature of capitalist accumulation.

First, while the market rate of interest is a definite nominal rate of return promised on future payments, the expected dividend yield contains elements of risk since future profits cannot be guaranteed in advance. Two types of risk are immediately relevant in this connection: first, risk due to the inherent variability of the unknown future profits and second, risk of company default. The expected dividend yield allows for risk by incorporating a certain risk premium in excess of the rate of interest.

Second, stock exchange investors also aim at capital gains resulting from future increases in share prices.[11] Thus the total expected yield of a share Y^e is the expected dividend yield plus the expected capital gains expressed as a proportion of the share price. If P_s^e is the expected share price at some point in the future, Y^e is

$$Y^e = [D^e + (P_s^e - P_s)]/P_s \tag{3}$$

The total expected yield of a share also incorporates a risk premium to cover the risks generated by the fact that future share prices are inherently unknowable. Expectations of capital gains, and their changes in the course of economic fluctuations, play an important role in determining both individual and general share prices. Generally rising share prices promote an optimistic perspective of the future in the capital market, and sometimes cause stock exchange bubbles by mobilising the flexible powers of expansion of the credit mechanism. The inevitable burst of such bubbles is often caused, and always worsened, by a swing of expectations toward pessimism. Both individual and general share prices are subject to instability induced by speculative expectations; this makes analyses of share prices that use a static demand and supply framework very problematic. Capital market price instability is an important source of monetary crisis both as an integral part of the industrial business cycle and quite independently of it. As the significance of joint-stock firms has increased in the twentieth century so has the potential for instability generated by the capital market.

Third, determination of the long-term rate of interest might become quite separate from that of the short-term rate. The short-term rate of interest is determined in the money market on the basis of the activities of banks, mostly in the short-term lending of money capital. The long-term rate of interest, on the other hand, is determined in the market for state (and company) bonds, which are typically promises to pay a fixed amount of interest at regular intervals over a certain period. Bond market transactions usually involve the lending of money over considerably longer periods of time. The total yield of fixed income bonds is determined along the same lines as the total yield of shares, and incorporates the expectation of future bond price changes. The important difference with shares is that future interest payments on bonds are known with certainty whereas dividend payments are uncertain. The price of bonds thus varies inversely with the market rate of interest, and is also subject to speculative increases and decreases. For the holders of idle money capital available for short-term investment the risk of the losses involved in bond transactions is usually forbidding. On the other hand idle money capital that is available for long-term lending is always available for lending to the short-term money market. The asymmetry in the demand and supply of loanable capital is the foundation for the generally higher long-term rate of interest compared with the short-term rate. The extent of difference between long-term and short-term rates of interest, however, cannot be theoretically determined *a priori*, and depends on the concrete historical and social circumstances of the country in question. The difference could also be reversed in favour of short-term rates during particularly critical phases of economic fluctuation.

It is intrinsic to its nature that the long-term rate of interest might become relatively independent from the short-term rate for certain periods of time. Were such relative independence of the long-term rate of interest to materialise, share prices might also be affected since the expected dividend yield is more naturally compared with the long-term rather than the short-term interest rate. Nevertheless, as both rates broadly relate to the motion of loanable capital, they generally move in the same direction driven by changes in the short-term rate. All other things being equal, a rise in the money market interest rate leads to a fall in bond and share prices; the opposite holds for a fall.

5.2.4 Founder's Profit

For Marxist political economy, determination of the profit rate is quite distinct from that of the interest rate. The general rate of profit is determined by factors reflecting the material and technical features of capitalist accumulation, namely the organic composition of capital, the turnover time of capital, the length of the working day and the value of the necessary means of consumption for workers. The general rate of interest, on the other hand, is determined purely by the balance between the demand and supply of loanable money capital in the money market; it does not reflect any aspect of the underlying material reality of capitalist accumulation. With the exception of some periods of financial tension and crisis, the rate of profit is generally higher than the rate of interest. Given the systematic difference between the rate of profit and the rate of interest, when a new company is established the money value of the capital invested in real accumulation per share is lower than the share price, as the simple formal presentation below shows. Hilferding (1910, p. 112) called the difference between the share price and the capital initially invested in real accumulation per share, 'founder's profit' (Gründergewinn).

Assume that the entire mass of profits is regularly paid out as dividends, and that share prices are the capitalised value of expected dividends. The following variables are relevant: the initially invested money capital in real accumulation, K, expected total profit, Π^e, expected dividend, D^e, rate of profit, r, and market rate of interest, i. The money capital invested per share in real accumulation is (K/N). If money capital flows between the money market and the capital market equalise the expected dividend yield with the market rate of interest (ignoring risk premia), the share price is given by,

$$P_s = (D^e/i) \tag{2}$$

Since all profits are paid out as dividends,

$$D^e = \Pi^e/N \tag{4}$$

Given the general rate of profit, r,

$$\Pi^e = rK \tag{5}$$

Hence

$$D^e = (K/N)r \tag{6}$$

Thus

$$P_s = (K/N)(r/i) \tag{7}$$

If $r > i$, the share price, P_s, exceeds the money capital initially invested in real accumulation per share (K/N). Managerial and other costs of financial transactions covered out of profits leave the substance of the argument unchanged.

Hilferding's own numerical example also helps to clarify the point. Suppose that an industrial enterprise is founded with a capital of 1 000 000 marks. Given a general annual rate of profit of 15 per cent, total profits equal 150 000 marks. Assuming that various costs (administration and directors' salaries) come to 20 000 marks, 130 000 marks are left for distribution among shareholders as dividends. Adding a risk premium of 2 per cent to the general rate of interest of 5 per cent capitalises the profit of 130 000 marks at roughly 19 000 000 marks, that is, 900 000 more than the initial investment. This excess might accrue to either the founders of the enterprise who made the initial investment or to 'promoters', who might purchase the enterprise at the initial investment price in order to reorganise and sell it as joint-stock capital. For shares that are not subsequently sold and continue to be held by the enterprise founders, 'founder's profit' is a fictitious estimate of monetary gain.

Based on Marx's argument regarding the qualitative division of total profit into interest and profit of enterprise, Hilferding also claimed that the promoter's profit of 900 000 marks is profit of enterprise accruing in a lump sum; the remaining profit is interest received by shareholders in the form of dividends. In this respect Hilferding's argument is problematic. There is no social mechanism restricting dividends to the notional 'interest' part of profit: dividends simply represent a form of distribution of total profit among shareholders. Founder's profit does not represent profit of enterprise but the redistribution of already existing money assets through share transactions. This holds for both newly founded enterprises and the share issues of established enterprises.

5.3   THE SOCIAL FUNCTIONS OF JOINT-STOCK CAPITAL

5.3.1   The Mobilisation of Capital and the Efficient Market Hypothesis

Joint-stock capital greatly facilitates the undertaking of joint investment by persons unknown to each other, it is therefore appropriate for mobilising idle money capital and constructing huge fixed capital in potentially profitable industries. Increases in the share capital of existing companies, or the issuing of shares by newly established companies, are an effective lever for the mobilisation of idle money capital. The difficulty that individual capitals face in creating big industrial enterprises employing huge fixed capital is thereby over-come. Joint-stock capital does not become universal across all branches of industry, including trade and services. Capitalism aims at the self-expansion of private capital, hence there is no necessity for capitalists to opt for joint-stock investment when either personal or partnership investment is adequate for a potentially profitable capi-talist project. Even in the twentieth century quite a few branches of industry exist in which small and medium-sized private firms continue to be appropriate for the technological characteristics of production; in such branches of industry joint-stock capital is either not dominant or does not exist at all.[12] In this regard joint-stock capital cannot be a universal form of economic organisation, even though it represents the most socially developed form of capital. This weakness of joint-stock capital ultimately derives from the historically limited nature of the capitalist economy, grounded as it is on private money-making.

Two implications for real accumulation follow from the fact that joint-stock capital facilitates the growth of new industrial branches with massive fixed capital, similar to the implications of the operations of the credit system for real accumulation. First, joint-stock capital can accelerate the accumulation of total social capital by transforming idle money capital into industrial capital in motion; the production of surplus value is intensified and the general rate of profit can be raised. Since it is idle capital that is turned to profit-making, the beneficial effect on the mass of surplus value is unaffected by changes in the organic composition of capital. Second, joint-stock capital allows the reallocation of capital and productive resources across industries in the direction of more profitable industries. The concomitant increase in the output supply of such industries leads to a lowering of their profit rate towards the social average. In this respect the social mechanism constructed on the basis of joint-stock capital broadly promotes equalisation of the rate of profit among industries.

The efficient market hypothesis, originally developed by Fama (1970, 1991), strongly emphasises the rational and socially beneficial functions of the capital market, particularly the efficient allocation of money capital according to the signals given by share prices.[13] If information is perfect and freely available to all investors, and if share transaction costs are negligible, share prices guide the allocation of money capital towards those industries and firms that can use the capital most efficiently. Capital market inefficiency, insofar as it exists at all, is due to the partial or imperfect nature of information available to investors. Three types of less-than-perfect efficiency are usually distinguished. First, under 'weak' efficiency share prices fully reflect the information content of past share prices, which is of course public knowledge. Second, under 'semi-strong' efficiency share prices reflect not only the entire informational content of past share prices, but also all other publicly available information, that is, company results, brokers' circulars, industry forecasts and so on. Third, under 'strong' efficiency all known information, whether publicly available or not, is reflected in share prices, for instance details of takeover bids, new product lines about to be launched and so on. Under weak efficiency investors cannot make extra gains by simply examining charts of past price movements. Under semi-strong efficiency no extra gains can be realised by utilising generally available information, such as the announcement of unexpectedly high earnings. Under strong efficiency no extra returns can be generated even if inside tips are available to investors. Since under the strong form share prices incorporate all available information, the best predictor of tomorrow's price is simply today's price, and the movement of share prices over time closely resembles a 'random walk'.

The efficient market hypothesis has very extensive limitations, apparent in the following three respects. First, the availability of perfect information to all investors is evidently an abstraction without a footing in reality. More damning, however, is the fact that the information dissemination patterns implicit in all three forms of efficiency also appear ideally abstract. In an anarchical capitalist economy based on private ownership of the means of production, it is impossible to distribute information about individual industries and firms uniformly and at the same time to all capital market investors. The property and power relations of capitalist society necessarily entail the existence of groups of investors with preferential access to information. Asymmetry in the availability of information, coupled with inherently different views and expectations about the future, contribute to speculative investment decisions.

Second, allocating money capital in the capital market according to security prices is not directly equivalent to allocating real productive resources across various industries. A rise in share prices, for instance, tends to channel money capital towards industries that can profitably expand production to meet strong social demand for their products. It is debatable, however, whether an actual expansion of productive plant and equipment also occurs rapidly as a result of the presence of profitable opportunities. It is very difficult to remove large fixed capital investment in certain industries and shift it towards other, potentially more profitable industries according to share price signals. Efficiency in the reallocation of money capital within the capital market does not necessarily translate into efficiency in the reallocation of productive resources.

Third, the capital market cannot be a comprehensive social organisation for all capitalist firms, since joint-stock capital, issued and transacted in the capital market, is not appropriate for all branches of capitalist industry. As argued above, considerable segments of industry exist in which firms are usually privately owned by individuals or partnerships. The credit system, which serves both these areas of industry and those characterised by joint-stock capital, is a more comprehensive social organisation for the reallocation of idle money capital than the capital market. For some capitalist countries, such as Germany and Japan, the reallocating function of the credit system has historically included long-term credit given to industry, further limiting the social functions of the capital market.

5.3.2   The Rate of Profit of Joint-Stock Capital and Monopoly Profit

The contribution of joint-stock capital to equalisation of the rate of profit, through the mobilisation of idle money capital, has complex and contradictory effects. Joint-stock capital facilitates the construction of huge productive capacity in potentially profitable industries, but the actual construction of such capacity normally takes quite a long time. The period during which the effective demand for means of production rises without a corresponding increase in their supply can be thought of as the gestation period of investment in very large fixed capital. During the gestation period the business prospects of the branches of industry that produce means of constructing large productive capacity appear better than they are in reality. Speculative profit expectations are thus encouraged, promoting the construction of massive competing facilities to produce means of production. The completion of rival productive facilities at the end of the gestation period tends substantially to increase the volume of existing productive capacity across the economy. Excessive capacity often materialises in some branches of industry, leading to unevenness and wide fluctuations in both the prospective and the actual profit rate among branches of industry that employ huge fixed capital.

Once excessive productive capacity in the form of fixed capital investment has been formed, joint-stock capital faces insuperable difficulties in significantly reducing it, short of inducing the sudden destruction of enterprises. The usual method is to wait for years while depreciation gradually turns the investment into fluid money capital. An important asymmetry exists in this regard: while joint-stock capital greatly facilitates the creation of massive fixed capitals, it cannot reduce the latter without risking the sudden death of enterprises. Insofar as excessive fixed capital persists in certain industrial branches, however, prolonged and severe pressure is exercised on their profit rate, which is not matched by the prospect of significant increases in the demand for their products. In this respect joint-stock capital makes equalisation of the profit rate slower and more difficult.

Using the example of railways, which seemed to operate with lower than average profit rates, Marx (1894, pp. 347–8) argued that joint-stock capitals investing in large productive enterprises 'do not enter into the equalization of the general rate of profit'. Thus it seemed to Marx that joint-stock capital counterbalances the tendency of the rate of profit to fall. Marx's argument, however, is problematic: joint-stock capital attempts to earn the highest rate of profit possible, as does private individual capital. Competition implies that the tendency towards profit rate equalisation is also present for joint-stock capital, even though it is slower and faces additional obstacles due to large fixed capital already in place. Industries with a lower than average rate of profit face a decline of additional investment, or even a complete stop; excessive productive capacity is eventually scrapped, even if that takes a long time.[14]

If a small number of giant corporations achieved control of a particular market they could put in place monopoly pricing, ensuring a higher than average profit rate. Monopoly profit implies that, through the monopolistic manipulation of prices, surplus-value transfers take place from competitive industries to the monopolistic industry. As a result monopoly profit systematically lowers the profit rates of competitive industries. To generate monopoly profits, monopoly organisations can be set up among giant corporations, such as cartels and trusts, or one company might be tacitly accepted by the rest as the price leader. Joint-stock capital facilitates the formation of giant monopolistic capitals and organisations. If domestic markets are protected from foreign competition by high import tariffs, expensive transport costs, and so on, the emergence of monopoly organisations is likely to be encouraged. Monopoly capitals distort the process of resource reallocation through the price mechanism and according to social demand. Monopoly pricing in an industry is often maintained by artificial restrictions on production, and is usually accompanied by increased levels of idle productive capacity and lower levels of employment. Since it allows idle capacity to persevere, monopoly pricing also tends to slow down technological innovation. When monopoly capitals dominate the economy they often reduce capitalist efficiency in the allocation of resources, and might further lead to persistent economic depression.[15]

The power of monopoly organisations to raise the price of their products is not arbitrary; rather it relies on forcing some productive capacity to lie idle, thus keeping the supply of output lower than it might have been.[16] Monopolists cannot always resolve their problems by raising prices. The sharing of profits among members of monopoly organisations notoriously lacks stable rules, and might lead to the break-up of the organisation. Moreover monopoly prices and profits often act as magnets for potential new entrants into the industry, and so undermine the quantitative limitation of output supply and the ability to maintain monopoly prices. The emergence of successful substitute products and competition by foreign firms might also threaten the viability of domestic monopoly prices. Capitalist rivalry and competition are not eliminated by giant joint-stock corporations, and constantly undermine monopoly prices and profit.

It was a tenet of Soviet 'orthodox' Marxism that monopoly capitalism operated on the basis of acquiring maximum monopoly profit rather than the proportionate redistribution of surplus value among all capitals.[17] However the development of joint-stock capital does not imply replacement of the law of equalisation of the rate of profit (as a concrete expression of the more fundamental law of value) by the law of monopoly profit. Profit rate equalisation still operates as giant joint-stock corporations continue to grow, but it is a more contradictory and slower process.

5.3.3 Instability Induced by Capital Market Speculation

In a capitalist economy speculative operations and outright swindling could potentially develop in any area of economic activity. It is implicit to the general formula of capital $M–C–M'$ (or purchasing commodities cheaply in order to sell them more dearly) that even industrial capitalists are always prepared to take advantage of opportunities for speculative gains. When the price of a certain commodity is expected to rise, all capitalists are tempted to buy and hold speculative stocks in order to make future profits.

Speculative transactions typically appear and grow massively under certain conditions in the capital market. Expectation of high future profits during the upswing of the business cycle especially encourages speculative purchases of shares, and leads to further temporary gains from share price rises; new share issues can be smoothly floated, for both potentially profitable projects and existing enterprises; and correspondingly large amounts of 'founder's profit' are realised. During the gestation period of large fixed capitals in particular, effective demand appears strong and durable, especially for firms engaged in producing the elements of fixed capital. For projects that lead to substantial increases in the productive capacity of an industrial branch, such as a new steel plant or a new heavy chemical plant, speculation starts at their inception and lasts for years.

The growth of joint-stock capital and the emergence of a capital market thus add a further element of instability to the capitalist economy. This instability is fully analysed in the subsequent chapters: suffice it to state here that during the upswing of the business cycle share prices rise not merely because of the actual increase of industrial activity and profits, but also because of expectations of strong demand and high profitability in the future. The credit system, particularly the money market, is also fully utilised to finance large share purchases. The combination of these factors can lead to the emergence of speculative booms in the capital market, which subsequently feed upon themselves. When the upswing turns into recession, speculative booms collapse and previously optimistic expectations about the future turn to pessimism. The rise in the rate of interest, which typically takes place at the time when the upswing turns to recession, accelerates the fall of share prices. Further speculation, but now in the opposite direction, might also worsen the fall in share prices and destroy the value of financial assets in the hands of banks, securities companies and individual investors.

6 Monetary and Financial Aspects of the Business Cycle

6.1 MARX'S ANALYSIS OF MONETARY CRISES

6.1.1 Instability in a Monetary Economy

In the work of the classical school the capitalist economy represents a natural and harmonious social order. For Marx, on the other hand, the capitalist economy is inherently unstable. Economic instability has several monetary and financial aspects. The following three levels can be identified in Marx's analysis of monetary and financial stability.

First, under conditions of simple commodity circulation, the possibility of economic instability arises purely from the social functions of money. Marx's argument in this connection coheres closely with his explanation of money's monopolisation of direct exchangeability with other commodities, as discussed in Chapter 2 above. Thus the functioning of money as means of circulation inevitably implies that 'No one can sell unless someone else purchases. But no one directly needs to purchase because he has just sold' (Marx, 1867, p. 209). The crude form of Say's Law, which asserts that the supply of commodities always generates an equal demand (on the implicit assumption of direct exchangeability among commodities) is simply incorrect for a monetary economy. Indeed in a monetary economy the antithetical form of sale and purchase themselves 'imply the possibility of crises'.

The functioning of money as means of payment in simple circulation also gives rise to the possibility of monetary crises. The interconnected series of promises to pay, as well as the 'artificial system for settling them', can break down when particular payment failures lead to a chain reaction and cause 'a general disturbance of the mechanism, no matter what its cause', (ibid., 1867, p. 236). On such occasions commodities have to be sold at 'sacrifice' prices in order to obtain money as means of payment. For the commodity owner these are trying times: 'As the hart pants after fresh water, so pants his soul after

123

money, the only wealth' (ibid.). The tribulations of the commodity markets thus necessarily result in the 'sudden transformation of the credit system into a monetary system' (ibid.).

Second, in an economy with a developed process of exchange backed by advanced credit and finance, monetary crises of quite a different order of magnitude and complexity become possible. Monetary crises might be caused by sudden breaks in the chains of industrial and commercial transactions prevalent in a particular country. Monetary crises might also be intensified by shocks to the chains of credit that run through industry and trade.

Third, in a capitalist economy monetary crises inevitably result from the essential motion of capitalist accumulation itself. Marx (especially in 1894, pt 5) offered several arguments regarding the logical inevitability of such crises, some of which shall be considered below. The key point is that in a monetary economy founded on industrial capitalist accumulation the inherent, but abstract, possibility of monetary crisis becomes an inevitability. This inevitability is particularly manifested in the cyclical crises that characterise capitalist accumulation.

In a note on the functioning of money as means of payment, Marx (1867, p. 236) remarked that:

> The monetary crisis, defined in the text as a particular phase of every general industrial and commercial crisis, must be clearly distinguished from the special sort of crisis, also called a monetary crisis, which may appear independently of the rest, and only affects industry and commerce by its backwash. The centre of movement of these crises is to be found in money capital, and their immediate sphere is therefore banking, the stock exchanges and finance.[1]

The note distinguishes between two kinds of monetary crisis: those which form a particular phase of a general industrial and commercial crisis (type 1), and those which appear independently of a general industrial and commercial crisis (type 2). According to the note, the analysis of the relationship between means of payment and monetary crisis in the text of *Capital* refer specifically to type 1 crises. However a close reading of the text reveals no reason why the analysis is inapplicable to type 2 crises (the later inclusion of the note in *Capital* is an implicit acknowledgement of this). After all, and as already quoted above, the text claims that a disturbance to the chain of promises to pay, 'no matter what its cause', can lead to a monetary crisis.

Neither monetary instability arising from the social functions of money nor type 2 monetary crises are specific to the capitalist economy. Chains of monetary transactions and interconnected promises to pay have characterised market economies long before the establishment of capitalism. However, as long as market processes have not yet penetrated the core of society's economic reproduction and remain a peripheral phenomenon, monetary instability has rather limited social repercussions. The social implications of a shock to the monetary mechanism are not comparable to those of bad weather, disease and war.

With the emergence and slow development of the capitalist economy in Europe after the sixteenth century, commercial and financial crises began to occur frequently in the large European trading cities, and acquired a broad social significance. In the early days of capitalism such crises were often related to the mercantilist wars, to speculative trading in particular commodities (such as the Dutch tulip mania of the 1630s) and to speculative operations in state bonds and stock market shares (such as the South Sea Bubble and John Law's 'System'). Early monetary crises lacked periodic regularity. Generally speaking, during the era of mercantile capitalism the burgeoning monetary assets in the hands of the bourgeoisie and the rich could not achieve systematic self-expansion through industrial investment. The social foundations for the latter were absent, particularly a large and skilled industrial working class. Inevitably monetary assets were channelled towards speculative trading in commodities and investment in bonds and shares, resulting in speculative booms and monetary crises of type 2. Mercantile capitalism simply lacked the social conditions necessary for the systematic generation of type 1 monetary crises.

6.1.2 The Theoretical Interpretation of Marx's Theory of Crisis

The classical school largely denied the possibility of the general overproduction of commodities, implicitly or explicitly accepting Say's Law. Marx's economic analysis, on the other hand, aimed at demonstrating the inevitability of economic crisis as evidence of the historically limited character of the capitalist economy. Nonetheless Marx's theory of crisis was not fully and consistently developed in his own work. Four different theoretical views on economic crisis can be identified in the corpus of Marx's writings, which could be classed into two separate groups.

The first group comprises excess supply theories of crisis, for which the ultimate cause of capitalist crisis is excess aggregate supply of commodities relative to effective demand. The imbalance between demand and supply could result either from the anarchical disproportionality among the branches of production (disproportionality theory), or the narrowly restricted consumption of the working masses (underconsumption theory). For excess supply theories, the difficulties that capitalists face in selling their commodity output during a crisis lead to a fall in the rate of profit.

The second group comprises excess capital (or overaccumulation) theories, for which the fundamental cause of crisis is excessive capital accumulation. The latter appears as a fall of the profit rate due to either the tendency of the organic composition of capital to rise (organic composition theory), or to labour shortage leading to a rise in wages (labour shortage theory). For excess capital theories, the difficulties faced by capitalists in selling commodities during a crisis actually result from more fundamental overaccumulation problems, which are also the ultimate cause of a fall in the rate of profit.[2]

Marxist economists have tended to stress one or other of the four types of crisis theory, often by selecting quotations from Marx's work. In the early years of Marxist economics, disproportionality theory was very influential and was typically found in the work of Tugan-Baranowsky (1913) and Hilferding (1910). Partly in opposition to disproportionality theory, underconsumption theory was subsequently asserted as the 'mainstream' Marxist theory of crisis, for instance in the work of Kautsky (1901–2, 1911), Luxemburg (1913), Varga (1937–8) and Baran and Sweezy (1966). The prestige of Marxist underconsumption theory grew during the long boom of the world economy after the Second World War because of its affinity with Keynesianism. After the early 1970s the failure of Keynesianism and the protracted difficulties of the world economy propelled overaccumulation theory to prominence within Marxist economics.

All the above strands of crisis theory can find some textual support in the work of Marx. Thus it is inappropriate for the adherents of one to condemn those of another as non-Marxist. Soviet 'orthodox' Marxists, for instance, endorsed underconsumption theory, and rejected other views as 'revisionist' or not truly Marxist. Similarly, it is not persuasive to characterise the labour shortage strand of overaccumulation theory as neo-Ricardian in order to stress the Marxists credentials of the organic composition strand.[3] In this light, two analytical approaches are open to the theorist, particularly as far as analysis of money and finance is concerned.

The first is to treat the various strands of crisis theory, including the three levels of Marx's analysis of monetary instability, as a toolbox from which concepts can be selectively employed to analyse historically specific instances of capitalist economic crisis. This approach is certainly appealing since it can deal flexibly with the historically specific features and immediate causes of capitalist economic crisis. It could also be useful for the historical study of economic crisis in the course of capitalist development. Mechanically applying one strand of theory in the face of the very diverse historical experience of capitalist crisis is not a satisfactory way to proceed. For instance the onset of the great crisis of the 1930s could be accounted for in terms of underconsumption, intensified by monopoly pricing and restriction of output supply. This combination of explanatory factors, on the other hand, seems irrelevant when attempting to explain the onset of protracted difficulties for capitalist accumulation in the 1970s, a point made clearer in Chapter 8 below. The weakness of this approach, however, is that it is essentially eclectic and cannot lead to a coherent theory of the capitalist business cycle that is fully articulated with an analysis of credit and finance. This is a serious deficiency because without a theoretical model of the business cycle it is impossible to show the necessity of internal contradictions of the capitalist economy erupting in the course of accumulation (and being resolved in practice). Furthermore, without an underlying theory of the business cycle the study of the historical transformation of crises during the course of capitalist development is essentially arbitrary.

The second approach is to adopt one of the strands of Marxist crisis theory and use it to develop a fundamental theory of the business cycle. The most developed Marxist analysis of the capitalist business cycle is that of the Japanese Uno school. The analysis of the business cycle is undertaken at the level of the basic principles of political economy, rather than being a concrete historical study of the stages of capitalist development, or an even more concrete empirical analysis of contemporary capitalism. For the Uno school, the labour shortage theory of crisis provides appropriate foundations for an analysis of the business cycle, that is compatible with both the law of value and the basic operations of the capitalist monetary, credit and financial mechanisms.[4] The emphasis of the Uno school on the role played by money and finance in the course of the business cycle is quite unique within the Marxist tradition.

6.2   FUNDAMENTAL THEORY OF THE BUSINESS CYCLE

6.2.1   Preliminary Theoretical Observations

It is possible to derive a theoretical model of the capitalist business cycle (and of economic crisis as an intrinsic part of the cycle) from a set of timeless axioms refering to the capitalist economy. However the methodological principle adopted in this work is that the abstractions of the model ought to possess a historical basis. The most appropriate basis is provided by the typical decennial business cycle of liberal British capitalism from the 1820s to the 1860s. This was also the classic era of competitive capitalism with minimal state intervention in the economy. The British cotton industry was the leading industrial sector at the time, and credit and finance were aimed largely at promoting cotton capital accumulation. Marx's theoretical discussion of the business cycle in *Capital* appears to have had the same historical basis, making it possible for us to use his insights throughout the discussion below.

The following initial conditions are necessary for the construction of a stylised schema of the business cycle. First, industrial capitals are mostly under sole ownership, competitive with regard to price and quantity, and self-financing with regard to long-term investment in fixed capital. Second, the credit system has the pyramid-like form analysed in Chapter 4. There is no large-scale branch banking system and the main business of banks is to discount bills of exchange; credit money circulates alongside commodity money (gold). Third, large joint-stock capitals do exist, but they are limited to few areas of economic activity; the capital market has a correspondingly limited size. Fourth, commodity and money capital transactions constitute a homogeneous order for both foreign and domestic economic activity. Foreign transactions do not qualitatively disturb the functioning of domestic capitalist accumulation but merely expand it quantitatively. Thus it is possible to derive the fundamental properties of domestic capitalist accumulation by adopting the assumption that all the means of production and consumption are domestically reproduced. The manner in which economic interaction with the foreign sector might quantitatively influence the domestic relations of capitalist accumulation will be occasionally indicated in the course of the exposition below.

Under these assumptions, economic analysis naturally begins with the upswing of the cycle as this phase represents a positive aspect of capitalist accumulation during which employment is expanding and harmony appears, more or less, to reign. Events towards the end of the upswing must be carefully and separately scrutinised in order to establish the necessary character of capitalist industrial and monetary crises. A highly stylised schema is presented below, which is neither a fully developed theory of the cycle nor an empirically supported account of the classical business cycle. The schema draws systematically on the work of Japanese political economy. Its aim is, quite specifically, to highlight the role of money and finance in the course of the business cycle, and to facilitate the drawing of relevant analytical conclusions.

6.2.2   The Upswing

The beginning of the upswing is characterised by the existence of a range of satisfactorily high profit rates in the vicinity of the general rate of profit. The driving element of our stylised account of the upswing is that firms will not abandon their existing fixed capital as long as they can make satisfactorily high profits and expand their reproduction easily. Substantial scrapping of valuable machines and equipment represents an absolute loss of capital invested, a fact that makes the introduction of new methods of production less attractive to the capitalist. Extra profits from the introduction of new technology may offset some of the loss. However there is significant risk attached to these extra profits since they disappear when similar technologies spread across a branch of industry. All other things being equal, the existence of a stock of fixed capital tends to limit the introduction of new technology in the initial stages of the upswing, encouraging capitalists to expand their production by using the existing machinery and equipment.

As a result employment tends to increase, even if not exactly in proportion to the expansion of accumulation. The existence of a relative surplus population (or an industrial reserve army of labour) is absolutely necessary for the upswing to unfold. Given the existence of untapped supplies of labour power, it is possible for employment to expand while real wages remain relatively stable. The stability of real wages and the unchanging production technologies imply relatively stable market prices. Some anarchical maladjustment of commodity demand and supply is unavoidable in the course of capitalist production and exchange, but the imbalances are rectified relatively smoothly through the motion of market prices. As long as reproduction continues to expand without the supply of labour power becoming problematic, the motion of market prices does not possess sufficient amplitude to provoke extensive speculative trading among capitalists.

Meanwhile the supply of idle money capital (formed in the turnover of industrial capital) increases as the scale of capital turnover grows both individually and socially. The greater availability of reserve funds among capitalists makes it easier to accept the deferral of payments and advance commercial credit. It is also possible for the circulation of bills of exchange to expand significantly because the steady enlargement of accumulation provides more scope for reliable future settlement of commercial debt and strengthens the credibility of joint liability. Thus as the upswing gathers steam, commercial credit expands and underpins accumulation independently of banking credit.

The proportion of bills of exchange brought to the banks for discounting remains limited in the early stages of the upswing. The increase in the demand for bank loans is small compared with the expansion taking place in commodity transactions and commercial credit. Banks, meanwhile, can easily augment their deposit liabilities since the available idle money capital is expanding. Banks can also safely rely on regular repayment of their loans, and on easy borrowing in the money market, in order to secure reserves. The central bank is in a similarly favourable position with regard to maintaining an adequate ratio of reserves to liabilities. These factors taken together result in a relatively low rate of interest compared with the rate of profit.

The gap between the rate of profit and the rate of interest further promotes the expansion of capitalist accumulation since it encourages increasing reliance on the credit system. The gap also facilitates the launching of new joint-stock companies with huge fixed capital, as well as expansion of the fixed investment of existing companies through the issuing of shares. Finally, the gap exacerbates the difference between share prices and real capital invested per share, leading to large 'founder's profits' (Gründergewinn). Given our assumptions, the course of the typical business cycle is mainly determined by the relationship between private industrial capitals and a credit system geared to providing short-term credit. Nevertheless investment in joint-stock capital could still play an important role in the development of the cycle by amplifying the swings of capitalist accumulation as a whole. With the development of capitalism the role of joint-stock capital in determining the characteristics of the business cycle has become increasingly important.

6.2.3 The Final Phase of the Upswing

An overaccumulation of capital relative to the existing labouring population occurs towards the end of the upswing, and radically alters the outlook for accumulation. The continuous demands on the reserve army of labour eventually lead to a labour shortage. In a capitalist economy, labour power is a special commodity: it is not produced capitalistically, but within the family, and its quantity is not capable of rapidly increasing according to demand. The difficulty of transforming the subjective human ability to work into a commodity like all others constitutes a fundamental weakness of the capitalist economy. The labour shortage towards the end of the upswing induces a rise in real wages and leads to a fall in the profit rate.[5]

For normal commodities a rise in the market price, caused by a deficiency of supply relative to demand, leads to an increase in production, which in turn lowers the market price. The rise of wages due to the shortage of labour power towards the end of the upswing, on the other hand, is not reversed. Individual capitals find it very difficult to limit their output even when overaccumulation is manifested as rising wage costs. Under competitive pressure, individual capitals continue to expand the scale of their reproduction, often by relying on overtime paid at higher wage rates. The first, and evident, corollary is that the rate of profit tends to decline. The second, and more complex, corollary is that a considerable number of commodity prices tend to rise. On the supply side, rising real wages mean that the cost of production tends to rise faster for industries with low organic composition of capital (labour-intensive industries) than industries with high organic composition (capital-intensive industries). Since profit rates move continually towards equalisation, the prices of labour-intensive commodities rise relative to the prices of capital intensive commodities. On the demand side, rising real wages imply increased demand for some consumer goods. This increase in demand often results in price rises for several important primary products (raw materials or energy resources), the supply of which is difficult to increase in the short term.[6]

As soon as several commodity prices begin persistently to rise, speculative trading and stockpiling of commodities take place in expectation of further price rises. Speculative stockpiling, accentuates the rise in prices by reducing commodity supply, while speculative commodity trading exacerbates the disproportionality among the branches of industry and gives rise to diverging rates of profit. The overall decline in the rate of profit meanwhile limits the expansion of production, and so delays and disrupts the readjustment of disproportionality. Speculative trading also appears in the stock exchange as the share prices of some industries begin to rise in response to the increase in their commodity prices. Joint-stock capital is characteristic of industries with very large plant and equipment needs, which usually require a long gestation period for their construction. Thus supply cannot respond promptly to the increase in prices, further intensifying the speculative trading in the capital market.

To maintain the expansion of production in the face of rising wages and to take advantage of the opportunities for speculation, the inherent elasticity of the credit system is put to full use during the last phase of the upswing. The pressure of rising wage bills (paid in cash) and the fall in the rate of profit reduce the idle money capital generated in the turnover of capital. Individual capitals tend to rely more heavily on bills of exchange and this leads to a corresponding rise in the volume of circulating bills. Large speculators, often wholesale merchants, are likely to increase their commercial debt enormously. At the same time the chains of commercial credit become shorter as the decreasing availability of idle money makes sellers less able to wait for deferred payment. This destroys 'the relative independence of commercial credit from bank credit' (Marx, 1894, pp. 626–7), leading to a greatly increased demand for bank credit in the form of bill discounts.

Banks respond to the greater demand for bank credit by raising their advances. At the same time, however, bank reserves tend to decline relative to liabilities: the inflow of deposits tends to decline, reflecting the slow-down in the generation of idle money capital in the turnover of industrial capital. Moreover the settlement of discounted bills of exchange, is delayed as the date to maturity tends to be prolonged. Bill settlement is now frequently completed with credit obtained by discounting new bills (particularly in the case of speculative operations), a process that might maintain a certain spurious regularity in the settlement of commercial credit obligations. The rate of interest tends to rise, reflecting the weaker supply of and intensified demand for loanable capital.

Thus the overaccumulation of capital relative to the labouring population leads to a rise in wages and a fall in the profit rate. Furthermore, the overaccumulation of productive capital, inevitably brings about a relative shortage of loanable capital, hence 'a rise in interest comes between prosperity and its collapse' (marx, ibid., p. 482).

The combined movement of wages, profit and interest generalises the difficulties for the accumulation of capital. The nature of these difficulties makes it clear that they cannot be overcome by the elastic expansion of credit, though the latter can sustain the growth of effective demand and the rise in prices. Similarly credit cannot overcome the shortage of labour power, which forces a rise in real wages. On the other hand the rising rate of interest contrasts sharply with the falling, and increasingly uneven, rate of profit. The opposite movement of the two impedes the process of real accumulation, hinders the growth of effective demand and destroys the potential profits from speculative commodity stockpiling. This is particularly so for wholesale merchant speculators who hold extensive stocks of goods.

6.2.4 Crisis

Under the conditions established above, the crisis phase of the capitalist business cycle typically begins with the collapse of speculation in stockpiled commodities by wholesale merchants. The rise in the interest rate and the weakening of effective demand force the sale of speculatively stockpiled commodities, leading to the collapse of prices and making the settlement of commercial debt very problematic. The bankruptcy of wholesalers also impacts negatively on the banks, which have advanced substantial amounts of credit for purposes of speculation. For Marx (ibid., p. 419):

> This explains the phenomenon that crises do not first break out and are not first apparent in the retail trade, which bears on immediate consumption, but rather in the sphere of wholesale trade, as well as banking, which places the money capital of the entire society at the wholesalers' disposal.

In general both industrial and commercial capitalists are involved in speculative overtrading. The overaccumulation of capital provides a natural field for speculation in the widened fluctuations of prices caused by the rise in wages. On the other hand speculative overtrading exacerbates the disproportionalities among the branches of industry. When speculation collapses the mood among capitalists takes a pessimistic turn, leading to a sudden drop in the expected future prices of many commodities. For the producers of these commodities, future demand appears significantly weakened.

The fall in demand provides objective grounds for analysis of cyclical crises in terms of excess commodity supply. It cannot be denied that disproportionalities or oversupply of commodities can exacerbate crises caused by overaccumulation of capital relative to the working population. This is especially so when disproportionality and overtrading are combined with speculation-induced instability in money and finance. However commodity overproduction cannot theoretically account for the logical inevitability of crises in the course of the business cycle. Potentially, commodity overproduction can be overcome without giving rise to a general crisis. For the excess capital theory of crisis, on the other hand, the overaccumulation of capital necessarily leads to the collapse of speculation by wholesalers and a general crisis.

Industrial capitalists also generally use commercial and banking credit to expand production and stockpile commodities in the expectation of higher prices in the future. Consequently the fall in commodity prices and the rise in interest rates make it very difficult for industrialists to settle bills of exchange on the due date. Business failures begin to occur among capitalists, resulting in a chain of insolvency. Company failures are exacerbated by the existence of joint liability for the endorsed bills, and by the accelerated fall of commodity prices due to 'sacrifice' sales. According to Marx (ibid., p. 363):

> The chain of obligations to pay at specific dates is broken in a hundred places, and this is further intensified by an accompanying breakdown of the credit system, which had developed alongside capital. All this therefore leads to violent acute crises, sudden forcible devaluations, an actual stagnation and disruption in the reproduction process, and hence to an actual decline in reproduction.

The emergence of insolvency creates great obstacles for the issuing of fresh commercial credit among capitalists. Bill discounting is also severely restricted since banks are concerned to secure their own reserves and avoid insolvency. The resultant credit crisis puts the central bank in a difficult position: it faces an increased demand for loans but cannot be certain of the creditworthiness of the assets offered for sale, and it is also losing its own reserves. Thus 'Interest ... reaches its maximum again as the new crisis breaks out, credit suddenly dries up, payments congeal, the reproduction process is paralysed and ... there is an almost absolute lack of loan capital along-side a surplus of unoccupied industrial capital' (Marx, ibid., p. 620).

In a crisis the rate of interest rises to its highest level while the rate of profit sharply falls, and often becomes negative. The radical change in profit expectations and the rise in the rate of interest induce a collapse in share prices: the speculative boom in the capital market is transformed into a crisis. Given that the speculative share trading of the last phase of the upswing relied on credit, the crisis in the capital market precipitates a wave of insolvencies among speculators who cannot settle their credit obligations.

Thus the typical cyclical crisis has a commercial, a credit and an industrial aspect. The crisis represents the eruption of the fundamental contradiction in a capitalist economy between, on the one hand, the unavoidable commodification of the human capacity to work, and, on the other, the necessarily incomplete nature of this commodification. The crisis also makes apparent the inherently unstable character of a monetary economy. In a crisis 'the antithesis between commodities and their value-form, money, is raised to the level of an absolute contradiction' (Marx, 1867, p. 236). To obtain money as a means of payment in 'the monetary famine', commodities and productive assets are sold at a large discount, their value being sacrificed. At the same time, real wages decline sharply and unemployment rises, annulling the improvements in workers' conditions that had taken place towards the final phase of the upswing.

If individual capitals are markedly similar across and within industries, a chain of successive and interconnected business failures could lead to the complete breakdown of the capitalist economy itself. However capitals are fundamentally dissimilar, and become even more so in the course of speculative expansion in the final phase of the upswing. As a consequence, how individual capitals fare during a crisis depends greatly on pure chance. While many firms go bankrupt under the weight of debt several times larger than their assets, some firms (often within the same industry as the bankrupt ones) are fortunate enough to receive return payments in time. Other firms might sell stocks of commodities at favourable prices at the right moment, and still others might have relatively small amounts of debt to settle. The fortunes of banks in a crisis are similarly uneven. Several industrial, commercial and banking capitals prove successful in maintaining their value during the upheaval of a crisis (often at the expense of others), but it is impossible to identify these at the outset.

A credit crisis arises, above all, from the difficulty of settling the commercial debt created towards the end of the upswing. Since trust evaporates, the issuing of fresh commercial credit becomes practically impossible. The pressure to obtain means of payment through 'sacrifice' sales, however, does not last long.[7] Intensive settlement of the outstanding commercial debt, paid mainly by the equally intensive sale of commodity stocks, leads to a mitigation of the pressure to obtain means of payment and ushers in the depression phase of the business cycle.

6.2.5   Depression

The tendency of wages to fall perseveres after the end of the crisis: it is not possible to reduce significantly the existing supplies of available labour power, despite the decline in production. The fall in wages, the rise in unemployment and the general reduction in working hours cause a precipitous decline in the total income of workers. Thus while the fall in real wages and the price of raw materials helps the rate of profit to recover, the reduced income of workers severely weakens effective demand. Fixed capital, on the whole, escapes significant physical destruction during the crisis. However, as effective demand declines in the depression, firms strive to reduce their idle productive capacity, intensifying competition among them. As a result market prices tend to fall, slowing down the recovery of the profit rate. For industries with steeply falling product prices, severe profitability problems arise that might lead to stagnation, further constraining effective demand across the economy. Some industries, however, find themselves in a particularly favourable position due to the typically uneven fall in prices, as happens for instance when the price of raw materials falls more steeply than the price of the finished product.

The chains of commercial credit begin slowly to reconstitute themselves as capitalist reproduction resumes after a crisis. The credit system, however, operates rather perfunctorily as long as industrial accumulation remains stagnant. During the crisis, some banks have actually – and fortuitously – received payments on a large part of their maturing assets, thus acquiring a healthy reserve position. They now have an advantage in collecting the idle money capital of industrialists in the form of deposits. On the other hand the demand for bank loans in the form of bill discounting tends to be weak. Strong supply and weak demand for loanable money capital result in a low interest rate in the money market.

At these moments, when the reproduction process has undergone a contraction (and after the crisis of 1847, production in the English industrial districts was cut by a third), when commodity prices stand at their lowest point, and when the entrepreneurial spirit is crippled, there is a low rate of interest, which in this case simply indicates an increase in loanable capital precisely as a result of the contraction and paralysis of industrial capital (Marx, 1894, p. 616).

The low rate of interest in the depression, however, can neither resolve nor mitigate the fundamental difficulties of real accumulation. These difficulties essentially arise from the generalised presence of idle fixed capital, and might be further compounded by the completion of very large projects by joint-stock capitals, the gestation period of which finishes in the course of the depression. Business failure does not significantly ameliorate the pressure of excess capacity as the plant and equipment of failed industrial capitalists is often bought cheaply by other capitalists and remains operational. Thus competition among firms is intensified, leading to further price falls and preventing the recovery of effective demand and the rate of profit. The capital market meanwhile remains inactive; low share prices reflect industrial stagnation and the dismal future prospects for profits. The low rate of interest is not generally successful in reactivating the capital market, though it could lessen the market's difficulties.

Confronted with the problems of depression, individual capitals begin to introduce new methods of production. Unlike the upswing, heavy competitive pressure during the depression forces industrial capitals to abandon and replace their existing fixed capital facilities. Under the pressure of depression, the temporary extra profit accruing from the introduction of improved methods of production proves an especially attractive incentive to innovate. The introduction of new technology becomes easier if substantial depreciation of the old stock of fixed capital has already taken place, limiting the capital losses from the scrapping process. The reserve funds accumulated in the course of depreciation help to finance the new investment. Thus in the depression, industrial capitals introduce new techniques of production that tend to raise the organic composition of capital. The drive to instal new technology becomes even more pronounced towards the end of the depression, since by then firms have generally succeeded in depreciating a large part of their fixed capital. Throughout this period cost economies are sought by capitalists in production and circulation. The 'rationalisation' of capitalist operations deepens as the scrapping and rebuilding of plant and equipment intensifies.[8]

It is both paradoxical and absurd, particularly from the standpoint of workers, that the drive to raise the organic composition of capital takes place at a time of high unemployment. Indeed the rising organic composition of capital adds further unemployment to the already swollen industrial reserve army of labour. The increased supplies of surplus labour power, however, enable capitalist accumulation eventually to surpass its previous peak (both in value and physical output), even when the size of the working population is given.

The industrial capitals whose technology has been renewed are now able to expand the scale of their production. In the course of replacing their fixed capital, firms have also been able to shift their operations towards more potentially profitable areas. The movement of capital across branches of production tends to eliminate disproportionalities among industries, despite the fact that the process is anarchically driven by the expected rate of profit. With improved methods of production across the economy, the rate of surplus value can be raised as the necessary part of the working day is further compressed. The elimination of divergences in the rate of profit, moreover, reconfirms the role of prices of production as the centre of gravity of market prices. Accumulation can now expand promptly, and the fluctuating market prices allow the emergence of satisfactorily high rates of profit in the vicinity of the general rate of profit. With renewed social relations of value corresponding to the new social powers of production, the process of accumulation can enter a new upswing.

In the capitalist business cycle the fundamental contradiction of a capitalist economy, rooted in the commodification of the human ability to work, erupts in a destructive and sharp crisis. The contradiction is resolved during the course of the depression that follows the crisis, and eventually the conditions for an upswing are put in place. The depression does not permanently remove the contradiction; rather it resolves the contradiction temporarily and in practice. Thus, a destructive crisis inevitably appears again as the upswing unfolds. In this manner a periodic business cycle materialises.

The replacement of fixed capital marks a decisive moment: the end of the depression and the beginning of a new upswing. Consequently the length of the economic life of fixed capital provides the material foundation for the amplitude of regular business cycles. Regarding the decennial cycle of liberal capitalism, Marx (1885, p. 264) remarked that the 'life-cycle' of fixed capitals in the main spheres of industry 'is one of the material foundations for the periodic cycle in which business passes through successive periods of stagnation, moderate activity, over-excitement and crisis'. However, neither the features of the capitalist business cycle nor the length of its periodicity are unchangeable. As the nature of the fixed capital employed in the leading industries of capitalist accumulation changes, so does the capitalist business cycle.

6.3   DETERMINATION OF THE VALUE OF MONEY OVER THE BUSINESS CYCLE

6.3.1   The Quantity Theory of Money and the Business Cycle

The movement of the price level in the course of the business cycle is complex: prices rise during the last phase of the upswing; they fall sharply during the crisis as 'sacrifice' sales take place; they stagnate at a low level during the depression. As a new upswing takes shape, two opposite price tendencies materialise. On the one hand the downward pressure on prices is removed because of the recovery of effective demand and the reduction in idle capacity during the depression. The establishment of a more balanced relationship between aggregate supply and demand tends to raise the price level. On the other hand the costs of production tend to decline because of the general improvement in the techniques of production as fixed capital is replaced. Hence prices of production tend to fall. When combined, the two tendencies might leave prices at a lower level compared with that of the previous upswing, but also that of the preceding depression.

The simple form of the quantity theory of money entirely fails to explain the price fluctuations of the business cycle. The rise in prices during the speculative last phase of the upswing occurs independently of changes in the circulating quantity of commodity money (gold). The expansion of commercial and banking credit, on the other hand, results in an increase in the quantity of credit money, mostly bills of exchange, banknotes and deposits. However the rise in real wages and the emergence of speculative overtrading are not due to the increase in the quantity of credit money, though the latter makes possible the overall rise in prices. Similarly the sharp collapse in prices during the crisis is not caused by a sudden reduction in the quantity of money relative to commodities.[9] Although a sharp reduction in the quantity of credit money usually accompanies the fall in prices, it is simply a result of the collapse and paralysis of the credit system induced by the overaccumulation of industrial capital. Finally, the low and stagnant price level during the depression might be accompanied by stagnation in the generation of credit money, but the ultimate cause of both is the weakness of effective demand and the intensification of competition among firms.

By the same token, control of the quantity of money by the monetary authorities – as was first attempted by the Bank Act of 1844 in accordance with the currency principle – cannot successfully stabilise the price level in the course of the business cycle. However this is not to suggest that the approach of the banking school is valid: banks are not able to discriminate between real and fictitious bills (that is, loans that might or might not be backed by real commodity transactions); similarly the regular reflux of bank liabilities as assets mature cannot guarantee the harmonious growth of the quantity of credit money relative to capital accumulation. Indeed in the last phase of the upswing and as overaccumulation appears, all capitals tend to use credit facilities in order to engage in speculation.

Marx criticised Ricardo's quantity theory of money because it ignores the full complexity of the functions of money and reduces the latter to means of circulation alone. For Marx, if the quantity of money exceeds the amount necessary as means of circulation, a part of it could become a hoard. The quantity theory, moreover, determines the exchange value of money (the inverse of the price level) purely in terms of quantities of money and commodities. This aspect of Ricardo's theory sits very uneasily with determination of the value of the money commodity as labour-embodied, and seems to apply only to the money commodity. By rejecting the quantity theory, Marx aimed at developing a more coherent theory of value. Finally, Marx's contributions to the theory of the business cycle, incorporating several of the economic functions of credit, constitute an evident critique of the tradition of the currency school.

Throughout *Capital* Marx examined the determination of the value of money on the same basis as the value of other commodities. In the first two volumes, equal exchange takes place between the labour embodied in the money commodity and in other commodities; in the third volume, the gold industry participates in the formation of the general rate of profit and of prices of production on the same footing as all other industries. Nonetheless Marx did not fully explore the peculiarities of the relationship between the value and the exchange value of money, particularly with regard to the balancing of the demand and supply of the money commodity. The social mechanism through which the law of value also applies to the money commodity remains a partially unresolved issue, some aspects of which are considered below.[10]

6.3.2 Balancing the Demand and Supply of Gold

Assume that the money commodity is gold, the gold industry participates in the formation of the general rate of profit and prices of production, and there is variable fertility of gold mines. Assume further that the organic composition of capital in the gold industry is equal to the social average. This assumption ensures that the rate of profit in the gold industry responds to changes in wages in the same manner as the general rate of profit. Relaxing it, that is, allowing for higher or lower organic composition in the gold industry relative to the social average, complicates the analysis without adding significant additional insight. The analysis rests on the fundamental observation that, since gold output is directly money, profitability of the gold industry moves in the opposite direction to the general price level. In the normal course of the cycle, prices rise in the final phase of the upswing, fall sharply in the crisis and stagnate at a low level in the depression.

Given unchanged technical conditions of production in the gold industry, higher input prices toward, the end of the upswing imply higher per unit costs in the production of gold. Hence the rate of profit in the gold industry falls.[11] The lower rate of profit and the general rise in the rate of interest toward the end of the upswing, compel the gold industry to stop expanding, and possibly to reduce production in the least fertile mines. If, moreover, the contracts that determine the magnitude of rent paid to the owners of land cannot be renegotiated in a short period of time (in response to the rising costs), the rate of profit of gold-producing capitalists in the more fertile mines also declines. Thus gold production tends to fall in both the less and the more fertile mines.

The reduction in gold output towards the end of the upswing has two effects. First, it reduces effective demand by the gold industry, thus partially countering the general boom unfolding at the time. This effect is analogous to the tendency of exports to decline due to a rise in domestic prices relative to foreign prices. Second, it further tightens the availability of reserves to banks and the central bank at a time when the issuing of credit has increased greatly. Though the decline in gold output is certainly not the main factor behind the reserve shortage in the credit system, it directly contributes to the rise in the rate of interest. Thus the price of loanable capital rises further as the exchange value of money declines.

The crisis and subsequent depression lead to a sharp fall and stagnation at a low level of both prices and wages. Thus the costs of production in the gold industry decline and its profitability is improved.[12] Marginal mines that could not be profitably operated previously now come on stream, and gold output rises. Provided that the rent contracts for the mines cannot be renegotiated in a very short period of time, the capitalists operating the more fertile mines also enjoy higher profits, and similarly tend to increase their production. The increase in gold output boosts the effective demand of the gold industry and partially mitigates the worst effects of the depression. The effect is, again, analogous to a rise in exports due to a fall in domestic relative to foreign prices. Increased gold production also helps augment the reserves of the banking system.

It is very unlikely that the mere rise in gold output in a depression is sufficient, in and of itself, fully to restore effective demand and raise the price level. Rather the price level recovers when depression turns to upswing, as correction of the imbalance between aggregate supply and demand removes the heavy downward pressure on prices. Prices might for a while remain below the level of the previous upswing, given that the techniques of production have improved during the depression. This is particularly so if productivity in the gold industry increases less than in other industries. As long the price level is below that of the previous upswing, gold output remains at a higher level since less fertile mines continue to come on stream and earn the average rate of profit. The increased supply of gold meets the sharpened demand of capitalist reproduction for gold, both as raw material in manufacturing and as money.

A point of critical importance in this respect is that gold is also used to hoard the absolute form of wealth and to make luxury ornaments. Furthermore, only a small part of the annual output of gold perishes naturally; the rest is added to the very large stock that is normally held by capitalist society, that is, circulating money, hoarded money, bullion, plate, ornaments and so on. Therefore the flow demand for gold in all periods, is not determined by the strict requirements of reproduction but can potentially rise beyond the latter. The instability the capitalist economy exhibits in the course of the business cycle, and the prospect of falls in the price level, encourage both the hoarding of gold among the wealthy and the creation of larger reserves among banks. The flow of the new production of gold per period, moreover, can be buttressed by parts of the social stock of gold, for instance by melting down plate and ornaments to supplement the circulation of money.

Consequently, even if low prices at the beginning of the new upswing encourage a supply of newly produced gold in excess of social demand, a fall in the exchange value of gold takes much longer to materialise than for other commodities. Still, as long as gold supply exceeds the demand for raw materials, additions to circulating money and planned additions to the hoards of individual economic agents, the excess is likely to lead to extra commodity purchases, partially boosting effective demand. This is likely to push the price level gradually upwards as the upswing unfolds. Furthermore the greater availability of bank reserves is also likely to promote the expansion of credit, contributing to the rising effective demand. Finally, wages will also rise as prices rise in the course of the upswing. The combination of these factors eventually reduces the rate of profit in the gold industry, resulting in a decline in the production of gold, starting with the worst mines. Gradually, the flow of new gold output adjusts to the flow of demand.

Given the large existing stock of gold, which can be flexibly employed to provide gold for several purposes, there is no rapidly operating social mechanism that balances the social demand and supply of gold. Equally there is no rapidly operating social mechanism that expresses the relative productivity changes between gold and other industries in terms of the exchange value of gold. The balance between the flow of gold demand and the flow of gold produced per period is adjusted slowly through the changes in the price level that occur in a typical upswing from one cycle to the next. The process might last for several business cycles, potentially leading to the emergence of protracted secular trends in the price level (or even long waves of prices).[13]

6.4 THE HISTORICAL EVOLUTION OF THE BUSINESS CYCLE

6.4.1 The Transformation of the Business Cycle

In a part of *Capital*, Marx (1867, p. 786) appeared to think that the decennial business cycle was destined to repeat itself, just as the motion of 'the heavenly bodies' repeated itself. However, several factors contributed to the transformation of the business cycle from the 1870s onwards. When the cotton industry reached technological maturity, the focus of capitalist accumulation shifted towards industries requiring very large fixed capital investment. Railways and steel, which had been rather marginal to capitalist accumulation and merely accentuated the features of the mid-nineteenth-century business cycle, began to lead capitalist accumulation in Britain and the world. The transformation of the business cycle was ultimately due to the emergence of leading industries with huge fixed capital requirements after the classical age.

It is impossible to expand the productive capacity of such industries on the basis of continuous incremental change by each firm. The construction of large plant and other productive facilities takes years, consumes large quantities of capital goods and keeps hundreds, or even thousands, of workers occupied without immediate productive results. Once completed, each firm's investment typically represents a significant addition to the existing productive capacity of the industry.

Since individual firms can no longer assume that their fixed capital investment adds only marginally to the capacity of the industry, it becomes absolutely necessary to form expectations about the future growth of demand. Thus speculation inevitably emerges in the field of real investment. During its gestation period, fixed capital investment tends to increase effective demand without increasing supply, encouraging speculative expectations about the growth of demand. These expectations lead to anarchical booms in the construction of large plant, which especially affect the capital goods industry. The upswing of the business cycle, led by the expansion of industries with huge fixed capitals, acquires an even more strongly speculative character, and may be highly uneven from the beginning.

Both joint-stock capital and idle money mobilised in the capital market play an important role in the construction of huge fixed capacity. Even in financial systems in which banks regularly advance long-term loans for fixed capital investment (typically in Germany and Japan), banks still expect to sustain their loans by promoting new share issues in the capital market. Thus banks obtain a part of the 'founder's profit' (Gründergewinn) from these issues. New shares can be issued with least difficulty as the upswing unfolds since future prospects appear at their rosiest, the gestation period of fixed capital is continuing and the rate of interest is low.

There are several reasons why the optimistic expectations emerging in the course of the upswing might prove incorrect: output demand might not grow as fast, productive capacity among rival firms might expand considerably, loanable money capital might prove unavailable at low interest rates, share prices might stop rising in the capital market. As a result expectations could take a sharp turn towards pessimism, leading to a break in the upswing long before the over-accumulation of capital relative to the labouring population can cause a rise in wages. In particular, as the upswing unfolds the speculative increase in fixed capital investment, accompanied by a rise in share prices, might lead to increases in the demand for loanable money capital and stringency in the money market. The concomitant rise in the rate of interest might cause a collapse of optimism.

Shoring up the expectations of capitalists with regard to the profit-ability of large fixed investment is one of the main problems of real accumulation. If pessimism appears, a collapse of share prices might take place, leading to a general financial crisis. The subsequent failure of large financial institutions, or of big speculators, might accentuate the demand for means of payment, leading to a further rise in the rate of interest. The combination of a failed investment drive, a collapse of the stock exchange and a rise in the rate of interest, could give rise to generalised difficulties for commercial and industrial capital, ushering in a depression.

The possibility cannot be precluded that, after a large speculative investment boom, a general collapse of the financial system might combine with a breakdown of commercial and industrial activities and lead to a fully fledged economic crisis. This sequence of events conforms with the experience of the crisis of 1929 and the subsequent Great Depression of the 1930s. For such a crisis to occur, it is not necessary that significant overaccumulation of capital relative to the labouring population should take place. However it is more likely that the collapse of a speculative boom in fixed capital investment, accompanied by a steep fall in share prices, would lead to a milder crisis, characterised by lack of determination fully to destroy excess capitals. The acute and total crisis of the typical business cycle is transformed into the unpredictable end of the upswing, which induces a depression. Business cycles as a whole become more speculative and unstable and their monetary phenomena acquire greater prominence.

In the depression phase, all the characteristics of the classical depression reappear but they are both more extensive and more persistent. Huge amounts of fixed capital remain in place and their value depreciates slowly. Excessive production capacity is further increased as plant and equipment comes on stream, the construction of which started during the upswing. The plant and equipment of failed firms is taken over by other firms (or by the same firms under new ownership and management), and does not reduce the excess capacity. The decline in the demand for loanable money capital lowers the rate of interest, but the process of accumulation is unlikely to be reactivated on this score alone. Moreover, as long as the profitability prospects of joint-stock capital are poor, the capital market remains depressed.

When the domestic economy is relatively well-protected and industrial technology changes rather slowly, monopoly organisation and pricing might emerge in order to mitigate the effects of the slowdown in accumulation. Monopoly pricing widens the profit margin of the monopolistic sectors at the expense of the competitive ones. However successful monopoly pricing relies on reductions in output and employment, and might lead to increases in the costs of non-monopolistic industries. Thus monopoly pricing might actually intensify and prolong the depression.

It is likely that widespread monopoly pricing contributed significantly to the extent and depth of the Great Depression of the 1930s. The prolongation of the depression phase of the business cycle, however, began historically with the Great Depression of 1873–96 and predated the establishment of monopolies at the turn of the century. A similar prolongation of depression has also been observed in the period after 1973, despite the significant intensification of capitalist competition that has taken place both domestically and internationally. Intractably excessive fixed capital investment in the major industries appears to be a more fundamental cause of the prolongation of the depression phase than the existence of monopoly (though the latter might compound the overall difficulties of accumulation).

New upswings are unlikely to begin at the core industries of capitalist accumulation as long as excessive fixed capital capacity persists. Thus upswings might be precipitated in peripheral industries, or in foreign markets, as partial, uneven and largely speculative phenomena. Such upswings tend to be short-lived and do not alter the keynote of persistent depression. In this manner a complex pattern of cycles emerges, including smaller and larger ones, as was evident in the Great Depressions of 1873–96, the 1930s and post-1973.

Attempts to alleviate and resolve the persistent difficulties of real accumulation in the major industries have historically taken many different forms. Narrowly economic methods have been widely employed, including innovation in industrial technology, the introduction of new products and the adoption of new methods of labour management. More broadly, the state has frequently attempted to deal with the difficulties of real accumulation by means of fiscal, monetary and austerity policies. At an even more general level, broad politico-economic developments have also contributed to the restructuring of capitalist accumulation, including imperialism, fascism and war. The attempts to deal with the problems of capitalist accumulation have often been at the expense of working people, and have frequently caused wholesale misery and the destruction of ways of life. Sustained upswings of accumulation, such as occurred during 1897–1913 and 1945–1973, are possible only after particularly determined and concerted attempts to restructure capitalist accumulation.

6.4.2 Long-Wave Theories

The historical transformation of the business cycle has led to the emergence of long wave theories of capitalist development, which assert that great cycles exist (long waves) punctuated by smaller cycles. It is usually assumed that the duration of each long wave is about fifty years, comprising a long upswing and a long downswing of roughly equal length.

Several Marxists, including Helphand (Parvus) (1901) and Kautsky (1913), explored long wave theory at the turn of the twentieth century in response to the transformation of the business cycle. However Kondratieff's (1935) later attempt to theorise long waves, stressing the role of money and finance, has proved more influential. For Kondratieff, a precondition for a long upswing is low prices together with abundant and cheap loanable capital. Long-term investment in large plant and equipment is thereby stimulated, land improvement proceeds and highly skilled workers are trained. On the other hand, long downswings begin when loanable money capital becomes relatively scarce and prices high, making long-term economic activity expensive and unattractive. The development of industrial technology, discoveries in gold mining, the incorporation of new markets into the world economy, wars and revolutions are not causes of long waves – though they often comply with the rhythms of the latter. Kondratieff thus advanced a theory that essentially located the causes of long waves within the order of the capitalist economy.

Schumpeter's (1939) appellation for long waves was 'Kondratieff cycles', but he actually proposed a different mechanism from

Kondratieff, though still essentially within the fundamentals of capitalist accumulation. For Schumpeter, in the course of the long downswing major industrial innovations appear and gradually induce a long upswing as they become diffused across industry; less significant innovations give rise to medium-term business cycles ('Juglar cycles', roughly decennial); and fluctuations in firm inventories give rise to short-term business cycles with an amplitude of about 40 months ('Kitchin cycles'). Schumpeter's theory suffers from the obvious weakness that the clustering of significant innovations at 50-year intervals is very hard to theorise using conventional economic analysis. Nevertheless Schumpeter's discussion remains a useful frame of reference for the analysis of long waves.

In contrast to the above theories, Trotsky (1941) asserted that long waves of capitalist development should not be treated as analogous to the classical business cycle. The major causes of long waves do not lie within the intrinsic dynamic of the capitalist economy. Rather, long waves are induced by the socio-political conditions that surround capitalist accumulation, such as the opening of new markets, the discovery of natural resources, wars and revolutions.

Mandel resurrected long-wave theory in the early 1970s in a manner heavily influenced by Trotsky, though his treatment was also eclectic.[14] Mandel (1975, ch. 4, 1980, pp. 21, 55) relied on Trotsky's argument to account for the turning point introducing the long upswing. At the same time he attempted to explain the turning point introducing the long downswing in terms of the intrinsic dynamic of capitalist accumulation, and stressed the tendency of the rate of profit to fall due to the rising organic composition of capital. If one disregards the stress on the law of the falling rate of profit, Mandel's asymmetrical theory offers considerable insight into the course of capitalist development after the Second World War. His argument, however, cannot deal satisfactorily with the long upswing that commenced around 1896: the latter appeared to be driven by the intrinsic dynamic of capitalist accumulation rather than socio-political events, and clearly ended with the outbreak of the First World War.

In more recent years, the French Regulation school and the Social Structure of Accumulation school in the United States explained the long-term movement of capitalist accumulation by analysing the socio-political framework of accumulation rather than the dynamic of accumulation itself. Both schools stress the importance of general social relations (not only economic) between capital and labour. Aglietta (1979) and Boyer (1986) of the Regulation school, for instance, argue that a critically important historical change has taken place in the development of capitalism: the earlier extensive mode of accumulation became the intensive, post-Second-World-War, Fordist mode of accumulation. The change strengthened the social power of workers and made possible rises in real wages roughly in line with increases in productivity. For the Regulation school, this was a key factor behind the continuous expansion of effective demand that characterised the 1945–73 period of high economic growth. The period of protracted accumulation difficulties after the 1970s signified the crisis of Fordism, and presented the capitalist countries with the challenge of appropriately restructuring their socio-political relations in order to regulate capital–labour relations. Gordon *et al.* (1982) and Bowles and Edwards (1985) of the Social Structure of Accumulation school, also stress the importance of the socio-political framework within which capital–labour relations develop. A period of initial proletarianisation lasted until the end of the nineteenth century and was followed by the period of homogenisation of labour in highly mechanised giant firms, which lasted until the 1930s. In turn this was followed by a period of segmentation of the labour market after the Second World War. According to this school, these distinctions are important for the explanation of long-wave phenomena in US history, and provide a background for analysis of the recent period of industrial restructuring in the United States, which has led to more flexible labour management.

As an heuristic device, long-wave theory is useful. However there are two important reasons why one should avoid the temptation of turning long-wave theory into a general theory of capitalist development. First, long waves are not particularly important for the explanation of the decennial business cycle and the periodic crises of the age of liberal capitalism. Similarly, in the age of mercantile capitalism, long waves of capitalist development were not as prominent as irregular speculative bubbles and crises. The historical basis for long-wave theory was actually provided by the transformation of the business cycle, which started with the Great Depression of 1873–96. Second, despite several attempts by Marxists, neoclassicals and others, it has proved impossible to advance a coherent explanation of the causes of long upswings and downswings. In practice, various concrete historical developments, specific either to the dynamic of capitalist accumulation itself or to the socio-political framework within which accumulation takes place, have proved critical for the emergence of long waves. Capital–labour relations have certainly played a vital role in the emergence of long-term patterns of capitalist accumulation. However to argue that changes in these relations (arising from the course of class struggle) are the ultimate cause of long waves is too simple and general an explanation. The complexity of capitalist accumulation, which has its own dynamic and unfolds in a definite historical context, cannot be reduced to the class struggle alone.

Finally, on the whole, Marxist long-wave theory after Kondratieff has tended, to neglect the role of money and finance. Nevertheless money and finance have often played an essential role in differentiating the historical features of long waves. Marx's theoretical legacy on the classical business cycle could offer many insights for analysis of long waves in this respect, without necessarily locating the causes of long waves in the phenomena of money and finance.

6.4.3   Non-Marxist Theories of Financial Instability and the Business Cycle

Wicksell (1898) has proposed an original and influential explanation of the business cycle. According to him, the 'natural' rate of interest is given by the marginal productivity of real capital while the nominal rate of interest is determined in the money market. At the beginning of the upswing, the supply of banking credit can be expanded promptly, thus lowering the nominal rate of interest below the 'natural' rate. As a result investment in real capital becomes more attractive and expands. This leads to cumulative price rises, starting with the price of capital goods, which further encourage investment. Taken together, the rise in prices, the concomitant increase in money incomes and an inevitable tightening of the reserve position of banks, eventually constrain the supply of banking credit and push the nominal rate of interest above the 'natural' rate. This reverses the cumulative process of investment and price increases, leading to deflation and depression.

Wicksell's theory rightly emphasises the significance of banks for capitalist accumulation. However the theory does not offer reasons why the dynamics of real capital accumulation allow banking credit to acquire such an important role. Wicksell's stress on the role of the money market in generating business cycles is essentially a reversal of the underlying process as that was analysed above. His monetary theory of the business cycle probably reflects the experience of the shorter-term business cycles that punctuate longer upswings and downswings, and often occur through speculative operations in the capital market. Wicksell's postulate of a 'natural' rate of interest, moreover, is very problematic. In Chapter 3 of this work it was argued that the rate of interest represents a conventional division of the surplus value produced and reflects no material, 'natural', aspect of capitalist accumulation. Despite these caveats, however, Wicksell's theory offers considerable insight into the role of banking credit in the course of the business cycle, and our earlier discussion has evident affinities with it.

Keynes' (1936) stress on expectations and speculation was an important contribution to the analysis of money and finance in the course of business fluctuations. For Keynes, the money rate of interest is determined by the demand and supply of money as a stock. The demand for money, or liquidity preference, arises from three motives: the transactions, the precautionary and the speculative.[15] The first two vary directly with income and the third varies inversely with the rate of interest. If the rate of interest is low, security prices tend to be high but more people expect them to fall in the future. The opposite holds for high rates of interest. The supply of money, on the other hand, is determined exogenously, that is, according to the essentially political choices of the monetary authorities.

For Keynes, the marginal efficiency of capital declines as investment increases. This is essentially because the expected revenue from increments to investment declines and the prices of the factors of production rise. Equilibrium investment emerges at the point at which the marginal efficiency of capital equals the rate of interest. The effective demand generated by equilibrium investment, which is added to the effective demand generated by consumption, may not be sufficient to generate full employment. In that case, state monetary policy could lower the rate of interest in order to promote further investment; fiscal policy could also directly expand effective demand, thus reducing unemployment. Above all, Keynes sought a theoretical explanation for large-scale involuntary unemployment that could help devise economic policies appropriate for the deep depression of the 1930s. He was less concerned with the role played by financial instability in business cycles and periodic economic crises. The recurrent economic crises since the 1960s, in which credit and finance have played a critical role, encouraged some of Keynes followers to develop theories of financial instability.

Minsky (1975, 1982) has advanced the most influential theory of financial instability and crisis within the Keynesian tradition. Minsky (1985) distinguished between capital asset prices, which reflect long-run expectations, and current output prices, which reflect short-run expectations. Firms can assume three types of financial posture: 'hedge finance', in which 'the cash flows from assets in position are expected to exceed the cash flow commitments on liabilities for every period'; 'speculative finance', in which 'the cash flows from assets in the near future term fall short of the near term contracted payments', implying the need to roll over or refinance the debt, but, 'the expected cash receipts in the longer term are expected to exceed cash payments commitments that are outstanding'; and 'Ponzi finance', in which the net income from receipts falls short of interest payments in both the short run and the long run, implying the need to borrow simply in order to cover interest payments and rapidly raising outstanding debt. A 'Ponzi finance' firm essentially hopes that a future bonanza will solve its problems.

An increase in investment raises gross profit, securing the principal and interest of debt. As a result capitalists form optimistic expectations about future profits, which serve to raise the price of capital assets and encourages further investment. In this favourable climate for accumulation (hedge finance predominating), banks can promptly expand their credit creation by relying on smooth return payments. However the rise in capital asset prices, combined with the ease of acquiring debt, eventually give rise to substantial investment funded by speculative or even Ponzi finance. Prices and profits begin to climb and as long-term investment also increases, there is a rapidly rising demand for finance. At the same time the internal workings of the banking mechanism (or central bank action to limit the possibility of inflation) constrain the supply of finance. A rapid rise in the short-term interest rate materialises.

For Minsky (1985, p. 46), 'Sharp increases in short-term interest rates increase the supply price of investment output, and also lead to a rise in long-term interest rates', as well as to a fall in the present value of gross profits. Consequently investment falls, as do current and expected short-term profits. Hence 'some hedge units become speculative units and some speculative units become Ponzi units' (ibid.) Since the expectations of profitability have become reversed, capitalists tend to 'sell-out of positions' rather than refinance them, and this makes 'asset prices fall below their cost of production as investment goods'. Whether the process develops into a fully fledged financial crisis depends on the promptness of the action of the central bank as lender of last resort, and on the effectiveness of government fiscal policy in maintaining effective demand. Business activity can be revived by means of fiscal and monetary policy, provided that long-term expectations have not become pessimistic. However if expectations have become pessimistic and long-term interest rates have risen, a protracted depression might follow a financial crisis.

Minsky's theory of financial instability has a clearly Keynesian pedigree since it stresses uncertainty, expectations and speculation. It has much in common with the Marxist theory of crisis, particularly because it attempts to identify inherent weaknesses of the capitalist economy. However Minsky completely ignores the contradictory and crisis-prone character of real capitalist accumulation, itself ultimately deriving from the class relations of capital and labour. With this critically important proviso, Marxist theory can benefit from Minsky's insight into uncertainty, expectations and speculation.[16]

It must also be noted that Minsky's emphasis on long-term expectations for the valuation of capital assets is appropriate only for capitalism that possesses a substantial capital market. Furthermore, financial instability was not particularly pronounced during the long upswing after the Second World War. Minsky's financial instability hypothesis appears most relevant for the period of accumulation difficulties that commenced in the 1970s. The specific changes in the historical conditions of capitalist accumulation in the post-Second-World-War period must be examined first in order fully to appreciate the significance of the relationship between long-term expectations and capitalist financial instability. Chapter 8 puts forth several analytical arguments in this regard.

7 Central Banking

Central banks possess and utilise an element of economic rationality in the anarchical world of capitalist finance and accumulation. Consequently they have long been the object of the reformist zeal of credit practitioners and political radicals. They have also been subjected to withering criticism by those who think that the inherent instability of capitalist accumulation originates in money and finance. This chapter argues that there are narrow limits to the effectiveness of central bank operations determined by capitalist accumulation. That is not to negate the element of conscious policy-making and the possibility of partial success of central bank operations. However the crisis-ridden character of the capitalist economy cannot be abolished by central banking, regardless of the experience of the central bankers and the erudition of their economic advisers.

7.1 THE NATURE OF THE CENTRAL BANK

7.1.1 Bank of Banks

The central bank is the apex of the pyramid-like capitalist credit system. Participation in the main money market enables ordinary banks to pursue their lending business flexibly, and without issuing their own banknote liabilities. In order to maintain the adequacy of their reserves, such banks rely on deposit accruals, regular debt repayment and borrowing in the money market. The efficiency and flexibility of their lending business can be further increased through the centralisation of their reserves. Just as industrial and commercial capitalists economise on their reserves of idle money by depositing funds with a bank, so banks economise on their reserves by depositing funds with a central bank. The most elementary function of a central bank as bank of banks is to hold a centralised reserve for the banking system as a whole. Several important implications follow from this function.

The existence of a centralised reserve enables individual banks systematically to turn their own reserves from accumulations of ready money into accumulations of claims on others (above all, on the central bank). This process is again analogous to the transformation of the hoards of individual capitalists into claims on banks (Marx, 1894, p. 600). As shown in Chapters 4 and 6, a spontaneously established capitalist credit system is underpinned by commodity money. Consequently the reserves of the central bank are a hoard of gold. Although individual banks, especially those in local areas, must also hold some quantity of gold coin to meet the requirements of local circulation, the largest part of a country's hoarded monetary gold becomes the reserve of the central bank. The main point of access to hoarded commodity money in advanced capitalist economies is provided by the liabilities of the central bank. Thus the gold hoard of the central bank can slowly assume a national character, it can become the national hoard of a capitalist economy.[1]

Given that it possesses the centralised banking hoard, the balance the central bank maintains between its liabilities and its reserves is critical for the operations of the banking system as a whole. As discussed in Chapter 4, the reserve requirements of individual banks are determined empirically and have an elastic relationship with the banks' lending operations. Insofar as ordinary bank reserves are claims on the central bank's gold hoard (that is, they are liabilities of the central bank), the size of the hoard inevitably has a significant bearing on the ability of individual banks to secure reserves and so expand their lending business. Concern about the size of its gold reserve, on the other hand, constrains the ability of the central bank to provide its own liabilities to individual banks. By the same token, it also constrains the ability of the private banks to provide their own liabilities to industrial and commercial capitalists.

Historical evidence that the relationship between reserves and liabilities influences the central bank's operations is provided by the so-called Palmer rule, which guided the Bank of England in the early 1830s.[2] This rule required that the Bank should keep no more than two thirds of its assets in the form of securities (the last third taken up by gold) against the whole of its liabilities (banknotes and deposits). As Clapham (1944, vol. II, p. 125) observed, in propounding this rule 'Palmer and Norman were describing the fair weather practice of a single decade, not promulgating a dogma'. The Palmer rule was the precursor of the Bank Act of 1844; the Act, however, removed whatever flexibility Palmer's rule possessed, and forced onto the Bank a rigid quantitative relationship between its gold hoard and its banknote liabilities.[3]

A closer look is necessary here at the relationship between the central bank's gold reserve and the ability of ordinary banks to extend credit. The balance between the demand and supply of loanable money capital across the economy translates, in the final instance, into changes in the ratio between the gold reserve and the liabilities of the central bank. More specifically, the flows of debt repayment, security purchases, loans and new deposits, which take place between the banking system and capitalists involved in real accumulation, are ultimately reflected in the ratio of the central bank's gold reserve to its liabilities. The central bank's gold reserve, in other words, acts as a reflection as well as a pivot for the extension of banking credit. This allows the price at which the central bank provides its own liabilities (mostly the rate of bill rediscount and the rate of short-term lending to banks) to become the benchmark rate for the money market rate of interest.

There is no reason to expect a stable relationship between the total quantity of credit money created by ordinary banks and the liabilities of the central bank, regardless of whether the latter are convertible into gold or not. For the operation of the banks what matters is an empirically ascertained minimum below which their reserve ratios should preferably not fall. The actual levels of bank reserve ratios, meanwhile, vary with the stage of the business cycle; they further depend on the particular institutional arrangements of both the credit system and real accumulation. If, for example, new borrowing instruments make it easier for banks to borrow funds in the money market, bank reserve ratios are driven downwards. Insofar as a money multiplier exists, that is, an algebraic relationship between the total quantity of credit money and the reserves held by banks with the central bank, it is an unstable magnitude that depends on the phase of the business cycle and the type of institutional framework in place.

Since they are the main means of access to the national gold hoard, the liabilities of the central bank are the preeminent form of a country's credit money. To sustain the circulation of bills of exchange as credit money it is necessary for a process of commercial debt clearing to be in place. Moreover the generalised clearing of various credit claims against each other is fundamental if banknotes and deposits are to function as credit money. By settling claims against each other banks can economise on their reserves, rely less on gold for payments, and secure a more rapid and smoother circulation of banknotes and deposits. The most important means of payment in the clearing process (or the money of large capitalist transactions) is provided by the liabilities of the central bank.

Despite central bank notes spontaneously becoming the preeminent form of credit money, state intervention is necessary for them to become legal tender, that is, a means of payment with obligatory acceptability. The state actively confers its own legitimacy onto the central bank notes, which are central to the operations of large-scale trade and of the credit system. The rise of state-backed credit money further limits the buying and paying functions of commodity money. However the latter does not spontaneously disappear from capitalist circulation. Small-scale payments, particularly for wages, the settlement of obligations among financial institutions remote from the money market and from the clearing process, and the requirements of international trade all continue to provide a residual role for circulating commodity money. For the complete disappearance of commodity money from advanced capitalist exchange there must be emergency action by the state.

It is well-attested historically that gold does not inevitably disappear from capitalist circulation, despite the continuing encroachments of credit money:

> During all this last Victorian era the nation's stock of coined money and notes remained extraordinarily uniform: nothing could better illustrate its insignificant function in daily business, in spite of the utility of that thin film of gold, on which a few notes and piles of cheques rested, in linking the currency of Britain with the world's other currencies (Clapham, 1944, vol. II, p. 299).

Clapham further noted, on the basis of estimates by Newmarch, that gold circulation in 1856 stood at about £75 million, while in 1895 it was thought to be £92.5 million, of which perhaps £30 million was in the hands of bankers, including the Bank of England. Meanwhile, the volume of banknotes in circulation in the United Kingdom, supplied by all the banks, hardly grew: from £39 million it rose to just below £40 million, despite the tremendous growth of commerce. Gold disappeared from British domestic circulation when the outbreak of the First World War imposed its own pressing requirements for national payments abroad in the money metal.

7.1.2 Bank of the State

Thorny analytical problems exist regarding the nature of the capitalist state and its relationship to accumulation. Suffice it to assume that a national state necessarily emerges in advanced industrial capitalism: it taxes, borrows, spends and provides a national character to money.

Unlike the feudal state, which could directly command labour and products, the bourgeois state uses money to employ people and generally perform its operations. Bourgeois state finance emerges slowly, with much trial and error, and has three prerequisites. First, a system of national taxation applying both to foreign trade and to the annual revenue of the economy. The system incorporates direct and indirect taxes, operates with a degree of predictability and is formed subject to the bourgeois democratic process. Second, the systematic calculation of forthcoming state expenditure on salaries and wages, the standing army, the purchase of commodities, subsidies to capitalists and welfare transfer payments to certain sections of the community. Third, a mechanism for bridging the gap between income and expenditure through borrowing.

Both the projected annual borrowing needs of the state and any sudden and extraordinary ones impinge upon the available loanable money capital. The state can borrow directly from the banks; it can also seek recourse to the money market or to the capital market, thus creating the national debt. For one financial institution to assume a pivotal role in meeting the borrowing needs of the state, two conditions are necessary: first, the existence of regular tax receipts and equally regular state expenditure;[4] and second, sudden bursts of expenditure, typically induced by war. Although it is not inevitable, a bank with regular and easy access to the money market is favourably placed to manage the borrowing needs of the state. The bank best able to marshal the available credit in the money market and place it at the disposal of the state (as well as lend on its own account) is the bank that possesses the main reserve of the banking system.

From the beginning central banking is concerned with the financing needs of the bourgeois state, particularly in times of war. Lending directly to the state and managing the issuing of its short-term borrowing instruments in the money market are on an equal footing with holding the aggregate reserve of the banking system. State debt provides depth and fluidity to the money market. Moreover, since the central bank manages the accounts of the state, collecting tax receipts and disbursing expenditure, the availability of temporarily idle money belonging to the state allows the central bank more easily and flexibly to intervene in the money market. Consequently the bank in charge of state finance is in a stronger position to dominate the money market and to lend directly to other banks. The national character of the central bank is further strengthened when the state proclaims its banknotes to be legal tender.

During the first century of its existence, the Bank of England's, strong connection with the state was more evident than its role as bank of banks. The bank was formed in 1694, mainly by London merchants as a joint-stock company to provide the new king of England with war finance:

> The establishment of the Bank of England can be treated like many historical events both great and small, either as curiously accidental or as all but inevitable. Had the country not been at war in 1694, the government would hardly have been disposed to offer a favourable charter to a corporation which proposed to lend it money (Clapham, 1944, vol. I, p. 1).[5]

The Bank of England remained technically a private concern for two and a half centuries, and had substantial private banking interests until well into the nineteenth century. In the characteristic English manner in which institutions are never abolished but become something entirely different in the course of their existence, the Bank became the bank of banks as well as of the state through the gradual loss of some functions and the accretion of others.[6]

Its public character gives to the central bank a role and a position in the economic reproduction of society that can partially transcend the narrow confines of capitalist accumulation. Capitalist credit involves the formation of expectations about uncertain future returns and some attempt at a rational analysis of economic decisions. For the central bank, these requirements apply at the aggregate level. In order to intervene in the money market, the central bank needs estimates of the borrowing needs of the various market participants, data on past behaviour and the performance of the market as a whole, and sound intelligence about the operations of the financial institutions. The central bank further needs to form projections about the state's borrowing needs and repayment patterns in the context of the overall cyclical and secular movement of capitalist accumulation.

The naturally pivotal role of the central bank in the supply of credit to real accumulation has historically engendered very diverse reactions. Social reformers have aimed at the transformation of capitalism through the operations of a nationalised central bank, while free banking supporters have advocated the abolition of central banks.[7] Both approaches exaggerate the ability of the central bank materially to influence the direction and pace of capitalist accumulation. It is argued in the rest of this chapter that the operations of the central bank are severely limited by the essentially anarchical nature of capitalist production and trade.

7.1.3 Holder of International Money

The bank of banks and bank of the state actually becomes the nation's central bank when it emerges as the guardian of the nation's hoard of international money. The capitalist world market comprises units of capital that compete internationally in several commodity and financial markets, but within a system of national states. These states impose their own character on laws, tariffs, subsidies, work practices and money. A precondition for an individual capital to enter and compete in the world market is that it has access to a hoard of internationally acceptable means of payment. Each national bourgeoisie seeks to secure its own position in the international division of labour and to defend its national interests in the world market. These interests include the ability to import and export key commodities for the operations of industry and the needs of the population. They also include the ability to borrow and lend in the global financial markets. Possession of a hoard of internationally acceptable means of payment is a precondition for the defence of national bourgeois interests in the world market. At the same time diplomacy, bribery, coercion, piracy and war are perfectly plausible methods of achieving the same aim. To employ such non-economic methods of defending the national interests in the world market, the national bourgeoisie again needs to possess a hoard of internationally acceptable means of payment, 'the sinews of war'.[8]

Under conditions of competitive industrial capitalism, discussed in Chapters 4 and 6, the internationally acceptable means of payment is gold. A country must possess a hoard of gold in order to participate in the world market. Thus the hoard held by the central bank for domestic purposes naturally begins to acquire an international role. Persistent or acute balance of payments deficits, a sudden need for purchases abroad, pressures of war and so on are reflected in the fluctuations of a country's gold hoard held by the central bank (though borrowing abroad can lessen the pressure on the hoard). The hoard continues all the while to reflect the domestic relationship between loanable money capital and real accumulation, and to support the movement of domestically circulating gold:

> The function of the metal reserve held by a so-called national bank...is threefold: (i) a reserve fund for international payments,

ie a reserve fund of world money; (ii) a reserve fund for the alternately expanding and contracting domestic metallic circulation; (iii) (and this is connected with the banking function and has nothing to do with the function of money as simple money) a reserve fund for the payment of deposits and the convertibility of notes...If notes are issued to replace metal money in domestic circulation...the second function of the reserve fund disappears (Marx, 1894, pp. 701–2).

In the central bank's hoard of means of payment the innumerable links between a national economy and the world market acquire one simple and thing-like representation. Thus, it is an overriding concern of the central bank to protect its hoard, thereby defending the foundation of the domestic credit system and the ability of the national bourgeoisie to participate in the international division of labour. Insofar as the domestic credit system functions with less and less reliance on commodity money, the domestic function of the gold hoard becomes weaker. As a result, fluctuations in the central bank's hoard mostly reflect the movement of the balance of trade and of loanable capital across the nation's borders. The fluctuations of the hoard are accompanied by corresponding exchange rate movements, though the latter are necessarily very narrow as long as credit money is freely exchangeable into gold.

A balance of payments deficit, whatever its cause, often leads to increased pressure to deliver payments abroad, a tendency for the exchange rate of the domestic currency to fall relative to foreign ones, and a drain of international money from the central bank. Under pressure to pay abroad, capitalists seek central bank liabilities by hastily selling securities or attempting to borrow from the central bank in order to obtain access to gold. In such a situation the central bank typically finds itself acquiring securities and other loan assets while losing reserve assets. To defend its reserves the central bank can adopt a number of policies, which can also be used in combination. One is to suspend the convertibility of its liabilities into the international means of payment. A less drastic option is rationing either of its loans or of access to the international means of payment. A further option is to raise the price at which it lends, leading to a general domestic rise in the rate of interest. This, if conditions in the world financial markets allow, encourages an inflow of loanable capital and so lessens the shortage of means of payment. Yet another option is for the central bank to borrow abroad from other central banks or financial institutions.

Protection of the hoard of international means of payment tends to constrain the ability of ordinary banks to find reserves, and limits the provision of fresh loans to industry and trade. In the course of the business cycle, if a pressing need to settle a balance of payments deficit coincides with the emergence of a commercial and industrial crisis, a fully fledged monetary crisis results. The existence of domestic and international pressure for means of payment might result in usurious rates of interest, even though the actual sums of international money flowing abroad might be very small relative to total output:

> [The gold drain] has this effect because it intervenes in circumstances where anything extra on one side or the other is sufficient to tip the scales...But it is precisely the development of the credit and banking system which on the one hand seeks to press all money capital into the service of production...while on the other hand it reduces the metal reserve in a given phase of the cycle to a minimum, at which it can no longer perform the functions ascribed to it – it is this elaborate credit and banking system that makes the entire organism oversensitive (Marx, 1894, p. 706).

Historically, it takes a long time for the third function of the central bank to emerge fully. The Bank of England, for instance, had neither the capability nor the technical knowledge successfully to defend its hoard through interest rate operations until the middle of the nineteenth century. While the Bank struggled against its bullionist critics at the beginning of the century, it was unwilling to admit that the issue of its banknotes had any relation to fluctuations in the exchange rate or the price of gold bullion. Furthermore the Usury Laws imposed a 5 per cent ceiling on its discounts until 1833. By the 1830s, however, the Bank certainly took the exchange rate into account when deciding its discount policy. This fact made it easier for the Bank Act of 1844 to formalise the link between banknotes and gold on the basis of the presumed signal that the exchange rate emitted on the state of 'circulation'.

Bank Rate policy, that is, raising the Bank of England interest rate in order to attract gold from abroad and so relieve the pressure on sterling, dominated the second half of the century and continued until the outbreak of the First World War. The ability successfully to undertake Bank Rate policy depended critically on London being the commercial and financial heart of the British Empire, as well as the greatest repository of loanable capital in the world. Only after the 1870s could Britain rely on attracting the necessary foreign inflows of gold by means of raising the rate of interest (Sayers, 1957, pp. 14–15). By the end of the century British financiers and bureaucrats were confident that Bank Rate policy would always allow extraordinary pressure on the Bank's hoard to be overcome.

How ill-advised they were, and how institutionally specific the effectiveness of interest rate protection was for the hoard of the central bank was revealed at the outbreak of the First World War. The sudden upsurge in foreign demand on the Bank's gold reserves led to a rise in the domestic demand for gold that could not be tackled even with a 10 per cent Bank Rate (Hawtrey, 1938, ch. 4). After the First World War and the collapse of convertibility of credit money into gold, Bank Rate policy never again recovered the significance it had had in the second half of the nineteenth century. In the twentieth century, protecting the hoard of means of international payments acquired a more complex meaning, some aspects of which are discussed in the remainder of this chapter.

7.2 OPERATOR OF MONETARY POLICY, OVERSEER OF THE CREDIT SYSTEM AND LENDER OF LAST RESORT

7.2.1 Monetary Policy

Given its position in the credit system, the central bank can enter the money market as a buyer or seller of bills and other securities, respectively lowering or raising the market rate of interest, all other things being equal. When the central bank buys securities, the banks acquire central bank liabilities; when the central bank sells securities, the banks lose central bank liabilities. The induced movement of the market rate of interest expresses easier or tighter conditions under which the banks can supply credit to real accumulation. Such open market operations are an indirect way of controlling the availability of credit. The central bank can also employ a more direct way of achieving the same result by altering the terms on which it is prepared to lend directly to banks. By making its liabilities less or more easily available to banks the central bank can raise or lower the rate of interest.

How effective the central bank is in influencing the rate of interest depends on the stage of the business cycle. During the recession phase loanable capital is abundant but lending opportunities are few and the rate of interest tends to be low: the central bank would find it difficult to raise the rate of interest in the unlikely event that it would wish to do so. Towards the end of the upswing, on the other hand, the rate of interest tends to rise as the supply of credit is stretched, hence the central bank would find it easier to raise the rate of interest. When accumulation reaches crisis point, credit dries up as the demand for means of payment soars: the central bank must increase its own rate of interest, forcing the market rate to rise.[9]

The ability of the central bank to influence the market rate of interest also depends on the relationship between its reserves and its liabilities within a given institutional framework. When gold circulates domestically and pays internationally, the discretionary manipulation of the rate of interest has to be reconciled with fluctuations of the central bank's gold hoard that reflect both domestic and international forces. The overriding need to defend the international hoard severely limits the ability of the central bank to pursue a low interest rate policy, even when domestic conditions allow it. A large and growing hoard, on the other hand, significantly increases the freedom of movement of the central bank. In any event, fluctuations of the central bank's reserve put objective limits on the bank's discretionary powers over interest rates.

Attenuation of the role of gold, both domestically and internationally, heightens the ability of the central bank to influence market interest rates. Under the Bretton Woods system, for instance, which prevailed from the end of the Second World War to the early 1970s, the US dollar, which served as the international means of payment, was convertible into gold at the fixed rate of $35 to the ounce in transactions among central banks. Dollars formed a substantial part of the international reserves of central banks, a fact that limited their ability to adopt discretionary domestic policies. On the other hand, as long as the liabilities of the US Federal Reserve System were internationally accepted as means of payment, the ability of the Federal Reserve to follow discretionary domestic policies was increased. The tenuous link with gold, however, provided some external discipline on the Federal Reserve given that persistent balance of payments deficits exerted downward pressure on the dollar exchange rate and the United States tended to lose gold reserves.

If the link between credit money and gold breaks down completely, as happened after the collapse of the Bretton Woods system, the ability of the main central banks in the world market to exercise discretionary power over the rate of interest increases greatly. It should be stressed, however, that the majority of the world's smaller central banks are still confronted with the need to defend their own reserves of international means of payment, even if these are simply foreign exchange. Monetary policy has assumed its present historical significance because of the attenuation, or complete absence, of reserve discipline on the central banks. The rate of interest has acquired some of the character of an instrument of public economic policy, and a multitude of often contradictory demands are placed on central banks regarding interest rate manipulation. Typically these demands include price stability (stability of the value of money), a satisfactory level of economic activity (perhaps also a low rate of unemployment) and a balance of payments outlook that is compatible with high growth and employment. The collapse of the Keynesian ideology of full employment, which characterised the post-Second World War boom, and the emergence of bouts of rapid inflation since the early 1970s caused price stability to become the primary objective of the main central banks. Raising the rate of interest and tightening the conditions for the advance of credit emerged as the main instruments for controlling price inflation. However the ability of the main central banks, including the Federal Reserve System, to adopt discretionary monetary policy has been circumscribed by the following factors.

First, removal of the link with gold lifted the constraint that used to limit the movement of the exchange rates of the main currencies. Since no commodity money need be paid in exchange for dollars, there is no automatic limit on the exchange rate of the dollar against other currencies. Persistent trade imbalances, temporary upsets in capital flows, and seasonal fluctuations of commodity flows result in movements of the exchange rate that appear gigantic in historical perspective. Such exchange rate fluctuations have significant costs for real accumulation since they affect import and export prices and increase business uncertainty. In practice no nation and no central bank can completely ignore the exchange rate when setting interest rates.

Second, complete removal of the link with gold removed the reserve discipline on central banks, and by extension lessened that on the ordinary banks. Consequently the spontaneous processes of credit advance and repayment are even less able satisfactorily to regulate the quantity of credit money at levels appropriate for the volume of circulating commodity capital. Inflation, partly caused and partly facilitated by credit money expansion, has characterised the post-Bretton-Woods world. The control of inflation via tight monetary policy works mainly through tightening bank credit, negatively affecting real accumulation and employment, and forcibly raising the exchange value of credit money relative to commodities. When setting the rate of interest, no central bank can ignore the contractionary aspect of counterinflationary policy.

Third, exchange rate instability and the tendency for inflation to occur increased the scope for speculative operations of finance. This is partly because the loss of the gold anchor inevitably increased the autonomy of the financial sector relative to real accumulation. The possibility of financial bubbles has become greater, though for such bubbles actually to materialise further conditions are necessary, which are discussed in Chapter 8 of this work. Since the burst of financial bubbles is harmful to real accumulation, central banks must form monetary policy with financial speculation in mind.

The complete removal of the link with gold appeared temporarily to free central banks from the slavery of the yellow metal, allowing them to set interest rates at will. However the absence of gold only served to emphasise the anarchical nature of the international capitalist system by encouraging exchange rate instability, price inflation and financial speculation. The disappearance of the mechanically operating gold anchor in practice accentuated the public role of central banks, also stressing the broad social limits within which they decide monetary policy. This has provided scope for theories to emerge advocating such opposite aims as complete central bank independence and the abolition of central banks.

7.2.2   Overseer of the Credit System and Lender of Last Resort

Any significant disturbance of the process of debt repayment and loan renewal might give rise to financial instability. The advance of credit involves the formation of expectations about the future, and affects the reallocation of the spare resources of society, but the process occurs on the basis of the operations of private financial capital at arm's length from production. Inevitably the operations of the credit system exacerbate the instability inherent to capitalist accumulation, and provide a natural breeding ground for speculation, rule-bending and outright fraud. Monetary crises of type 2, arising purely as a result of the operations of the credit system are distinct from monetary crises of type 1 which are an integral part of the broader industrial and commercial crises that arise in the course of the business cycle.

Goodhart's (1985) theory of the origin of central banking is based on the assumption that banks know more about each other than the public knows about banks. It is too expensive for the public to collect information about the creditworthiness of individual banks (ibid., ch. 5). Banks that are imprudent therefore get a free ride on the efforts of the rest of the banks to maintain a public image of uprightness. Furthermore banks as financial intermediaries are obliged to issue liabilities (deposits) and buy assets (loans) of a fixed monetary value. This is because lenders know less than borrowers about the projects for which their money is lent. Hence, as discussed in Chapter 3, the contract between lenders and borrowers cannot have a variable value that is contingent on the actual outcome of the project (Goodhart, 1987). Thus the fixed monetary value of deposits is supported by the value of bank assets, but the latter is in practice variable and market-determined, a fact that gives rise to instability.

Depositors who are worried about retrieving the full monetary value of the bank liabilities they hold and are unable to distinguish among banks, might precipitate contagious bank runs that threaten the stability of the credit system. Therefore the banks assign the role of overseer to a 'good' bank among their number. The overseer bank is not able to continue with its private operations for long as its new position results in conflict between its public and its private interests. Eventually the overseer bank becomes a public, non-profit, central bank (Goodhart, 1985, ch. 8). In order to protect the value of the depositors' assets, the central bank provides lender of last resort facilities, that is, it lends flexibly to banks in the event of bank runs.

Goodhart's stress on the spontaneous emergence of central banks is intuitively appealing, and his argument that the public cannot normally tell a 'good' bank from a 'bad' one is persuasive. It is important, however, more sharply to distinguish between the general overseeing of the banking system and the function of lender of last resort. Goodhart essentially interprets all instances of acute financial instability as type 2 crises, that is, as crises arising purely from the processes of credit. However, type 1 monetary crises do not originate in the imprudent decisions of some banks but in the interaction of the banking system with real accumulation in the course of the business cycle. Monetary crises of that type reflect and exacerbate but do not cause the inherent instability of capitalist accumulation. Type 1 crises are more likely to threaten the stability of the credit system as a whole as they are combined with commercial and industrial crises. The central bank, as the possessor of the central reserve of the banking system and banker to the state, is the natural source of the requisite means of payment when type 1 crises materialise.[10]

By policing the credit system the central bank can indeed reduce the danger of type 2 crises. Even then, however, the intrinsic tendency to bend rules and the necessarily precarious nature of a structure of promise and counterpromise leave scope for crises due to the activities of rogue banks, plain rumour or natural disasters. On such occasions the central bank is still called upon to provide the requisite means of payment in order to avoid wholesale bankruptcies and the collapse of the credit system as a whole. However the historical importance of the lender of last resort arose primarily because of the role of central banks in credit crises of type 1. Such crises are not merely, or even primarily, a banking problem. Ultimately type 1 crises result from the inability of merchants and industrial capitalists to continue to produce and sell at the same levels as before, thereby becoming unable to honour their past debts. The resultant credit crisis exacerbates the underlying commercial and industrial crisis.

Central banks are certainly concerned with the stability of the credit system as a whole, and so they attempt to weed out 'bad' banks. More than this, however, central banking requires the ability to provide means of payment when full-blown capitalist crises occur. In order to function effectively as lender of last resort the central bank relies on holding the national reserve (domestic and international) and on having access to the credit of the state. Moreover the central bank is not always able to protect its reserve against external pressure and at the same time act as lender of last resort: the institutional and historical conditions under which this action is possible have to be specified in advance.

Bagehot (1873, p. 79) famously argued that:

> What is wanted and what is necessary to stop a panic is to diffuse the impression that though money may be dear, still money is to be had. If people could be really convinced that they could have money if they wait a day or two, and that utter ruin is not coming, most likely they will cease to run in such a mad way for money. Either shut the Bank at once, and say that it will not lend more than it commonly lends, or lend freely, boldly, and so that the public may feel you mean to go on lending.

The context in which he argued this, however, was that of the classical industrial, mercantile and monetary crisis of *laissez-faire* capitalism:

> The problem of managing a panic must not be thought of as mainly a 'banking' problem. It is primarily a mercantile one. All merchants are under liabilities; they have bills to meet soon, and they can only pay those bills by discounting bills on other merchants. In other words, all merchants are dependent on borrowing money, and large merchants are dependent on borrowing much money... If the bankers gratify the merchants, they must lend largely when they like it least; if they do not gratify them, there is a panic (ibid., p. 73).

The ability of the Bank of England to satisfy the pressing need for money on such occasions, and so rescue not only bankers but also merchants and eventually industrialists, derived from its possession of the ultimate banking reserve and its access to the credit of the state. Nonetheless, for the Bank effectively to apply Bagehot's prescription more was required than possession of the centralised reserve, access to state credit and the accumulation of experience. As Bagehot (ibid., p. 75) himself pointed out, the practice of lender of last resort often contradicted the simultaneous need to defend the Bank's gold hoard against external pressure. Only after the establishment of the City of London as the centre of the financial mechanism of the British Empire was the Bank of England able successfully to undertake last resort lending in times of crisis. These conditions were not present during the first two thirds of the nineteenth century.

To be sure, Bagehot (ibid., p. 80) also argued that centralisation of the reserve was 'anomalous', but as a practical Englishman he proposed to make use of what existed rather than aim at some 'natural or many reserve system of banking' (ibid., p. 80). Bagehot's treatment of the centralised reserve as 'abnormal' is often quoted by the advocates of free banking, who prefer to consider as 'natural' a system of decentralised, individually held bank reserves (Smith, 1936, pp. 133–44). It is, however, a rather peculiar view of reality that treats what actually exists as abnormal and reserves the term 'natural' for the models theorists construct in the quiet of their study.

7.3   CENTRAL BANK INDEPENDENCE AND FREE BANKING

The heightened importance of central banking operations in the post-Bretton-Woods world has led to renewed debate about the role of central banks in a capitalist economy. In this debate, the antithetical proposals for central bank independence and for free banking have commanded much attention.

7.3.1   Central Bank Independence

The theory of central bank independence is a relatively recent development, a product of the profound monetary instability following the collapse of the Bretton Woods Agreement. The theory bears the distinctive hallmarks of the conservative turn taken by economics since the early 1970s, further discussed in Chapter 9 below. Its origins lie in Kydland and Prescott's (1977) analysis of the conflict between rules and discretion in economic decision-making, but its analytical framework was developed by Barro and Gordon (1983a, 1983b). The theory adopts the assumption (prevalent in contemporary macroeconomics) that the actual rate of unemployment of a capitalist economy cannot diverge from a 'natural' rate in the long run. Expansionary monetary policy by the government might reduce unemployment but only in the short run and by generating inflation in excess of that expected by workers (that is, by reducing real wages). However, as soon as expectations adjust, unemployment returns to the 'natural' rate and the sole result of monetary expansion is a higher rate of inflation, which is 'bad' for social welfare.

The 'natural' rate of unemployment is also assumed to be higher than the desired level of unemployment. Why that should be so is not very clearly explained, but it is often claimed that 'distortions' in the functioning of the capitalist economy, such as trade unions, might result in a 'natural' rate higher than otherwise. Thus, in formulating monetary policy the government aims to minimise the social loss caused by inflation and unemployment above the desired rate. Within the framework of the theory the optimal monetary policy is to aim at zero inflation and not to attempt to reduce unemployment below the 'natural' rate since that is pointless. The problem is that, though such a policy might be announced, the government is always tempted to create unexpected inflation, temporarily reducing unemployment. A variety of reasons are normally adduced for this course of action

(Alesina and Tabellini, 1987), but the message is the same: governments are inherently dishonest in implementing monetary policy and attempt to bribe the electorate. However, workers will eventually ascertain the true character of the government's actions, adjust their expectations of inflation upwards (building them into their wage demands, hence into actual inflation), and refuse the government the opportunity of generating unexpected inflation and temporarily reducing unemployment. The final outcome of the government's dishonest use of monetary policy is a permanently higher rate of inflation, while unemployment remains at the 'natural' rate.

Into this framework Rogoff (1985, 1989) inserted the 'conservative' central bank, a public institution that assigns a greater weight than the government to the 'bad' of inflation. Why the central bank should be more 'conservative' on inflation than the government is never explained but simply taken for granted. Given this assumption, it is evident that monetary policy operated by the central bank independently of the government generates milder inflationary surprises, leading to a smaller upward adjustment of inflationary expectations and a permanently lower rate of inflation. Society thus appears to benefit from an independent 'conservative' central bank. The more recent developments of the theory, associated with Persson and Tabellini (1993) and Walsh (1995), have concentrated on devising contracts between the government and independent central bank which would completely eliminate any inflationary bias. If the transfers made by the government to the central bank for the payment of salaries, running costs and other expenses were made to vary inversely with the actual rate of inflation, it is possible, in principle, to induce an independent central bank to adopt monetary policies that result in zero systematic inflation while unemployment remains at the 'natural' rate.

A considerable volume of empirical work has attempted to substantiate the theory's claims regarding the superior inflation performance of independent central banks. Typically, these are econometric studies relating indices of central bank independence to inflation. Grilli *et al.* (1991) report that for a group of developed industrialised countries there is a significant negative relationship between the two. Similarly, Alesina and Summers (1993) also find a clear negative relationship for industrialised countries, as well as the absence of a positive relationship between the variability of output and central bank independence. The last result is contrary to the theory's predictions: if the independent central bank is relatively less concerned than the government about unemployment, it is less likely to undertake output stabilisation by means of monetary policy; hence output variability is probably higher. However, since the finding claims that the stability of output (mysteriously) does not suffer from central bank independence, the result is normally treated as an unexpected bonus rather than as a problem for theory. Finally, Cukierman (1992, ch. 20) reports that the vaunted negative relationship between inflation and central bank independence collapses as soon as the sample is broadened to include less developed countries.

The construction of indices of central bank independence is a completely *ad hoc* exercise. Legal (or formal) independence is normally distinguished from actual independence: the former is a matter of the law governing the operations of the central bank while the latter is a matter of informal arrangements with the government, the capability of the central bank for economic analysis, even the personality of the governor (Cukierman, 1992, ch. 18). The literature typically opts for measures of legal independence since actual independence is evidently impossible to quantify. Even so, the point at which legal arrangements render a legally independent central bank actually independent cannot be precisely identified. This is obvious, when some of the relevant issues are considered: Should there be no government appointees on the committee deciding monetary policy? Independence in choosing the goals of monetary policy? Full financial self-sufficiency for the central bank? Control over exchange rate policy? Unable to provide a precise formulation for independence, the empirical studies result to grossly unsatisfactory proxies for the disparity between actual and legal independence, such as the actual turnover of governors or the ratio between their actual and legal tenure. Even worse, empirical work is undertaken on the basis of questionnaires which ask central bankers how independent they feel at a particular point in time.

The difficulties faced by the empirical literature in constructing indices of independence are not simply the inevitable difficulties of attempting to apply theoretical concepts to empirical analysis. They are rather an indication of how inappropriate the concept of independence is for the analysis of the operations of the central bank. The bank of banks is connected with the participants of the money market through a dense web of professional, informational, educational, and even personal relations. It cannot avoid becoming exposed to the institutional and personal influence of industrial and commercial capitalists since the supply of its own credit underpins the supply of bank credit to real accumulation. A central bank is a creature of the financial system: the range, type, and manner of its operations are determined by its underlying character as a bank. Analogously, the bank of the state, even if it does not directly lend to the latter, necessarily becomes entangled with the state personnel overseeing and planning the borrowing of the government. Even more importantly, the holder of the international reserve cannot become 'independent' in taking monetary policy decisions that might affect the international interests of the national bourgeoisie. It is inherent to the nature of the central bank to be a public institution, an arm of the state.

The problems of the empirical work derive from the fact that in the theoretical literature on central bank independence the central bank has no banking functions at all, indeed there is no financial system in these models. The institution assumed to be in command of monetary policy is not a central bank but a social planner armed with a single instrument (the supply of fiat money) in pursuit of a single aim (monetary stability). With this in mind, 'independence' acquires meaning: it is, above all, the independence of the monetary planner from the executive branch of the state. Given that its exposure to the electoral process makes the government inherently mendacious and untrustworthy, social welfare is increased when a monetary planner takes complete control of the supply of money. Ultimately, it is best for society to appoint a benevolent monetary dictator with the task of achieving price stability.

Significant problems emerge at this point regarding the internal consistency of the theory. First, as McCallum (1995, 1997) argues, if the 'conservative' central bank is concerned about inflation, and realises, as it must, that expansionary monetary policy cannot shift unemployment below the 'natural' rate, why should it be satisfied simply with a lower inflationary bias instead of aiming at zero systematic inflation? Analogously, if there are no means available to force the government to adopt the optimal monetary policy, who is going to enforce the contract between the government and the central bank? McCallum's critique thus identifies a contradiction within the theory: the 'independent' central bank is a wise monetary planner with complete discretion over the supply of money but somehow remains satisfied with merely an improvement of the economy's inflationary performance rather than the optimal zero systematic inflation. Second, if indeed an inflationary bias results from the government's monopoly over the supply of fiat money, for theorists in the neoclassical tradition, who generally accept the optimal welfare and efficiency properties of free markets, it seems more consistent to demand a free market in money rather than the establishment of a monetary planner. It is certainly not at all evident within the theory's own parameters that social welfare would be higher under a benevolent monetary dictator than under free trade in money.

If society is to have a monetary planner, however, a further set of important problems emerges. Why should the planner's remit be limited to price stability? Control over money, and influence over the generation and allocation of credit, affords considerable power to promote capitalist accumulation in certain areas and restrict it in others. It also affords power to influence the distribution of income through consumption and housing credit. There is no *a priori* reason for a monetary planner to ignore these powers, other than the arbitrary assumption of a 'natural' rate of unemployment. Moreover, what should be the processes of appointment and accountability for such a powerful institution? The advocates of central bank independence want to entrust monetary policy to experts with sufficient stability of tenure and freedom to pursue what they deem optimal for society. In their view, the economy is a mechanism obeying its own logic that is disturbed by collective decision-making, rather than a set of social relations over which people are able to exercise conscious control in their collective interest. Hence the monetary planner ought to be independent of even the limited expression of popular will that takes place in elections. That is a profoundly undemocratic view of economic activity in general and monetary policy in particular. It is pure ideology to claim that society cannot employ monetary policy consciously and in its own interests, instead entrusting it to an elite of high priests. The design and execution of monetary policy ought to be subject to democratic participation by broad swathes of the people whose lives are directly affected by it.

Finally, at a deeper level the advocacy of central bank independence in theory and practice is a response to the increase in financial and monetary instability in the post-Bretton Woods world. As mentioned earlier in this chapter, the abolition of the link with gold has led to the attenuation of reserve discipline on banks and ushered in a period of exchange rate volatility, price inflation and financial speculation. The failure of monetarist policies in the late 1970s, for reasons discussed extensively in Chapters 8 and 9, has discredited the idea of controlling price inflation by the simple quantitative regulation of the money supply. Thus faith is now placed in a 'conservative' monopolist of legal tender freed from the pressure of elections, who can apply wise and discretionary regulation over the supply of money, keeping inflation in check. Meanwhile, the social discontent associated with anti-inflationary monetary policy and the inevitable reductions in output and rises in unemployment would be deflected from governments and attributed to unelected monetary experts. Central bank independence, far from severing the links between the central bank and politics, is likely to provide politicians with an additional cushion in confronting the social stresses and tensions created by tight monetary policy.

7.3.1 Free Banking

Free banking has a much more substantial theoretical pedigree than central bank independence, despite being much more tendentious as a practical proposition. In its present form the theory owes much to Hayek (1976a, 1976b), though it can trace its ancestry at least to Parnell (1827, 1832).[11] Free banking proponents essentially believe in the inherent harmony of capitalist markets, and seek to extend it to the realm of money. The control and monopoly influence that the state has historically exercised over money is presumably the ultimate cause of economic instability and crises: '*The past instability of the market economy is the consequence of the exclusion of the most important regulator of the market mechanism, money, from itself being regulated by the market process*' (Hayek, 1976b, pp. 79–80, emphasis in original).

Thus it is necessary for free banking supporters to argue that central banks are not a spontaneous and natural development of the financial system. Rather, central banks are monopolies issuing legal tender, and are extremely useful in supplying the state with cheap finance. While providing such finance, and by merely using their powerful monopoly position in the financial markets, the central banks become a source of economic instability:

A central bank is not a natural product of banking development. It is imposed from outside or comes into being as the result of Government favours. This factor is responsible for marked effects on the whole currency and credit structure which brings it into sharp contrast with what would happen under a system of free banking from which Government protection was absent (Smith, 1936, p. 169).

It is important to note that, in the opinion of free banking supporters, mere convertibility into gold is not enough to guarantee stability of the value of money since the role of central banks was also profoundly destabilising throughout the nineteenth century. Consequently, to provide stability for the value of money (indeed for the whole of the market economy), a banking system with a central bank should be replaced by 'natural' free banking.[12] No special regulations should be imposed on entrants to the banking business other than those that generally apply to all companies. Banks should be allowed to go bankrupt. A reserve asset should be designated, which could be gold but also a commodity bundle, and the liabilities of banks should be immediately convertible into it.[13] All banks should possess their own reserves of this asset, and a clearing system should be constructed to allow the mutual settlement of claims. No bank liabilities should be legal tender.

For free banking supporters, under the above conditions the existence of competition among banks will prevent the overissue of liabilities by an individual bank. If an individual bank overissued it would rapidly lose reserves in the clearing process (White, 1984, ch. 1; Dowd, 1989, ch. 1). If the bank wished to maintain an excessive amount of outstanding liabilities it would face rising costs in securing reserves. To earn a competitive rate of profit, banks have to issue liabilities prudently, thus also gaining and retaining the confidence of the public. The more the public becomes accustomed to the operations of a free banking system the more difficult it will be for an individual bank to hoodwink its customers into keeping its liabilities away from the process of clearing. Competition and the profit motive, based on convertibility against an asset that cannot be created at will, are sufficient to ensure stability in the value of credit money, and so facilitate broader economic stability.

The theory of free banking is right to concentrate on the principles of self-regulation of bank-issued credit money. It has been consistently argued throughout this volume that the quantity and the value of credit money are not arbitrarily determined but result from the practices of banks in sustaining capitalist accumulation. At the same time, however, free banking theory erroneously asserts that harmony naturally exists in the determination of the quantity and value of credit money. The claim of free banking supporters that central banks are the ultimate source of capitalist instability is an inversion of the historical and the logical process. On the contrary, central banks could contribute to the amelioration of capitalist crises, and are forced to do so in the midst of anarchical credit operations that determine the quantity and value of credit money. In this connection, three criticisms can be levelled against free banking theory.

First, as established in Chapter 6, the capitalist economy is characterised by monetary crises, whether these are related to the underlying instability of production and exchange (type 1), or simply result from the independent and speculative operations of the credit system (type 2). The view that credit processes fundamentally contribute to capitalist instability has a longer ancestry than free banking. Tooke of the banking school, an arch free trader and defender of the concept of self-regulation of credit money, famously dismissed the idea of free banking: 'As to free banking, in the sense in which it is sometimes contended for, I agree with a writer in one of the American journals, who observes, that *free trade in banking is synonymous with free trade in swindling*' (Tooke, 1840, p. 206, emphasis in original). The 'swindling' mentioned by Tooke relates to what we have called a type 2 crisis. The banking school also recognised 'overbanking' as a source of crisis, that is, the overextension of banking credit that characterises the last phase of the upswing. In contemporary economic literature, the inherent instability of the structure of credit (a chain of promise and counterpromise) is also widely accepted. A currently influential argument claims that panics and runs on banks might occur simply because of self-validating rumours about the solvency of particular banks (Diamond and Dybvig, 1983).[14]

There is no natural harmony between credit and real accumulation. Commercial credit has an objective foundation in the buying and selling activities of capitalist firms, but it can also be hugely expanded without the underlying transactions changing significantly in value. Similarly, banking credit has an objective foundation in the idle money systematically generated in the turnover of capital, but its advance is based on the anticipation of future returns and overlaps with the extension of commercial credit. Thus no rigid controlling influence by real accumulation exists over banking credit. Both forms of credit are inherently elastic, and that is precisely the reason why credit can support and stretch real accumulation. Real accumulation ultimately does set limits to the operations of credit, but such limits might well take the form of a sudden contraction of the overextended structure of claim and counterclaim. For banks, as well as industrial and commercial capitalists, the existence of a central bank to act as lender of last resort is vital in these circumstances.[15]

Second, the centralisation of reserves is a spontaneous process based on the economic benefits it brings to banks. As established earlier in this chapter, by depositing their reserves with one institution banks can pursue their business more flexibly and cheaply. By holding a claim on a centralised hoard instead of holding the reserve commodity itself individual banks are able to reduce the size of their reserves, all other things being equal. The banking system as a whole, moreover, needs to maintain a smaller reserve of commodity money for all levels of operation. The centralisation of reserves, a tendency heightened by the possibility of panics and bank runs, is a condition for the further expansion of the credit system. The international role of money further contributes to the centralisation of the national reserve of means of payment. To participate in the world market and the international division of labour, a national bourgeoisie must possess a hoard of international means of payment. Whatever the commodity bundle that comprises the reserves of a free banking system, it has to be convertible into foreign money. Even if national denominations of money were abolished, each national bourgeoisie would still have to possess an internationally oriented hoard of means of payment. Balance of payment crises, national emergencies and wars inevitably lead to the concentration and centralised management of the national hoard. In the history of capitalism war has in practice proved the strongest force for concentration of the gold hoard. There is no reason to assume that a free banking system, constructed under the present political conditions, would reverse the tendency towards centralisation of international means of payment.

Third, the argument that the quantity and value of credit money can be stabilised by the process of bank competition and clearing is a contemporary version of the law of the reflux. Free banking supporters on the whole, recognise the affinity between their own analysis and the law of the reflux, the latter being treated as a broad statement about the behaviour of credit money (Glasner, 1989, ch. 3). At the same time they usually differentiate between their version of the law and that of Adam Smith, whose analysis relied on the real bills doctrine, or of the banking school, which also discussed the importance of debt repayment to banks. The putative effectiveness of the law of the reflux in stabilising the value of credit money is exaggerated by free banking supporters. The most that clearing can do is ensure that banks issue liabilities in step with each other in order to avoid losing reserves. Even that is not certain, however, if certain banks can sustain a different pricing of their liabilities from that of their rivals for significant periods of time (Goodhart, 1985, p. 30). Assuming that banks do issue liabilities in step, there is still the well-known and very old criticism of this approach to credit money, namely that competition and clearing by themselves cannot guarantee that the total quantity of credit money is not excessive. If banks were collectively to lower the price of their liabilities they could continue to increase the total quantity of credit money, albeit in step with each other.[16]

According to Selgin (1988, pp. 81–2), if banks were to continue to expand their issues in step, the variance of clearing of debits and credits would increase, exacerbating the need for banks to hold higher precautionary reserves and resulting in a self-correcting equilibrium. This is an unwarranted assertion. More persuasively, though still cursorily, White (1984, pp. 17–18; 1989, pp. 33–4) stated that, if overissue were to occur, the country as a whole would lose reserves abroad and this would correct the problem. This is similar to bullionist/currency school arguments but the conclusion of the Ricardians was that the issue of credit money ought to be regulated by the movement of the exchange rate and the centralised gold hoard, which is not exactly in sympathy with the conclusions of the free banking supporters. The Ricardian proposal had several weaknesses, as we have already seen, but at least it revealed a clear sense of national priorities in the world market. Consider now the following argument by White (1989, pp. 140–1):

> Contrary to what the headlines lead us to think, there is no cause for alarm at the international money flows or resulting trade 'deficits' and 'surpluses' in a world of purely metallic currency. Indeed, there is no special reason even to keep track of national aggregates. One might as well keep track of net money shipments from left-handed to right-handed persons. Money moves across national borders as easily and inconsequentially as it moves from one side of Main Street to the other. The concept of a national money supply is irrelevant, because the world's money is homogeneous.

If money had no national denominations the problem of exchange rates would indeed not exist. The national bourgeoisie, however, would still need to hold an international reserve to be able to buy and pay abroad as extraordinary needs arose. The movement of international money would never be as 'inconsequential' as shifting cash from one pocket to the other. While national denominations persist, furthermore, the relation between the total quantity of domestic credit money and the external requirements for money cannot be simply dismissed but must be theorised explicitly. It is not at all clear that the free issue of credit money could be reconciled with protecting the national hoard and defending the exchange rate. On the contrary, the domestic role of credit money is much more likely to be in constant conflict with its international role.[17]

Competition and clearing by themselves – that is, a simple version of the law of the reflux – cannot harmoniously regulate the total quantity of credit money relative to real accumulation. To claim the latter with any degree of persuasiveness further arguments are necessary regarding the operations of banks in the course of capitalist accumulation. It was not accidental that the real bills doctrine (that is, the suggestion that banks ought to lend short-term and on good bills alone)[18] kept appearing among theorists who were attracted to the notion that the domestic quantity of credit money is automatically regulated through the operations of the credit system. It is necessary to show that the advance and the repayment of bank credit as a whole also possess a natural harmony relative to real accumulation. That individual banks cannot overissue under the pressure of competition is not an answer to this problem. The real bills doctrine is of course a fallacy, but this is evidence less of poor theorising and more of the objective absence of bank practices that provide the much-desired natural harmony. It is true that, strictly speaking, this is not an argument in favour of central banking: the same absence of harmony in domestic determination of the total quantity of credit money also exists when the credit system possesses a central bank. Nevertheless the point is especially problematic for free banking supporters, who essentially hold that capitalist instability would be impossible if the central bank were removed.

The law of the reflux and convertibility into gold could indeed provide an anchor for the value of credit money, but the anchor would operate in complete absence of harmony. Capitalist credit periodically overexpands and contracts as real accumulation goes through the business cycle, and the value of credit money falls and rises as a consequence. Gold provides an anchor for these fluctuations, but only in the sense that overexpanded bank credit suddenly collapses as borrowers rush to obtain means of payment, thus inducing falls in commodity prices. The need to defend the national hoard and protect exchange rates is also a decisive factor in sudden fluctuations of credit, in practice making gold the anchor of the value of credit money. In this context the lender of last resort can ameliorate the worst side-effects of violent readjustments of the value of credit money to the value of gold.

Both independent central bank and free banking theories recognise that central banks possess some aggregate organising capacity in the capitalist economy, and both are partial representations of capitalist reality. The credit system naturally tends to possess a centralised reserve of domestic and international means of payment; in this respect the credit system tends to have a central bank that underpins credit money. It is not surprising that this bank also tends to be the bank of the state, as long as the latter needs a bank. The central bank takes over the hoard of international money and is forced by its position to supervise the credit system and to lend in times of distress. However there are clear limits to what central banks can do imposed by, first, the fact that credit is about forecasting the unknowable future, and second, the anarchy of the underlying process of real capitalist accumulation.

The historical experience since the collapse of the Bretton Woods system has revealed increasing confusion and anarchy in capitalist production and trade. The proposal for central bank independence, aims at introducing harmony through the powers of the central bank. This exaggerates what the central bank can do and in practice amounts to promoting the interests of capitalist accumulation at the expense of working people. Free banking on the other hand, aims at introducing harmony by abolishing the central bank, the presumed cause of disharmony. This proposal, apart from its doubtful practical feasibility, turns effect into cause. The central bank, though it cannot abolish instability, can at least ameliorate some of instability's worst aspects. Free banking would not only fail to introduce harmony in economic life but would probably result in more instability in capitalist trade and production.

Part III

Postwar Realities and Theories

Money and finance are highly contradictory economic phenomena. They evolve spontaneously and anarchically out of private transactions, but in the capitalist mode of production they give rise to a set of tightly woven social mechanisms. The mechanisms put idle money to use, thus mobilising spare resources and expanding capitalist accumulation, but they can also disturb and harm society's economic reproduction. Money and finance tend passively to follow the essential movement of capital accumulation, but at times they take the initiative to stop accumulation, or alternatively to stimulate it out of its torpor.

The contradictory character of money and finance is rooted in the historically specific nature of the capitalist economy itself. Precisely because it treats capitalism as a timeless form of social organisation, mainstream economics tends to develop one-sided theories of money and finance. Its underlying assumption that the capitalist economy is a natural and harmonious economic order prevents a thorough investigation of the contradictory totality of money and finance. Thus price instability, recurrent crises and depressions are frequently attributed to disruptive intervention by the state and the central bank in the operations of money and finance.

Control and increasing socialisation of money and finance are both possible and desirable even under capitalist conditions. Nevertheless capitalist instability cannot be eliminated, though the course and eventual outcome of economic crises can be materially altered. In this connection, the role played by historical circumstances and by the institutional structure of a given country cannot be overemphasised. Finally, while state monetary and financial policies might be beneficial to capitalist accumulation, they could also be deeply damaging to the welfare of working people.

8 Loss of Control over Money and Finance

From the end of the Second World War to the end of the 1960s the capitalist world economy enjoyed relatively stable growth. The profound instability of the interwar years, including the Great Depression of the 1930s, were not repeated, despite fears to the contrary immediately after the war. Although recessions occurred, for instance, in the US economy in 1953–4, 1957–8, 1960–1, 1966–7 and 1969–71, they were neither particularly severe nor persistent. Such recessions were often called 'growth recessions' since only the rate of growth and not the absolute level of real GDP declined. Economic growth was not merely stable but also rapid in historical terms. Annual output growth of the seven most advanced capitalist countries (the United States, France, Britain, West Germany, Italy, Japan and Canada) averaged an estimated 4.9 per cent in 1950–73, compared with 2.2 per cent in 1820–70, 2.5 per cent in 1870–1913 and 1.9 per cent in 1913–50 (Armstrong *et al.*, 1984, p. 167). As a result the total output of these countries was almost three times as large in 1973 as it had been in 1950. Remarkably, throughout the high economic growth of this period prices remained relatively stable. There were isolated episodes of rapid inflation immediately after the war, but on the whole inflation remained subdued. Low inflation prevailed despite the predominant ideological belief that expansionary state economic policies could sustain effective demand. Annual consumer price inflation for the same seven countries was only 2.7 per cent in 1960–8, but it climbed to 5.5 per cent in 1968–73 and 9.8 per cent in 1973–79 (OECD, *Historical Statistics*, various issues).

8.1 RELATIVE STABILITY UNDER THE BRETTON WOODS SYSTEM

The political economy of the postwar period of rapid growth accompanied by low inflation has been extensively debated, and is not directly relevant to our purposes.[1] In this section we simply summarise the four most salient factors behind the emergence of such an extraordinary period in the history of capitalism.

8.1.1 Four Main Causes of Relative Stability

US Economic Hegemony and the Bretton Woods System

First, the Bretton Woods system, established in 1944, underpinned the relative stability of prices (the exchange value of money). The system fixed the rate of exchange between the US dollar and other currencies on the basis of an undertaking by the US authorities to convert $35 into an ounce of gold upon request by foreign governments or monetary authorities. Consequently the capitalist world tended to hold US dollars as a stable international means of payment. The Bretton Woods system relied on the existence of overwhelming US economic hegemony. Immediately after the war the US economy accounted for roughly two thirds of mining and manufacturing output, a third of wheat production and two thirds of the official gold reserves of the capitalist world. The competitive strength of the United States in both manufacturing and agriculture allowed it to enjoy substantial and recurrent trade surpluses. As a result the rest of the capitalist world tended to be short of the international means of payment (dollars). To protect their reserves and to avoid worsening their export strength in the world market, other countries were obliged to keep price inflation under control. Typically, when inflation accelerated in the course of more rapid accumulation and credit expansion, aggravated dollar shortages forced the monetary authorities to implement counterinflationary policies. The system retained a substantial element of the stabilising role of gold, as discussed in Chapter 7. Given that capitalist accumulation did expand steadily, the Bretton Woods system was able to prevent inflation from becoming a serious problem.

During the long boom the United States undertook large expenditure abroad, comprising mostly grants for reconstruction and military spending necessitated by the Cold War against the USSR and its allies. This development was completely different from the isolationist policy of the United States after the First World War. In addition, private foreign direct investment by US companies rose significantly as large corporations increasingly internationalised their activities in the 1960s. Large-scale US public expenditure abroad and rising US private foreign direct investment allowed other capitalist countries to obtain necessary reserves, and ameliorated the prevalent shortage of dollars. It was possible to expand money and credit across the capitalist world, while both the rate of interest and inflation remained low. Substantial US foreign aid and military spending abroad, moreover, strengthened effective demand for US products abroad and facilitated the smooth transition of the US economy from a war to a civilian footing.

A Wave of Technological Innovations

Second, a wave of industrial technological innovations, which had begun in the United States in the interwar years, continued in the postwar period. Technologies were developed (often in relation with one another) for the more efficient production of thin steel, cars, various types of improved electrical appliances, ships, tankers, jet planes and petrochemical products. Scientific discoveries and new technologies were extensively applied to the mass production of consumer goods. The output of consumer goods, especially durables, found an expanding market in the advanced capitalist countries as both employment and real wages steadily increased. The strength of the trade unions significantly contributed to the steady rise of real wages, more or less in line with the rise in productivity.[2] The postwar period was characterised by the proliferation of industries that consumed oil heavily, and by the spread of car ownership, which also contributed to the heavy use of oil. Oil rose from roughly one fifth of the world energy supply at the end of the war to two thirds in 1974. Oil was also an important raw material for the petrochemical industry.

The Low Prices of Primary Products

Third, it was essential for the sustained economic growth of the advanced capitalist countries that oil remained relatively cheap. The price of crude oil stayed below two dollars per barrel throughout the period, while supplies from the Middle East greatly increased to meet the expanding demand. Compared with the gently rising export price of manufactures, oil became progressively cheaper. The availability of cheap and abundant oil led to the substitution of several manufacturing raw materials, for example rubber, cotton, wool and wood, by synthetic petrochemical products. As a result the less developed countries, which often relied heavily on the exportation of such raw materials, were confronted with unfavourable prices. Furthermore the price of agricultural products fell, particularly the price of foodstuffs, as productivity rose rapidly in the agricultural sector of the advanced capitalist countries. Protectionist trade policies by the advanced countries frequently added to the difficulties of the less developed world.

The terms of trade of primary products relative to manufactures actually fell by 32 per cent from 1951 to 1970 (Armstrong *et al.*, 1984, p. 171). The share of less developed countries in total world exports declined from roughly a quarter in 1955 to a fifth 1970, marking their failure to secure a firm place in the world division of labour (with the exception of the exporters of mineral resources). The political liberation of old colonies and their transformation into independent nation states did not guarantee economic growth within the liberal world market order. However the availability of cheap primary products from the less developed world provided a vital foundation for high and stable profitability in the advanced countries. During the long upswing, less developed countries were not a significant market for the products of the advanced countries.

The Abundant Supply of Labour Power

The final necessary condition for the extended postwar boom was the availability of inexpensive and relatively compliant labour power. The enormous pressures exerted on the labour movement in advanced capitalist countries during the quarter of a century before the long boom contributed to the decline in workers' militancy. In the Axis countries, oppression by the fascist regimes, war mobilisation, confrontation with the occupation forces and the subsequent revival of capitalist confidence, stemmed the militant current in the labour movement and confined the trade unions to narrowly economic demands. In the victorious countries, nationalism during the war and postwar welfare policies similarly contributed to the greater compliance of workers with the demands of capital. The anticommunist witch-hunt during the early years of the Cold War, particularly in the United States, also helped subdue the radical communist influence.

Labour market conditions also became favourable to capital. The demobilisation of armed forces and the running down of the arms industries released significant quantities of labour power into the labour market. Subsequent population growth, and migration from the countryside and the agricultural sector, further increased the supply of labour power in the urban industrial sector. In the seven major capitalist countries, annual population growth in 1955–68 was of the order of 1 per cent, while annual employment growth in industry and services averaged roughly 1.5 per cent and 2.0 per cent respectively. It would have been very difficult to maintain this disparity without the annual decline of agricultural working population of 3.8 per cent. Substantial immigration of workers from less developed countries also took place. Up to ten million immigrants were added to the working population of Western Europe in 1950–75. Finally, the rise in the participation rate of women in the labour force was also an important factor in expanding the supply of labour power.

The labour power employed by firms in the seven most advanced countries rose by about 60 million between 1950 and 1970, roughly equal to three fifths of the total number of civilian wage workers in 1950. Output, however, grew even faster as labour productivity rose at about 3.8 per cent annually. While it is very probable that there was a rise in the technical composition of capital (the physical ratio of constant capital to living labour) both reflecting and causing the rise in labour productivity, the value composition of capital (the value ratio of constant to variable capital) appears to have remained relatively stable as the value of capital goods per unit declined. The rate of surplus value, or the share of profits in value added, also tended to be stable as workers shared the rewards of improved productivity. In all, the profit rate in the advanced capitalist countries remained at a high and stable level during this period. According to a composite estimate for the seven major capitalist countries in 1950–68 the profit rate was roughly 20–25 per cent in manufacturing and 15–20 per cent more generally (Armstrong *et al.*, 1984, p. 171).

8.1.2 Money and Finance in the Long Boom

In sharp contrast to the profit rate, the rate of interest remained low throughout the period. Between 1960 and 1967 the long-term nominal interest rate in the major capitalist countries (measured by the yield of long-term government bonds) was 4–6 per cent, or just over 2 per cent in real terms (if inflation is taken into account).[3] As argued in Chapter 3, the general rate of profit in a capitalist economy need not be equalised with the rate of interest; indeed the former tends to lie above the latter. The systematic gap between the two allows room for the state to influence the rate of interest through monetary policy. Throughout the long boom, the rate of interest was manipulated to favour increases in industrial and other investment.

Monetary policy in the major economies (above all the United States) contributed significantly to keeping the rate of interest (nominal, and especially real) relatively low, in sharp contrast to the high profit rates. An abundant supply of loanable money capital was also generated during the long boom by banks and other financial institutions, sustained by the idle money of individuals and corporations, and by the smooth repayment of debt. The wide gap between the rate of profit and the real rate of interest promoted long-term capital investment in plant and equipment through direct finance in the United States and Britain (the issuing of shares and bonds in the capital market) and through indirect finance in Japan and Germany (bank loans).[4] Nevertheless, given that the causes of the high and stable rate of profit during the long boom were independent of the low real rate of interest, state monetary policies were a supplementary rather than a fundamental factor of the long boom.

In the recessions that occurred, expansionary fiscal policy operating through budget deficits was neither particularly substantial nor lasted very long; typically, the promptly ensuing upswing eliminated the budget deficit by raising tax proceeds. The vigour imparted to capitalist accumulation by the fundamental conditions discussed above was more important than government fiscal and monetary policies. It is misguided to claim (particularly under the influence of Keynesian ideology) that the contribution of such policies was the decisive factor behind the long boom. The most that can be argued in this respect is that US politico-military expenditure in the early years of the postwar period probably boosted effective demand and supported accumulation. In the course of the long boom, however, such spending became less significant, and eventually undermined the boom itself.

8.2   THE INFLATIONARY CRISIS AND THE LONG DOWNSWING

8.2.1   The Inflationary Crisis and 'Stagflation'

The postwar boom ended with an inflationary crisis that opened a period of 'stagflation', a word composed from stagnation and inflation. At the beginning of the 1970s the annual rate of inflation in the major capitalist countries climbed rapidly, especially following the sharp rise in oil prices after the first oil shock of 1973–4. The annual increase of the GDP deflator in the seven major capitalist countries was 3.1 per cent in 1960–8, 6.0 per cent in 1968–73 and 8.6 per cent in 1973–9. In the years 1973, 1974 and 1975 the measure stood at 7.3 per cent, 11.6 per cent, and 10.3 per cent respectively (OECD, *Historical Statistics*, 1986). Inflation remained high throughout the 1970s and picked up again during 1978–81, the years of the second oil shock. Very high annual rates of inflation, often around the 20 per cent mark, were not unusual in the advanced capitalist world after 1974. The growth rate of the major economies, meanwhile, fell sharply. Annual growth of real GDP in the seven major capitalist countries declined from 5.1 per cent in 1960–8 to 4.6 per cent in 1968–73, to 0.1 per cent in 1974 and -0.4 per cent in 1975. It recovered to above 4 per cent in 1976–8 but fell again after the second oil shock. During 1979–84 growth was as low as 1.9 per cent, and even registered −0.7 per cent in 1982 (OECD, ibid.). For some countries the absolute decline in real GDP was considerably greater than these averages for the seven most advanced countries.

During the long boom, increases in the rate of inflation typified periods of strong effective demand. From the late 1960s onwards, however, more rapid inflation tended to aggravate the rising difficulties of capitalist accumulation. Expansionary fiscal and monetary policies in the 1970s not only proved incapable of bolstering effective demand, but actually worsened the plight of accumulation by exacerbating inflation. The seemingly anomalous coexistence of inflation and recession resulted from the disappearance of the fundamental conditions that had favoured the accumulation of capital during the long postwar boom. In the course of the long boom capitalist accumulation undermined those favourable conditions and prepared the ground for its own crisis.

US economic hegemony, which had underpinned the stability of the Bretton Woods system, was eroded during the long boom as rival capitalist countries, particularly West Germany and Japan, restored and strengthened their competitive power. The uneven advance of productivity growth significantly altered the relative costs of production among the developed capitalist countries. Consequently fixed exchange rates, which had initially benefited US exports, began to favour rival countries such as Japan. Advanced US technology was transferred and successfully employed by rival countries, while innovation dried up in US industries. This further weakened the competitive power of large US industrial firms, and from the 1960s onwards encouraged them to internationalise their activities by increasing their foreign direct investment. As a result of these trends the US trade surplus decreased sharply in the 1960s and had disappeared by 1970. Meanwhile foreign spending by the US government escalated due to the Vietnam War. Government spending abroad, foreign direct investment and declining trade surpluses led to increasing deficits in the US balance of payments in the 1960s.

The ability of the United States to fulfil its official undertaking to convert $35 into an ounce of gold upon request by foreign monetary authorities became increasingly problematic. Dollar crises repeatedly occurred in the foreign exchange markets, typically caused by speculative pressures on the United States gold reserves. In August 1971 the United States was forced to abandon the convertibility of the dollar into gold, signalling the collapse of the Bretton Woods system. An attempt to replace Bretton Woods with a system of exchange rates fluctuating within fairly wide bands (the Smithsonian Agreement) failed to stabilise the relative value of dollar, and broke down in March 1973. A floating exchange rate system has prevailed among the main currencies of the capitalist world since then.

The turmoil in the international monetary system encouraged substantial outflows of dollar funds from the United States in order to make speculative gains against the falling dollar, or simply to avoid losses. The funds further swelled the dollar reserves of other advanced industrialised countries. Easier acquisition of international reserves facilitated the implementation of expansionary monetary policy to ameliorate the recession of the 1970s. In Japan, for instance, the government intentionally stoked up 'adjustment inflation' hoping that the rise in domestic prices would mitigate the rise of the yen against the dollar. In the United States itself, the disappearance of the requirement to maintain substantial gold reserves also removed the gold anchor from domestic prices.

Boosted by laxer monetary policy made possible by the collapse of the Bretton Woods system, inflation accelerated throughout the advanced capitalist world. As the annual rate of inflation rose above 10 per cent, the real rate of interest often became negative. Low real rates of interest led to an explosion of speculative stockpiling of primary products and raw materials. The speculative explosion of the 1970s resulted from the changed monetary and financial conditions of the period, but also from the overaccumulation of capital in the advanced countries relative to the tighter supply of labour power and primary products, discussed immediately below. The phenomenon was similar to the speculative overtrading and stockpiling of commodities funded by cheap credit that used to characterise the last phase of the upswing of the classical business cycle.

8.2.2 Overaccumulation and the Transformation of the Capitalist Crisis

During the long postwar boom there was intensified mobilisation of the labouring population in the advanced capitalist countries, as well as heightened consumption of primary products. In the final stages of the boom the advancing overaccumulation of capital generated a shortage of labour power and primary products, thus removing these fundamentally favourable conditions for capitalist accumulation. Tighter labour market conditions contributed to a wage explosion in the second half of the 1960s and the early 1970s. Between 1965 and 1973 nominal wages in manufacturing rose by more than 50 per cent, 100 per cent, and 200 per cent in, respectively, the United States, several key European countries and Japan. The strengthened negotiating power of the trade unions played a significant role in bringing about these increases, but only within the favourable conditions created by the tighter labour market. Moreover workplace discipline had become laxer as it was relatively easy for workers to obtain jobs in the labour market. Well before the first oil shock, profits in the major capitalist countries were being increasingly squeezed by the rise in wages.[5]

The world market prices of primary products such as corn, wood, cotton, wool and minerals also began to rise rapidly in the late 1960s, reflecting the relative shortage of these products. The quadrupling of the price of crude oil within a few months in 1973–4 owed much to the fourth Arab–Israeli war, but was also integral to the general shortage of primary products due to the overaccumulation of capital in the advanced countries. The terms of trade of primary products relative to manufactures were raised by more than 10 per cent in 1970–3 and by nearly 70 per cent in 1970–4. The price of raw materials for manufacturing nearly doubled within the year prior to the first oil shock.

Together with the decline in labour discipline, such price increases led to a fall in the ratio of output to capital of the order of 10–20 per cent in the United States, Europe and Japan. In turn, the combination of declining profit share and a falling output to capital ratio led to a fall in the profit rate in the major capitalist countries: by 1973 profit rates in the major capitalist countries had declined by 20–40 per cent relative to their long boom peak. According to one estimate, three quarters of the decline was due to the squeeze of the profit share and one quarter to the fall in the output to capital ratio (Glyn, 1988). In short, the underlying overaccumulation of capital worsened the conditions for the production of surplus value in the major capitalist countries and resulted in a fall in the profit rate. The problems of accumulation were caused neither by underconsumption nor by a shortage of effective demand.

In the classical business cycle, overaccumulation leads to a falling rate of profit accompanied by growth in speculation and a shortage of loanable capital. A sharp deflationary crisis occurs as the falling rate of profit crosses the rising rate of interest. In contrast, after the collapse of the Bretton Woods system overaccumulation accompanied by speculative explosion led to an inflationary crisis. There was no shortage of money capital to force 'sacrifice' sales of superabundant commodities. Rather the superabundance of money led to rapid inflation, which, together with the shortage of primary products, severely disturbed productive activity in 1974–5. Industrial firms often had to reduce production because of the difficulty of obtaining raw materials, which were being speculatively bought and stockpiled. In these circumstances monetary and fiscal policies tended to exacerbate the economic crisis, contrary to the claims of Keynesian ideology. The inflationary crisis did not result simply from poor (or too much) government policy, but from the intrinsic limitations of the capitalist economy expressed as the overaccumulation of capital.

8.2.3   The Long Downswing

More than two decades have elapsed since the inflationary crisis of 1973–5. Though economic activity recovered in 1976–8, severe recession took a grip again in 1979–83 as the second oil shock and the austerity policies of the turn of the decade struck real accumulation. Since the recovery was not particularly strong, total unemployment among the OECD countries rose steadily from 7.9 million in 1973 to 15.0 million in 1975, 21.5 million in 1980 and 31.8 million in 1983. Recovery in 1983–9 was again unstable and weak, and the total number of unemployed in the OECD countries remained about 30 million. In several European countries in particular, the rate of unemployment continued to exceed 10 per cent even during recovery. When financial speculation of the late 1980s collapsed in several major capitalist countries, severe recession followed for the third time since 1973. Real wages remained stagnant or even slid downwards in several industrial countries including the United States.

The annual growth of real GDP in the seven major capitalist countries declined from 4.8 per cent in 1960–73 to 2.8 per cent in 1973–9, remained at 2.6 per cent in 1979–89 and fell further to 1.7 per cent in 1989–95 (OECD, *Historical Statistics*, 1997). Firms in the advanced capitalist countries have faced intensified competition in both the domestic and the world market, as well as stagnating profitability. Short-term recessions and recoveries, combined with the overall difficulty of sustaining robust capital accumulation, indicate that the capitalist world entered a long downswing in 1973–74. This long downswing is historically comparable to the Great Depressions of 1873–96 and the 1930s, and has forced the restructuring of capitalist economies in several respects, some of which are discussed in the next section. Given that the pressure to restructure has not abated for more than two decades, the duration of the present downswing appears longer than that of the previous two, giving it the character of a rather chronic disease of capitalist accumulation.

8.3   INCREASED FINANCIAL INSTABILITY

8.3.1   Increased Economic Instability

The introduction of floating exchange rates in 1973 was generally expected to facilitate the smooth and gradual adjustment of exchange rates in line with the competitive power of different countries. Harmful speculation against the dollar in the foreign exchange markets would become, it was presumed, a thing of the past. Without the requirement to build foreign exchange reserves and defend the exchange rate, it was hoped that domestic fiscal and monetary policies, the mainstay of the Keynesian orthodoxy of the time, would become more effective.

Fiscal and monetary policy, however, did not prevent the inflationary crisis and were not able to reverse the long downswing and the rise in unemployment. Indeed such policies proved harmful as they stoked up inflation. The expansionary policies of the 1970s also led to a substantial increase in government borrowing as public expenditure climbed higher. Countries that had relatively low levels of government debt at the beginning of the downswing saw outstanding debt as a proportion of GNP rise significantly. Between 1973 and 1979, for instance, the proportion rose from 11.6 per cent to 34.4 per cent in Japan, and from 6.7 per cent to 14.5 per cent in West Germany. In contrast, countries that already had high levels of government debt at the beginning of the period, such as the United States and Britain, did not face the same problem as rapid inflation destroyed the value of old debt. However this was not Keynes' 'euthanasia of the rentier', but rather the cause of a broad and uneven destruction of the value of the savings of working people. At the same time, given the fixed nominal schedule of taxes in several countries, the increases in nominal income due to inflation resulted in a heavier tax burden on working people (fiscal drag).

Keynesian orthodoxy in economic policy was abandoned at the end of the 1970s since it had failed to solve the problems of capitalist accumulation, indeed it had exacerbated them. Government resort to expansionary policies became less popular among working people and political parties. The official swing towards economic neoliberalism and monetarism began with the election of Thatcher in Britain and was confirmed with the election of Reagan in the United States. Neoliberalism is essentially an economic ideology that stresses the harmonious and efficient functioning of the market. Neoliberal policies aim at limiting the economic role of the government, and strengthening the dynamism of the free market through reductions in the marginal rate of income tax for the wealthy. Monetarism, on the other hand, is the contemporary form of the quantity theory of money, the main policy recommendation of which is tight control of the money supply in order to deal with inflation. Neither neoliberal nor monetarist policies worked as intended in dealing with recession and rapid inflation after the second oil shock. In practice the United States' massive military expenditure in the final phase of the Cold War led to a tripling of the (already large) US budget deficit in 1981–6, and a significant increase in government borrowing. The consequent rise in the real rate of interest attracted a huge inflow of loanable money capital into the United States from across the world. As a result the exchange rate of the dollar rose against the main currencies, worsening the US trade deficit and further damaging the competitiveness of US industry.

It was ironic that the recovery of the US economy after 1983 was spurred mostly by the huge deficits of an avowedly anti-Keynesian administration. Much of the increase in US effective demand, however, leaked abroad. As long as the United States continued to expand domestic demand by accumulating domestic and foreign debt based on an appreciating dollar, Japan and other Asian countries were able greatly to increase their exports to the US markets. Consequently trade friction between the United States and Japan was heightened. European countries, in contrast, failed to participate in the recovery and continued to suffer from historically high unemployment in terms of both rates and numbers. Less developed countries, with the significant exception of several Asian countries, experienced deeper difficulties as the price of primary products declined and real rates of interest escalated.

Neoliberal policies in the 1980s failed to restore stability and harmony to the world economy. On the contrary such policies led to substantial US government and balance of payments deficits, historically high real rates of interest in the United States and exceptional strength for the US dollar. At a meeting of the finance ministers of the so-called G5 (the five major capitalist countries) in September 1985 it was agreed that steps had to be taken to reverse the rise of the dollar. The resultant fall in interest rates led to a broad reversal of exchange rate patterns, attended by much speculation in the foreign exchange markets.[6] Massive speculation also followed in the stock exchange and the market for real estate in the major capitalist countries, intensified by lax monetary policy and low interest rates in the late 1980s. Such financial 'bubbles' contributed to a partial recovery of domestic demand and economic activity for a short while, but their burst led to a serious financial crisis and renewed recession in the 1990s. Nothing daunted, however, the US capital market has been riding the crest of another great wave of speculation since the middle of the 1990s, raising the spectre of a new collapse and international financial crisis. There is no end in sight to the instability attendant to the present long downswing.

8.3.2 The Impact of the Information Revolution

Important developments in information technology have taken place in the course of capitalist restructuring precipitated by the long downswing, which have resulted in a veritable information revolution. Advanced silicon-based integrated circuits (ICs) have tremendously increased the ability of computers to deal with many different types of information. Combined with the further development of telecommunication systems, the information revolution has revitalised the competitive functioning of the world market since the mid 1970s. Money and finance have also been profoundly affected, both directly and indirectly.

Compared with the huge investment in industrial plant that typified industrial capitalism until the end of the 1960s, investment in automated factories and offices using the new information technology has tended to be smaller. Furthermore the introduction of computer control has allowed the flexible production of several different models of the same product from the same line. This increase in the production flexibility of firms has led to intensified competition. The introduction of automation technology, moreover, has encouraged the hiring of relatively cheap part-time workers on flexible hours (often women), whose proportion in the labour force consequently rose. Trade union membership, traditionally based on male full-time workers, has declined, as has the unions' negotiating power. Thus labour market changes have also led to the intensification of competition among firms. At the same time, state economic intervention in the advanced countries has declined as a result of the failure of expansionary policies and rising budget deficits. The increasing internationalisation of firms, moreover, has intensified competition in the world market and further limited the scope for economic intervention by each nation state. Taken together, these changes indicate that the course of capitalist development since the late nineteenth century has perhaps been reversed. The material foundation for the ideological shift from Keynesianism to neoliberalism was provided by the restrengthened competition in the domestic and world markets.

Credit and financial mechanisms have also been greatly affected by the information revolution. Financial institutions can pursue their business more efficiently as the costs of making necessary calculations, receiving money, recording transactions and transmitting funds have declined significantly. Sophisticated on-line systems and automated cash dispensers have been increasingly installed within and between banks. The use of credit cards to make payments has spread widely, and so has the payment of workers' salaries and wages directly into banks through deposit transfers. It has become possible, therefore, for a part of the monthly revenue of workers to remain with the banks as deposits, thus boosting the supply of loanable money capital.[7]

Increased efficiency has made it possible for financial institutions to expand their business beyond their customary sphere and enter the traditional territory of other institutions. The demarcation lines between banks, securities firms, savings associations, credit cooperatives and other institutions of the credit system have become increasingly blurred. New financial transactions are constantly devised to overcome restrictions on financial investment and saving. All this both contributed to and took advantage of the increasing deregulation of financial markets in the 1970s and 1980s. Financial institutions now have increased legal and technical room cheaply and flexibly to channel funds into domestic government bonds, foreign securities, consumer credit and loans to firms; they can also further speculate in foreign currency, real estate and the stock market.

To recap, the information revolution has allowed the financial system to expand its activities while increasing its efficiency. It has become possible for the financial system to enjoy bouts of robust expansion of its business relatively independently of stagnating real capital accumulation. This seems a new development in the history of capitalism, completely contrary to Keynes' advice to embark on the 'euthanasia of the rentier' in order to rejuvenate industrial investment.

Increased efficiency in financial transactions and intensified competition in the financial markets, however, have not contributed to the emergence of harmony in capitalist accumulation. The introduction of information technology has allowed large industrial corporations to improve labour productivity without undertaking gigantic investment in plant and equipment. As a consequence they have not accumulated large amounts of debt during the long downswing. Moreover they have been able to take advantage of direct finance by cheaply issuing shares, convertible bonds, warrants and a host of other securities in capital markets across the world. Large industrial firms' reliance on bank loans has tended to decline: self-financing and the emergence of large firms as net lenders rather than borrowers have become much more commonplace.

Consequently banks and other financial institutions, which are now able to deal more efficiently with rising volumes of loanable capital, have been encouraged to seek opportunities for lending outside the process of real accumulation. Helping to finance rising state budget deficits through the purchase of government bonds has offered one avenue of investment. Speculative trading in foreign currencies and securities also became increasingly important in the 1980s.[8] In his influential work on Japan, Miyazaki (1992, pp. 9–11) estimated that annual turnover in the four major foreign exchange markets in 1986 was about twelve times the annual volume of international trade in goods and services; by 1989 the same annual turnover had doubled compared with 1986, and stood at more than twenty times the annual volume of international trade.

In the late 1980s trading in shares and real estate encouraged the formation of speculative bubbles across the developed world, leading to vertiginous increases in share and real estate prices. Instead of lessening the anarchical fluctuations of the capitalist economy, advanced information technology has encouraged the emergence of enormous speculation.[9] The automated, computer-based buying and selling of financial instruments has tended to swell speculative bubbles, only to heighten the pressure to sell when the direction of prices turns downwards. Similarly, cheaper trading in the enormous markets for financial derivatives, based on the availability of the new information technologies, appears to have increased the instability of the capitalist economy by providing banks and other financial institutions with more scope for pure speculation. Sophisticated information technology has thus intensified the inherent difficulty of controlling capitalist money and finance.

8.3.3   The Limitations of Economic Policy

The introduction of floating exchange rates after the collapse of the Bretton Woods system was supposed to stabilise the markets for foreign exchange and to make domestic monetary and fiscal policies more effective. The reality was completely different: the fluctuations of exchange rates in the subsequent two decades have been gigantic in historical terms, often in the region of 50–100 per cent. The attempt to operate Keynesian expansionary policies in the 1970s, on the other hand, did not halt the recession, but instead stoked up inflation. The switch from Keynesianism to monetarism in the early 1980s in the United States and Britain failed even to control the money supply, but inflation was brought down as real accumulation was subjected to the heavy recessionary pressure of tight monetary policy. However monetary policy could not prevent the emergence of disastrous speculative bubbles in the late 1980s, which caused considerable damage to real accumulation when they burst. Lax monetary policy and lower interest rates in the 1990s did not lead to a resurgence of robust capitalist accumulation.

Monetarism, the contemporary version of the quantity theory of money, had limited relevance to the high rates of inflation in the early 1970s. The high price of crude oil, the relative shortage of other primary products and the shortage of labour power were at least as significant as the increased supply of money in igniting inflation. The resurgence of inflation in 1979–82 was also related to the second oil shock. Attempting to control the money supply in the late 1980s was not a realistic policy option, considering the growth of direct finance and the by-passing of banks by other financial institutions in the provision of finance (disintermediation). Furthermore, increased efficiency in the management of financial assets seems to have accelerated the velocity of money.

The increased efficiency and flexibility of the credit system, coupled with low interest rates, did not lead to inflation in the late 1980s but to the emergence of speculative bubbles exclusively concentrated in real estate and share prices. The emergence of substantial part-time labour, the considerably weakened power of the trade unions under pressure from recession and technological change, and the depressed prices of primary products in the world market were important factors in suppressing of inflation. The same factors were probably important in the failure of inflation to surge when the speculative bubbles burst in the 1990s.

Under floating exchange rates the monetary authorities have more room to manipulate the rate of interest and the supply of money. In this regard, money and finance have become more amenable to social and political management. Consequently the policy of the central bank with respect to its own rate of interest and the supply of reserves to banks has become a matter of heated controversy. In Chapter 7 of this work, however, it was established that there can be no objective rule with which to guide the operations of central banks. Even when the international money was gold, central banks had considerable room for discretion on interest rates and the supply of their liabilities. They have much more under floating exchange rates. To replace discretion with, say, the monetarist principle that the supply of money should be kept growing at a steady rate in accordance with long-term economic growth, is actually a recipe for greater instability as it denies flexibility to the money supply. Moreover the categories included in the 'money' whose growth is to be kept steady have become very unclear: the rapidly changing financial system has given rise to new financial instruments that can be used as means of purchase or hoarding.

It is one of the paradoxes of the long downswing that as floating exchange rates made social control of money and finance more feasible, the mechanical theory of monetarism became prominent. Nevertheless the practice of governments has demonstrated that it is not possible to achieve harmonious economic growth by controlling the supply of money. As the downswing has progressed, exchange rate instability and the emergence of temporary speculative bubbles have intensified. This was certainly not imagined by the advocates of monetarism or neoliberalism. Meanwhile working people have had to bear the burden of austerity policies, unemployment and a more unequal distribution of income and wealth encouraged by financial speculation and instability in the economy.

8.3.4 Can Stability be Restored?

Lessening the remarkable instability of the post-1973 world is a particularly intractable problem. Five broad options for greater stability are briefly considered below.

A World Central Bank

One possibility is the establishment of a world central bank. This idea was originally floated by Keynes during the Bretton Woods negotiations in 1944, only to be rejected by the US side, which was mainly responsible for the final form of the Bretton Woods system. In contemporary capitalism, advancing economic internationalisation, led by the activities of huge multinational companies, has reduced the ability of the monetary authorities of national states to adopt effective economic policies. In these circumstances a global monetary authority, perhaps drawing legitimacy from some notion of global citizenship, could potentially undertake global policies to tackle monetary instability. The same authority could also perhaps tackle other socioeconomic problems, such as poverty and ecological crises in many parts of the world.

However an effective global monetary authority would inevitably impose severe restrictions on the ability of each nation state to formulate economic policy, and it would require close and harmonious cooperation among nation states. Given the tremendous heterogeneity in economic and political power among the existing capitalist nation states, this is a very unrealistic prospect. Even if some progress towards the establishment of such an authority were to be made, it is likely that the hegemonic capitalist powers would dominate the decision making process to promote their own interests. Monetary policy formulated by mechanisms dominated by the hegemonic capitalist powers will not serve the interests of working people across the world, particularly those living in weaker countries.

Regional Integration

A more feasible path to greater stability is the regional integration of several countries, as typified by the European Union (EU) and the North American Free Trade Agreement (NAFTA). Regional groupings of countries can attempt to form a common monetary authority, which would then make efforts to stabilise the regional monetary order, even to the extent of creating a common means of exchange and payment. The current policy aim of the EU, for instance, is to establish within the near future a European central bank managing a single currency. Considerable opposition to the scheme has already emerged at the grassroots level, often led by socialist and workers' organisations. Contrary to what is often maintained, such opposition is not backward-looking. Control of monetary policy by a single EU authority would significantly hamper the ability of the nation state to reduce unemployment locally, or to adopt fiscal and monetary policies favouring the economic welfare of working people. Meanwhile, the capitalist class, which would have countless ways of directly and indirectly influencing the policies of the single monetary authority, would enjoy greater investment choices in both productive capacity and financial assets.

Regional unification, moreover, is unlikely to promote harmonious economic growth, and would probably intensify uneven development and the inequitable distribution of the costs of integration. Differential inflation rates, and variable success in increasing competitiveness among capitalist countries, typically result in fluctuations of exchange rates and changes to monetary policies. Integration would block both of the latter, forcing the strains of uneven development within the grouping to emerge locally as reductions in productive capacity and increased unemployment. This would in turn exacerbate uneven development. The resulting unevenness in the welfare of workers within the regional group would be much more difficult to tackle by employing the power of the nation state. Since, moreover, multinational workers' organisations able successfully to defend workers' interests within regional groups do not exist at the moment, the present opposition of European workers to monetary union is a natural development. Far from revealing nationalist backwardness, it reflects the profound anxiety of working people that there might be a complete loss of control over policy-making that directly affects their interests.[10]

A Return to Gold

A further possibility is the full return to gold as the international means of payment, or to a system partially based on gold with fixed exchange rates, similar to Bretton Woods. The anchor of gold has historically provided capitalist economies with relatively stable exchange rates and price levels. A return to gold is not as anachronistic as might appear at first sight, particularly if one bears in mind the tendency for the reversal of the historical development of the capitalist economy in the direction of greater market competition. However, to restore gold as the international means of payment requires the prior resolution of the following fundamental difficulties.

The existing stock of monetary gold would have to be enlarged in order to match the tremendous expansion of financial transactions and the smaller, but still substantial, expansion of international trade. The United States, moreover, would have to eliminate the huge deficit in its balance of trade and reverse its tendency to borrow from its main capitalist competitors. The experience of the Bretton Woods system has shown that sustaining the convertibility of the dollar into gold would otherwise be very problematic. More broadly, the effective functioning of gold as the international means of payment in the past has rested on the economic and political hegemony first of Britain and then the United States (*Pax Britannica* and *Pax Americana*). The erosion of US hegemony, which led to the collapse of the Bretton Woods system, has not yet been made good. The long downswing appears to represent an interregnum in world hegemony. As long as US economic hegemony is not reestablished, it is not clear when and how the interregnum will end. Though the possibility of a return to gold cannot be excluded, its feasibility is clearly problematic at the moment. Finally, even if it were feasible to instigate a return, it is far from clear that it would be desirable for working people. A monetary system based on gold operates automatically, and stabilises prices by severely and adversely influencing real accumulation. There would inevitably be strong political opposition to a proposal to stabilise economic life by resorting to the callous blindness of the yellow metal.

Free Banking

The abolition of central banks, of national denominations for money and of bank-created legal tender has also been proposed as a means towards greater stability, as examined in Chapter 7. The persistent failure to control credit and finance in the long downswing has allowed free banking arguments to gain popularity. For the advocates of free banking, the ultimate cause of financial instability, inflation, and general economic upsets lies with the distortions to the operations of the market that are brought about by government monopoly of the issue of legal tender. However the free banking school's faith in the inherent harmony of the free market is unconvincing on several scores. First, as established in Chapter 7, it is a natural tendency of the banking system to concentrate reserves and to assign prominence to one type of bank money over others. Second, nation states would not abandon their control over the issuing of money without significant political and other resistance. Third, the free issue of competing monies by several institutions is likely to create more, not less, room for inflation, intensified speculation, and severe financial crises. At the same time, the abolition of central banks, would remove precisely the institutions that could take some steps towards ameliorating the worst symptoms of capitalist crises.[11]

Piecemeal Reform

Finally, piecemeal and gradual improvements might be wrought to the current system, implicitly acknowledging that no dramatic transformation in the direction of greater stability is possible. Possible improvements, with some limited potential to reduce fraud and speculation, include the increased availability of information about the operations of financial institutions, and more efficient prudential regulation by the central banks of the practices of financial institutions. Increased international cooperation among central banks could reduce the fluctuations of exchange rates; in this respect it is essential for the United States to tackle its balance of trade deficit and its enormous borrowing requirements. Somewhat more drastically, a so-called 'Tobin tax' on trading in foreign exchange could be imposed globally on foreign exchange transactions.[12] The tax could also be extended to other internationally traded financial instruments. Considering that speculators typically engage in several frequent transactions, even a low rate of tax on each transaction could substantially increase the total cost, thus helping to reduce speculative activity in the foreign exchange and the financial markets.

Piecemeal and partial changes to the international monetary order are the most realistic prospect for greater stability in the capitalist world market for the foreseeable future. This is far from an ideal and desirable prospect. Shoring up the ailing international monetary order, after all, is not an end in itself. The destructive repercussions of its anarchic functioning on the lives of working people are not usually prominent in technical analyses of the system's weaknesses. In reconstructing the international monetary order the issue of democratic control of monetary processes in the broad interests of working people must be more central. The incorporation of these aspects, moreover, should start at the level of the national economy. It is perfectly within the powers of the vast majority of people to comprehend the key issues involved in controlling money, credit and finance, and to take appropriate action.

9 The Rise and Fall of Keynesianism

John Maynard Keynes has been by far the most eminent economist of the twentieth century. When he was very young he was admitted into the most influential circles of economic theorising in Britain and the world, and soon began to shine in economic policy-making in the global arena. Keynes was first and foremost a monetary theorist who was not afraid to be polemical in defending the practical implications of his work. In the 1930s this fully paid-up member of the British intellectual and political elite launched a frontal assault (or so he thought) on economic orthodoxy. Elements of the tradition of Steuart, the banking school and Marx resurfaced in Keynes' attack on the orthodoxy: the complexity of the functions of money in a capitalist economy, particularly the importance of money hoarding; the inherent tendency of capitalist accumulation to move towards disequilibrium and crisis; and the role of uncertainty and expectations about the future in shaping the path of capitalist accumulation. These elements taken together provided the rationale for Keynes' support of government economic intervention, both fiscal and monetary.

The rise of Keynesianism to prominence after the Second World War was the result of the historical and institutional transformation of world capitalism after 1945, not merely the intellectual power of Keynes. The Keynesianism of the long boom, the so-called neoclassical synthesis, which introduced elements of Walrasian general equilibrium into, and removed the radical content from, Keynes' work, was not the same system of ideas as Keynes' *General Theory*. For the neoclassical synthesis, so long as prices were flexible capitalism would remain crisis-free, or could be rendered so by means of judicious economic policy. The international inflationary crisis of the 1970s destroyed postwar Keynesianism in a remarkably short period of time. Since then, no school of thought has dominated economic theory, though several competing currents have returned to the premises of pre-Keynesian orthodoxy. The revolutionary aims of Keynes' mature work have completely vanished from contemporary mainstream economics.

The end of postwar Keynesianism was championed by monetarism, a current of economic thought that represents the resurgence of key concepts from Hume, Ricardo and the currency school, and advocates stabilisation of the capitalist economy through control of the money supply. The failure of monetarist policy prescriptions to bring stability quickly led to the theory's loss of prestige and its retreat. In its wake, influential neoliberal (new classical) analysis has stressed rational expectations and continuous market clearing, and theorised instability in terms of unforeseen monetary shocks delivered by governments to the course of real accumulation. The evident narrowness of the new classical emphasis on sudden monetary shocks as an explanation of capitalist instability has further led to the emergence of real business cycle theory. The latter also accepts rational expectations and market clearing, but attempts to theorise the business cycle in terms of unforeseen changes in the technology of production. Finally, the persistence of instability and disharmony in the operations of the free market has encouraged the emergence of new Keynesianism. The optimality and efficiency of the free market is generally accepted by the new Keynesians, but they also attempt to establish microeconomic reasons for market failure. For new Keynesians, price rigidity lies behind market failure. Price rigidity arises for reasons such as an economic agents' attitude to risk and the peculiarities of the employment contract.

9.1   THE RADICAL CONTENT OF KEYNES' *GENERAL THEORY*

9.1.1   Rejection of Say's Law

Keynes wrote the *General Theory* in 1936 in the midst of the interwar depression. In order theoretically to account for persistent disequilibrium in the labour market, represented by severe unemployment, Keynes rejected Say's law. Keynes (1936, pp. 18–21) attributed this law to all the 'classical' economists, amongst whom he also included neoclassicals such as Marshall. Keynes' rejection of Say's law was a radical step in his critique of economic orthodoxy, but lumping together classical political economy and neoclassicism was problematic for the following reasons.

For the Ricardian classical tradition, money is primarily a means of exchange, a plain facilitator of commodity transactions. Goods are essentially bought with goods, and so money can be disregarded for the purposes of analysing the substantive content of capitalist exchange. It was also clearly understood by this tradition that planned expenditure by an individual (purchases, or planned demand) must be matched by the planned supply of commodities of equal value (sales). If this were not so, the individual would be irrationally anticipating that either he/she or some other individual would supply more commodity value than that received in every period. The same holds at the aggregate level: for all individuals the planned aggregate demand for commodities (purchases) must equal the planned aggregate supply (sales). At the aggregate level, of course, this principle need not hold for each commodity, the imbalance between demand and supply leading to changes in relative prices which readjust supply and demand until the market is cleared.

The peculiarly important and disputatious position of Say's law in economics arises because, based on the necessary equality of planned aggregate demand and supply, the law asserts that there is also equality of effective (that is, backed by money) demand and supply. A true statement about the direct exchange of commodities, or about planned demand and supply, is turned into a tendentious assertion about demand and supply backed by money. If Say's law holds true, then excess demand (valued in money terms) in some markets is always and exactly offset by excess supply (valued in money terms) in other markets. The implications of this for economic theory are profound. Above all, overproduction of all goods in a monetary economy – a 'general glut' – is impossible. A 'glut' is equivalent to an excess of aggregate supply over aggregate demand, that is, a positive aggregate excess supply, which directly contradicts Say's law. By this token, if the planned output of producers is at the full employment level, the whole of this output is taken up by effective demand. In principle there is no systematic reason why national production and national income should diverge from the full employment level.[1]

A precondition for Say's law to hold is that money is a pure means of exchange, that is, no money hoarding takes place. If sellers were to opt to hold onto the money form of their sold commodities, it would be trivially true that effective demand need not equal supply in each period.[2] This aspect of Say's law was criticised by Marx on several scores (1905, pt II, pp. 500–2; 1867, pp. 210–20). At one remove, money splits purchase from sale, and no-one needs to buy because he or she has sold: monetary exchange is qualitatively different from direct exchange. At a further remove, capitalist production and exchange systematically generate money hoards, that is, systematically give rise to selling without buying. Moreover, under capitalist conditions much of the selling and buying of commodities is done by merchants, who certainly do not have to buy because they have just sold. In short the sale of commodities for money (these commodities already containing surplus value generated in production) is a qualitatively different process from simple barter. Hoarding of money regularly takes place under capitalist conditions.[3]

Two related points can now be made with reference to Keynes' rejection of Say's law, and his claim that the denial of the possibility of disequilibrium applied equally to all economists ('classical') up to and including Marshall. First, Say and even Ricardo, recognised the possibility of gluts in the short run (Sowell, 1974, pp. 38–52).[4] For Ricardo in particular, the validity and significance of Say's Law must be understood in the long run: capitalist production is not limited by demand but by the rate of profit, which depends on the distribution of revenue between wages, rent and profit (Harris, 1981a, pp. 97–101). In contrast Keynes was much more concerned with the determination of total output in the short run.

Second, for Ricardo, capitalist accumulation exhibits a tendency to stagnate in the wake of population pressure on cultivable land, which reduces marginal returns from agriculture, raises the value of food, increases real wages and so reduces profits. Say's law is relevant only as long as the rate of profit is at a satisfactory level for capitalist accumulation; in the course of the latter, partial imbalances of demand and supply are regularly corrected. In contrast, according to neoclassical theory, so long as labour is paid the value of its marginal product the Ricardian analysis is incorrect. Factors of production can, and will, be substituted for each other if their relative prices change. Therefore rising wages lead to the displacement of labour by capital. If labour is unemployed that must be because wages are too high, and for no other reason at all (Fine, 1980, p. 35). The very different analytical apparatuses employed by classical and neoclassical theory imply that they could not have the same view of Say's law.

Keynes clearly rejected the claim that aggregate excess supply is equal to zero in a monetary economy, though the precise content of his rejection has been much debated in the postwar period. The analytical interpretation of Keynes' rejection of Say's law that is closest to Keynes' letter and spirit is that offered by the 'reappraisal of Keynes' group of the 1960s (Clower, 1965; Leijonhufvud, 1967, 1968). Essentially these economists argued that Keynes rejected

Say's law by postulating the sequential character of purchase and sale, and by using the concept of quantity responding to quantity rather than quantity responding to price. For each individual transactor, supply and demand are separated in space and time. The equality of aggregate planned demand and supply can be translated into equality of effective demand and supply only if individual demands and supplies are correctly sequenced. For instance, if workers find themselves unemployed they might not be able to purchase the full output of consumption goods, leaving capitalists unable to purchase the full output of production goods, and so perpetuating unemployment. Under such conditions, and as long as quantities and prices are not responsive to each other, effective demand is necessarily insufficient. Hence there is excess supply of goods and unemployment is involuntary. Were effective demand to increase (say, through an autonomous rise in investment in production goods) extra incomes would be generated; increased income would lead to additional expenditures swelling effective demand and so further increasing income. This chain reaction, the well-known multiplier, would continue until the full effect of the initial increase in effective demand on income had revealed itself.

Keynes (1936, ch. 19) insisted that involuntary unemployment is unrelated to money wages being above their market-clearing level. Unemployment is due to insufficiency of effective demand, making it impossible for workers to achieve their desired level of employment and so limiting their effective consumption. The interpretation of his work by the 'reappraisal' group makes much of the primacy of the response of quantity to quantity rather than quantity to price. For this group of theorists, an initial deficiency of effective demand leads to disequilibrium, which far from being self-corrected, becomes amplified as incomes decline. For Keynes, full employment equilibrium does not generally characterise the capitalist economy, the reason being not a disturbance of the price mechanism but the systemic weakness of effective demand.

9.1.2 Money and Interest

In a capitalist economy, if overproduction and an excess supply of goods materialise, some capitalists must be hoarding money, that is, there must have been selling without buying. Capitalist overproduction crises are typically characterised by the interconnected elements of unsold stocks of commodities, involuntary labour unemployment and stocks of idle money. Conversely, if commodity flows are never interrupted in the aggregate, money hoarding is an insignificant aspect of economic theory. By this token, Say's law and the quantity theory of money, which ignores money hoards, were essential complements. Keynes' rejection of Say's law necessarily led to the rejection of the quantity theory of money.

Keynes (1936, ch. 15) identified three motives for the holding of money: for transactions (individuals and firms), as a precaution, and for speculative purposes.[5] Of these the first is simply the traditional function of money as means of exchange; thus, money held for transactions purposes varies directly with commodity output, all other things being equal. The second is the similarly well-understood reserve function of money in the face of unpredictable shocks to production and exchange. The third represents a theoretical innovation by Keynes, and is the foundation of his original theory of liquidity preference, or money hoarding.

Liquidity preference recognises that money is a store of value, an adequate representation of social wealth that can be exchanged for commodities or make payments in the future. By making this function of money central to monetary theory, Keynes directly rejected the Ricardian tradition of emphasising the exchange function and positing money as a plain veil over the process of commodity exchange. The innovative element in Keynes' treatment of hoarding was to associate the latter with speculation. Money, which is the most liquid of assets and can always buy, can be held in the expectation that commodity prices or financial asset prices will fall in the future. By moving into money, capitalist speculators can retreat from commodities and financial assets if there is a danger of prices declining. Equally, by moving into money speculators can prepare for their eventual return to commodities and financial assets in order to realise speculative gains. Speculative liquidity preference complements Keynes' rejection of Say's Law on the basis of insufficient effective demand.

A theory of the rate of interest is necessary to sustain the postulate of speculative money hoarding. For the classical economists the rate of interest is unrelated to the quantity of money – interest is a share of total profit. Interest is also the price at which saving out of revenue (understood as real output not consumed) becomes equal to investment (again understood as spare resources ploughed back into production). Keynes (1936, ch. 13), on the other hand, postulated that interest is the price at which the demand for money, driven by liquidity preference, is equal to a given supply of money. Keynes' theory of interest, unlike classical political economy, is a monetary theory of the rate of interest. This innovation has critical theoretical implications in Keynes' work, and in order to appreciate this fully we should first consider Keynes' views on uncertainty and expectations. Marx's analysis differed from both the classical theorists and Keynes in this respect. Marx accepted that interest is a part of total profit, but argued that it is also the price at which the supply of loanable capital equals the demand; such capital typically assumes the money form, and is not equivalent to real resources saved and reinvested. As for Ricardo, however, interest is unrelated to the quantity of money: the latter is determined by entirely separate factors, which we examined in Chapter 2. Marx proposed a monetary theory of interest that pivoted on money capital rather than money.

9.1.3   Expectations and Effective Demand

Keynes' attempt to form a new theoretical system in economics is inseparable from his philosophical views on uncertainty and the role of expectations in economic intercourse.[6] Keynes was profoundly concerned with the philosophical nature of probability, and related probability to the fact that the future is fundamentally unknowable. Economic activity takes place in historical, irreversible time, thus economic agents must form expectations about the future. Expectations, however, are not formed on an entirely rational basis. Moreover, they are not the typical expectations allowed for in contemporary economic theory, that is, the average value of a parameter within the context of a well-defined probability distribution (Keynes, 1973, pp. 112–15). For Keynes, expectations contain an irreducible psychological element due to human nature. Expectations, furthermore, are not only about the future as such but also about what others expect, and what others expect still others to expect.

Given expectations of this nature, Keynes' treatment of the rate of interest, the value of capital, liquidity preference and effective demand gave rise to distinctly non-orthodox results. Capitalists invest in real assets according to the marginal efficiency of capital (MEC). The MEC is partly a technical result of production possibilities over time, but also depends on expectations about effective demand in the future since output must be sold in the future. Thus the MEC incorporates an irreducible element of 'animal spirits', an instinctual confidence about the future that makes capitalists invest; the MEC declines with the volume of investment. Capitalists also invest in financial assets; for our purposes the purchases of capitalists in the financial markets can be thought of as eventually financing real investment by other capitalists. Real investment takes place up to the point at which the MEC equals the rate of interest that can be earned by purchasing financial assets.

Expectations in the financial markets and liquidity preference play a critical role in determining investment. The rate of interest is inversely related to the value of financial assets through present value discounting. If capitalists expect the rate of interest to rise, they avoid investing in financial assets and they hold money instead. Hence liquidity preference rises. The implication is that even if the rate of interest equalled the MEC, investment might not be at the full employment level as capitalists hoard their capital as money. At very low rates of interest this effect might prove decisive in limiting investment; capitalists hoard liquid money as they are worried about the losses that will be sustained if interest rates rise. This is the 'liquidity trap', a concept that supports the view that low interest rates are not necessarily successful in increasing effective demand.

Furthermore individual consumption, quantitatively the most significant element of effective demand, is subject to the psychological law that as people become wealthier they tend to consume a progressively smaller proportion of the increases in income. The diminishing marginal propensity to consume weakens effective demand precisely as the social capacity to produce becomes greater. This psychological propensity makes it even more important to rely on investment (which also depends on psychological 'animal spirits'), and makes the influence of liquidity preference on the rate of interest (another psychological magnitude) decisive for achieving full employment. Price flexibility is entirely irrelevant to the core of Keynes' analysis.

9.1.4   An Assessment

Keynes' analysis of effective demand and unemployment clearly set him apart from Ricardian classicism, which is mostly concerned with the determination of long-run output on the basis of technical conditions of production, wages, the rate of profit and rent. It also set him apart from neoclassicisism, for which involuntary unemployment has no meaning as long as factors of production are paid their marginal product. When explaining the tendency of the capitalist economy to generate unemployment, Keynes accorded a central role to money hoarding. The emphasis on the deficiency of effective demand and on the role of money, moreover, provides a rationale for the conscious intervention of government in capitalist accumulation. Direct government spending (financed by taxation, borrowing or the issue of fiat money) can bolster effective demand and increase employment. Monetary policy, particularly a rise in the supply of money, which in the *General Theory* is typically assumed to be under the control of government, can also reduce the rate of interest and induce increases in investment, further bolstering effective demand. Thus a theoretical foundation was provided for the government to respond actively to the disaster of the interwar depression.

Keynes, however, claimed to have written a general theory of employment, interest and money, and it is in this respect that his contribution should be assessed. One remarkable aspect of his work is that he constructed a macroeconomic theory in which the behaviour of the aggregate magnitudes is different from that of the sum of the individual magnitudes. With the exception of Marxism, economic theory before and after Keynes has not been able to reconcile itself with the view that aggregate regularities in a capitalist economy might be contrary to what is suggested by individual economic behaviour. Keynes also rightly emphasised the essentially unpredictable and unknowable character of capitalist production and exchange, and identified it as a source of instability.

Nevertheless it is clear that Keynes did not succeed in developing a theory of the capitalist economy comparable to that of classical political economy.[7] Keynes' reliance on the subjective theory of value of neoclassicism is a fundamental reason for this failure. Ricardo was able to construct a monumental logical structure in a slim volume not only because he was a giant of economic thought but also because his analytical constructions were based on value as labour embodied. Whatever one thinks of Ricardo's conclusions regarding the laws of distribution there is no doubt that they had sound foundations in his value premises. Keynes attempted to construct a radical macroeconomics based on marginalism, pretending that the latter's conclusions about the remuneration of factors of production according to marginal productivity were not important for his results. In the postwar period marginalism eventually won the day, and reasserted the supremacy of price flexibility over Keynes' stress on quantities and effective demand.

As for Keynes' incorporation of expectations and uncertainty into macroeconomic theory, welcome as it is, it has two fundamental weaknesses. First, his analysis contains a wholly psychological element that is neither explicable within the framework of economic decision-making nor amenable to analysis using economic categories. That is not a satisfactory foundation for economic analysis. Second, Keynes' view of expectations bears the heavy imprint of the operations of the financial markets. This is evident in his stress on expectations about expectations (particularly in determination of the rate of interest), typical of capital market speculation. However, the capital market provides a very narrow social basis from which to derive conclusions about the formation of expectations by economic agents. To theorise the formation of economic expectations among industrialists and workers, economic theory needs a broader and more socially informed treatment of uncertainty and its psychological implications.

9.2   THE NEOCLASSICAL SYNTHESIS

The long upswing after the Second World War was based on objective conditions favourable to capitalist accumulation, as was established in Chapter 8. Keynesian demand management by the governments of the major capitalist countries was largely incidental to the boom. Early instances of demand management in the 1930s appear not to have had much success in shoring up capitalist accumulation (Mattick, 1969, ch. 12). Broadly speaking, the state had already begun to play a significant role in economic activity before the war, steadily increasing the share of government expenditure in the gross domestic product and nationalising several key industries across the developed capitalist world. The Second World War markedly accelerated this tendency and in the process resolved the depression of 1930s. Furthermore the popular demand for the establishment of a welfare state after the war, particularly in several European countries, did not result from the influence of Keynesianism but from a surge in popular aspirations for a more egalitarian society.

Nevertheless, in the confident and euphoric climate of the 1950s and 1960s the myth of Keynesianism took root. A profoundly academic theoretical system was constructed in economics, based on Hicks' (1937) pedagogical summary of Keynes' *General Theory* and systematised by Hansen (1949, 1953), Modigliani (1944), Samuelson (1947) and others. It was natural in the circumstances of the time to imagine that the new 'scientific' and increasingly mathematical economics had enabled the authorities to eliminate economic crises and depressions. The rapid demise of this confident ideology after the global crisis of the early 1970s is a remarkable demonstration of the claim that ideas always have a material foundation.

The mainstay of postwar Keynesian economics was the IS–LM model, taught to generations of economists. A closed economy is analytically dichotomised into the goods market and the money market. The IS, a downward-sloping schedule in interest–income space, represents equilibrium in the goods market, and comprises all points at which investment equals savings. The IS becomes steeper the lower the interest elasticity of investment spending and the smaller the value of the multiplier. Similarly the LM, an upward-sloping schedule in interest–income space, represents equilibrium in the money market, and comprises all points at which the demand for money equals the supply of money. The LM becomes steeper the higher the income elasticity and the lower the interest elasticity of the demand for money. Overall equilibrium emerges at the intersection of the two curves. Whether actual equilibrium theoretically coincides with full employment depends on the assumptions one makes about prices. If they are assumed to be fully flexible, it is practically impossible to allow for unemployment, unless one also argues that quantity constraints operate on capitalist firms. With full price flexibility and no quantity constraints, unemployment inevitably leads to falls in real wages, which restore equilibrium in the labour market. Falling real wages encourage the expansion of capitalist production and restore the deficiency in aggregate demand. If, however, prices are inflexible, especially if nominal wages are 'sticky' in a downward direction, unemployment cannot be eliminated by falls in real wages. The deficiency in aggregate demand remains and equilibrium at less than full employment persists.

State management of effective demand looms very large in this schema. If the economy has become lodged at less than full employment due to the deficiency of aggregate demand and 'sticky' prices, the state could adopt expansionary fiscal policy, that is, increase its own spending, directly boosting aggregate demand. Alternatively the state could adopt expansionary monetary policy, that is, increase the supply of money, lowering the rate of interest, thus promoting private investment and boosting aggregate demand. Within the confines of the model, there is no reason why a judicious mix of fiscal and monetary policies could not always assuage the deficiency of aggregate demand and result in full employment. Considerable complexity arises when one considers the financing of expansionary policy, that is, the implications of tax, borrowing or money creation, but the substance of the case is not altered.

For further analytical results it can be assumed that on the approach to full employment prices begin to rise, and rise even faster if full employment is exceeded. Expansionary fiscal and monetary policies thus appear to be able to eliminate unemployment at the cost of some inflation. If the degree of expansion is misjudged, or if effective demand is particularly robust anyway, inflation could become relatively severe. On such occasions the government has to reverse course and adopt contractionary fiscal and monetary policies. This perception of the capitalist economy as a manageable entity, and of the government as facing a choice between unemployment and inflation, is further strengthened by the concept of the Phillips curve. Originating in the work of Phillips (1958), the curve purports to capture a key empirical regularity of the capitalist economy, namely the higher the rate of inflation the lower the rate of unemployment, and *vice versa*. Thus governments appear to have both the tools and the empirical information necessary to guide the economy towards the desired combination of unemployment and inflation.

The fundamental issues of full employment and the prevention of accumulation crises presumably having been resolved, economic theorists devoted enormous energy to the largely pointless debate of the slope of the IS and the LM curves. The flatter the IS and the steeper the LM, the less effective fiscal policy is in influencing aggregate demand, an argument that found favour with the critics of official Keynesianism. On the other hand, the steeper the IS and the flatter the LM, the more effective fiscal policy is in raising aggregate demand, and so Keynesians generally supported this view of the IS–LM. At the extreme, the LM could be argued to be perfectly flat at very low rates of interest. This is the 'liquidity trap': capitalists are so concerned that a rise in the (very low) rate of interest will result in heavy capital losses on their financial assets that they are prepared to hold unlimited amounts of money. Monetary policy becomes entirely ineffectual in the 'liquidity trap'.

The theoretical results derived from the IS–LM model regarding the effectiveness and importance of fiscal policy depend on the assumptions made about the flexibility of prices. This is very much contrary to Keynes' intentions: he tried to develop a macroeconomics of capitalist unemployment that does not rely on real wages being above a presumed market-clearing level. The official Keynesianism of the postwar era implicitly accepted that it was impossible to combine Keynes' theory of involuntary unemployment with the standard analysis of market clearing under the capitalist price system. In the most developed abstract formulations of the capitalist economy, further-more, it was explicitly argued that, as long as some downward price flexibility is allowed for, the capitalist economy will always move towards full employment equilibrium by itself. As prices fall in the presence of unemployment, the real wealth of individuals rises, whether this is measured by the value of money balances or of financial assets relative to prices. If individual consumption depends on wealth as well as income, rising real wealth implies rising con-sumption, hence a rising effective demand. The real balance (or Pigou) effect, fully analysed by Patinkin (1965), claims that a capitalist economy could never be permanently lodged in unemployment equi-librium, even if liquidity trap interest rates prevailed. Keynesian unemployment is at most a special case arising from the downward rigidity of prices and wages.[8]

9.3   THE RETURN OF A FRAGMENTED ORTHODOXY

The combination of high inflation and rising unemployment after 1973–4, which were not only impervious to government policy but probably exacerbated by it, proved the death-knell of the official Keynesianism of the long boom. The crisis, as discussed in Chapter 8, was due to capital overaccumulation relative to the available labour power, compounded by high prices for primary products and the financial instability attendant to the collapse of Bretton Woods. The end of the long boom marked the beginning of protracted difficulties for capitalist accumulation: a long downswing commenced, charac-terised by advancing financial instability. In this context, several strands of economic theory began to vie for the mantle of official Keynesianism. Despite their apparent differences, these strands of theory share much common ground. Above all, they accept the inher-ently harmonious and equilibrating nature of capitalism. In the face of persistent mass unemployment, low rates of growth and stagnant real wages, mainstream economic theory has retreated into an ideological bunker, restating the supposedly beneficial effects of freely function-ing capitalism. In this respect the present downswing has been very different from the interwar depression, which produced Keynes' radi-cal challenge to economic orthodoxy.

Monetarism is rightly associated with Milton Friedman, who was already proclaiming its main message in the late 1950s. Friedmanite monetarism represents the resurgence of the tradition of the quantity theory of money in the conditions of postwar capitalism. The most important part of Friedman's theoretical work on money is the formulation of the quantity theory as a theory of the demand for money. For Friedman (1956), the demand for real money balances is a function of many variables, including real income, wealth (both human and material) and several rates of return on different assets. Moreover, monetarists assert that the demand for real money balances is empirically stable; it can be estimated using a relatively small number of variables and does not exhibit abrupt fluctuations. At the same time the supply of nominal money balances is assumed to be autonomous since the central bank controls (or could control) the supply of reserves to the banking system. Since the supply of nominal money is determined by the authorities, and the demand for real money balances is independent and stable, changes in nominal income have to be proportionate to changes in the nominal supply of money. It follows that 'inflation [is] always and everywhere a monetary phenomenon' (Friedman 1970), that is, inflation arises from the more rapid growth of the money supply relative to output growth.

Friedman's (1953) methodological approach to economics is unabashed positivism: the internal coherence of the theory matters not at all, so long as its conclusions and predictions can be empirically validated. In this vein Friedman and Schwartz (1963, 1982) undertook an extensive study of the history of monetary phenomena in the United States and the Britain, seeking to substantiate the main monetarist contention that changes in nominal income are mostly driven by changes in the autonomous supply of money. Not surprisingly they claimed to have established their point. Friedman and Schwartz's work has been subjected to withering criticism for its superficial view of financial institutions and history (for instance Tobin, 1970).[9] The validity of much of the empirical work of the monetarists has also been extensively disputed (Desai, 1981, ch. 4).

Friedman (1968) also threw a challenge to the official version of the Phillips curve, denying the existence of a stable trade-off between inflation and unemployment. For Friedman, adaptive expectations are a critical component of wage determination: the expected wages for the next period diverge from current wages by a proportion of the difference between last period's expected wages and current wages. In the long run no trade-off takes place between inflation and unemployment, but instead unemployment settles at the 'natural' rate, a term that has become standard in contemporary theory despite its ambiguous meaning. Expansionary demand management along Keynesian lines could be effective in reducing unemployment below the 'natural' rate, but only in the short run. Policy essentially works by fooling workers into thinking that real wages are higher than their actual level. However as soon as workers' expectations begin to catch up with reality, unemployment starts to return to the 'natural' rate. Unemployment in this context can only be voluntary. In effect, workers choose to leave their jobs as soon as they realise that the actual level of real wages is not what they think it ought to be. The only permanent result of expansionary policy is a higher rate of inflation.

The practical proposals of the monetarists included the abandonment of demand management and the adoption of a steady rate of growth of the annual money supply, leaving everything else to the free operation of the capitalist markets. By the mid 1970s, given the discredit into which official Keynesianism had fallen and the emergence of rapid inflation, monetarism temporarily gained enormous influence in the advanced capitalist countries. The policy of tightly controlling the money supply was briefly adopted in the late 1970s and early 1980s by the Thatcher and Reagan governments in Britain and the United States respectively. The policy was a failure, particularly in Britain, where, in the new environment of financial instability and innovation, the government systematically failed to meet its money supply targets. Faced with the failure of monetarist policies, Friedman (1981) predictably replied that there was nothing wrong with monetarist theory: it is just that central banks were incompetent at putting it into practice. Nevertheless inflation did fall in the early 1980s, aided by the heavily recessionary effect that tight monetary policy had on real accumulation.

The loss of prestige of Friedman's monetarism, caused by the failure to control the money supply, laid the ground for the ascendancy of the so-called new classical economics, which is associated above all with Robert Lucas. New classical economics rejects the adaptive treatment of expectations and argues strongly in favour of 'rational' expectations, first analysed by Muth (1961). There are different formulations of this concept, perhaps the broadest being that economic agents use all available information in forming expectations, and do not systematically make mistakes. New classical economics typically pushes this claim to extremes, arguing that, in equilibrium, the subjective expectations of rational agents coincide with the 'true' expectations of the mathematical economic model formulated by the theorists themselves. On average, so to speak, agents' expectations about economic variables are correct, as attested by the properties of the theoretical model of the economy. This astonishingly narrow view of economic rationality, which essentially claims that the formulations of new classical economics are not only correct but people know them so to be, has become the dominant approach to analysing economic expectations in contemporary theory. Keynes' complex and philosophically profound expectations, as well as Friedman's adaptive expectations, have been banished to the fringes of mainstream theorising.

The new classical school further stresses the existence of continuous market clearing, that is, the absence of systematic disequilibrium. Essentially prices are perfectly flexible and the elimination of disequilibrium in all markets is rapid, indeed instantaneous. This particular form of a resurrected Say's law is again in stark contrast to the old official Keynesianism, and even to Friedman's monetarism, which accepts that disequilibrium is possible for significant periods of time. Continuous market clearing necessarily implies that unemployment is entirely voluntary, a remarkable assertion in the face of persistently high unemployment during the last two decades. The combination of rational expectations and continuous market clearing allows the derivation of the following very strong conclusions regarding the supply of output and the role of state intervention in the economy.

For Lucas (1972, 1973), firms know the prices of their own goods but discover the movement of other prices only with a time lag. Firms must consequently decide whether price changes reflect a real shift in demand for their products, necessitating a supply response, or whether these are merely aggregate movements, to which supply ought not to respond. Firms might mistakenly take the latter for the former, and alter their output from its 'natural' level. Eventually, however, firms recognise their mistake and restore 'natural' output. Since firms do not systematically make mistakes, they are unlikely to change the level of their output when they observe aggregate prices moving due to some cause of which they have had prior experience. This has profound implications for role of the state in the economy: if it is to have an effect, state policy must constantly 'surprise' economic agents.

The prior announcement of expansionary monetary policy, for instance, makes agents anticipate inflation and take appropriate action with regard to wages and the prices of the goods they sell. As a result, actual inflation materialises and there is no effect on unemployment and output. Only sudden monetary shocks, resulting in unanticipated inflation, can bring about a change in output and unemployment from their 'natural' level. The effect, however, does not last for long as agents eventually realise their mistake. In short, new classical economics claims that state economic policy is entirely ineffectual in influencing output and employment (Sargent and Wallace, 1975, 1976).[10] Indeed the observed instability of capitalist economy is largely the result of misguided past monetary policy. The best that the state can do is to abstain altogether from intervening in the operations of capitalist accumulation, which is a harmonious and self-equilibrating process. Faced with the profound and worsening problems of capitalist accumulation in the 1970s and 1980s, mainstream economic theorising could only come up with the neoliberal argument that capitalism is best left alone.

By the middle of the 1980s, however, continuing instability across the heartlands of capitalism made the emphasis of new classical economics on unanticipated monetary shocks (and the resultant conclusions about the ineffectuality of policy) unappealing to economic theorists. After all, the essential message of new classical economics is that economics itself is a rather pointless intellectual pursuit. One response was the development of the theory of real business cycles, associated with Kydland and Prescott (1977, 1982) and Long and Plosser (1983). Much common ground is shared with new classical economics, particularly the emphasis on rational expectations, continuous market clearing, the voluntary nature of unemployment and the irrelevance of monetary policy. In these respects real business cycle theory is very much in the neoliberal tradition, for which freely functioning capitalism is naturally harmonious and self-equilibrating. Nevertheless the theory argues that sudden changes in technology could deliver a shock to production and aggregate supply, and impart some elements of fluctuating behaviour to the economy as a whole.

It should be stressed that real business cycle theory is not a theory of capitalist cycles as such, since it accepts the inherent harmony of the capitalist economy. The theory merely formulates the fluctuations that real accumulation will necessarily exhibit if subjected to some random shock, particularly in the technology used in production. For real business cycle theorists, moreover, monetary factors play an entirely subsidiary role in capitalist instability, indeed the monetary aggregates are endogenous to the essential relations of real capital accumulation. The truly neoliberal credentials of this school become even clearer when its policy prescriptions are considered. Since the fluctuations of output and unemployment are ultimately due to the rational responses of economic agents to random shocks (especially to the technology of production), the state should do nothing about them. The astonishing conclusion is reached that, though mass unemployment might be present, the observed levels of employment actually represent full employment, which happens to move along a particular secular path in response to external shocks.

The evident theoretical narrowness of both new classical economics and real business cycle theory, together with their intrinsic inability to offer governments meaningful policy prescriptions, have contributed to the partial resurgence of Keynesianism, the so-called new Keynesian economics. This approach hardly deserves to be called a school of thought as yet, being primarily a reaction to the utter hopelessness preached by the neoliberal tradition. The main feature of new Keynesian economics is the argument that prices are not fully flexible, and therefore markets do not clear continually and instantaneously. Nominal wage and price rigidities have been much theorised by the new Keynesians, relying above all on the institutional features of the contract of employment. Wage contracts tend to last for relatively long periods of time, a condition that is favourable to economic activity since wage negotiations are costly and tend to break down. Downward price rigidities may also exist in markets that are oligopolistic: the lowering of prices by firms might improve raising sales but it also reduces revenue (Akerloff and Yellen, 1985). Other rigidities, for instance in the movement of real wages and output, have also been discussed. When combined with market failure arising out of asymmetries of information, externalities and the fragmentation of markets, rigidities might result in suboptimal levels of output and employment (Mankiw and Romer, 1991).

The new Keynesian current, quite apart from its rather inchoate character, is profoundly conservative compared with the official Keynesianism of the postwar boom, and to Keynes himself. It does not challenge the prevalent ideological assumption that the freely operating capitalist system is a naturally harmonious social order, but merely seeks to establish partial conditions under which the tendencies to harmony would not exhibit themselves. The policy prescriptions that follow from this approach are similarly partial and piecemeal, such as reforming labour laws and wage legislation in order to reduce the rigidities of the labour market. Demand management aiming at full employment is not among the proposals of the new Keynesians. The radical and profound legacy of Keynes in the field of money and finance has been abandoned.

In conclusion, the persistent post-1973 downswing has resulted in fragmentation in the realm of economic theory. Postwar Keynesianism disappeared rapidly, to be replaced by an array of competing theories, none of which carries especial weight in a historical sense. Confronted by mass unemployment, instability and the stagnation of living standards, mainstream theory has spent the best part of the last two decades stressing the harmonious, beneficial and altogether optimal characteristics of industrial capitalism. Where Keynes had tried to develop a theory of mass unemployment allowing for the evident fact that the unemployed are prepared to accept jobs at the going market rate, contemporary economists expend an enormous amount of energy in attempting to persuade each other that the unemployed mostly choose not to work. The assertions of economic theory have, however, provided ideological cover for various governments in their efforts to introduce austerity and attack real wages. Meanwhile the pronounced disharmony that has characterised capitalist accumulation since the middle of the 1970s, particularly in the sphere of money and finance, has continued unabated. The impact of this instability on the lives of working people has been of little interest to economic theory. To compensate for its paucity of ideas on the state of economy and society, contemporary economic theory has plunged headlong into the development of increasingly sophisticated mathematical techniques. The comparison with pre-Copernican astronomy, at once enormously complex and utterly erroneous, is appropriate. Political economy, particularly its Marxist strand, might not possess the technical sophistication of contemporary mainstream theory, but it remains a social science that can shed much light on the monetary and financial instability of contemporary capitalism.

10 Post-Keynesian Monetary Theory

Official postwar Keynesianism largely ignored Keynes' original emphasis on uncertainty, the capitalist entrepreneur's 'animal spirits' and the psychological elements of money holding. In Britain, where the radical milieu in which Keynes had moved remained much in evidence, it became common practice to differentiate between the economics of Keynes and official Keynesianism. Moreover the tradition of the banking school had also retained a strong influence in British policy-making and academic life. These strands of economic thought were instrumental to the emergence of post-Keynesianism.

Post-Keynesianism has become a significant current of economic thought since the mid-1970s, with a vary varied intellectual output.[1] It has attracted economists who see themselves as the true heirs of Keynes, as well as the more radical followers of Kalecki's approach to macroeconomics, Sraffa's neo-Ricardianism and Marxism. The range of post-Keynesian analysis has become very wide, including the analysis of economic methodology, the theory of investment and saving and the theory of distribution.[2] The disparate nature of the components of the current, however, has prevented the emergence of coherent and clearly recognisable post-Keynesian policy proposals.[3] Post-Keynesianism has remained mostly a critique, reflecting the profound disillusionment of many economists with the formalism and conservatism of mainstream economics. However, despite the relative paucity of alternative proposals regarding the future of the capitalist economy, post-Keynesianism has provided vital breathing space for various radical currents of thought and alternative economic analyses of capitalism in the Anglo-Saxon world.

Post-Keynesianism first made its mark in monetary theory in the 1970s and 1980s, at the time when Nicholas Kaldor clashed with Milton Friedman's ascendant monetarism. In his seminal contributions, Kaldor (1970, 1980, 1982, 1985), one of the leading lights of the Radcliffe Report (1959) in Britain, explicitly associated monetarism with the tradition of the currency school. The present chapter examines post-Keynesianism as a distinctive critique of mainstream monetary theory, concentrating particularly on the points of similarity with and difference from Marxist monetary theory.[4] The theoretical under-pinnings of the post-Keynesian treatment of money and credit are considered first, followed by a discussion of the post-Keynesian claim that the money supply is endogenous.

10.1 UNCERTAINTY, TIME AND MONEY

10.1.1 The Critique of General Equilibrium Theory

In the first of his three well-known lectures on money and inflation, Hahn (1982, p. 1) claimed that:

> The most serious challenge that the existence of money poses to the theorist is this: the best developed model of the economy cannot find room for it. The best developed model is, of course, the Arrow–Debreu version of a Walrasian general equilibrium. A world in which all conceivable contingent future contracts are possible neither needs nor wants intrinsically worthless money.[5]

Hahn further argued that a minimum requirement for modelling a monetary economy is that there should be trading at every date. The model should be one of a 'sequence' economy rather than of a Walrasian economy in which all transactions are completed at one point in time. This in turn implies the need to have a theory of how price expectations are formed. In such a model, money can find a place as a store of value, functioning as a link between the present and the future. As Hahn also pointed out, however, even under these conditions a unique equilibrium is not guaranteed. The theorist may further allow for uncertainty, positing money as a precaution against uncertainty and a store of value, but a unique equilibrium is still not guaranteed. No firm place for money can be found in general equilibrium models, as long as it is not theoretically established that money possesses some special property relative to other goods.

The problem of logically incorporating a medium of exchange in formal general equilibrium analysis is particularly intractable, as Menger (1892) recognised a long time ago. A solution was proposed by Clower (1967), namely to impose the special property that only money buys goods, that is, that goods do not buy goods. However it is not at all clear how this postulate can be included within the confines of general equilibrium analysis. Hahn's (1982, p. 21) preferred solution was to claim that money reduces the transactions costs of trading: money buys goods more cheaply than goods would buy goods. Combining sequential trading with the minimisation of costs has become a standard way for general equilibrium theorists to introduce the means of exchange in their models; (for instance Kiyotaki and Wright, 1989, Iwai, 1996). As Hahn further admitted, however, general equilibrium theory has no fundamental way of showing how transactions costs are generated within the process of exchange itself (Hahn, 1982, p. 23). There is therefore no analytically satisfactory way of showing why the general acceptability of money should arise in the first place. The most that can be shown is that, if everyone accepts money, money-using agents can acquire goods more cheaply than agents who trade directly. This is a fundamentally circular argument: why is money special? Because it is money.

The post-Keynesian discussion of the economic role of money stresses precisely the aspects of money that Hahn argued were lacking from general equilibrium analysis. For Davidson (1972a, chs 2, 3), who has provided much of the post-Keynesian theory in this field, the world is characterised by uncertainty in the profound sense that the future is unknowable. Entrepreneurs and households formulate production, investment and consumption plans in the context of such uncertainty. At the same time the economy exists in historical, irreversible time; therefore the unalterable past is the backcloth against which economic plans are made. Money as a store of value, on the one hand, and the stock of durable investment goods in existence, on the other, are methods of bridging the present and the future. According to Davidson, however, the most significant expedient for bridging the unalterable past and the unknowable future is the institution of contracts denominated in money. Thus money also functions as a means of payment (a broad means of exchange) in facilitating the clearing and eventual settlement of contracts. Davidson has returned several times to the importance of this approach (for example 1982, ch. 2; 1972b, 1978), and has used it to attack general equilibrium analysis. The 'real world' is characterised by monetary relations and lacks any tendency towards full employment equilibrium. Money can be anything that has negligible elasticity of production, negligible elasticity of substitution with other goods and negligible transfer costs between medium of exchange and store of value.

Dow (1984) has attempted to incorporate the key elements of Davidson's approach into a overall critique of the methodology of general equilibrium analysis. For Dow, the theoretical foundations of Keynes' radically different approach to economics were provided by money as store of wealth, the formation of expectations under uncertainty and historical rather than logical time.[6] Each one of these elements, moreover, necessarily implies the other two. Societies exist in historical time, which means that uncertainty must exist in decision-making, and uncertainty is partly expressed in money. 'The fact that almost every society employs some form of money is in itself a response to uncertainty. Denominating contracts in an intermediate commodity money allows a sharing of uncertainty between the buyer and the seller (Dow 1984, p. 19). According to Dow, money can separate transactions in time and space, postponing their completion until the uncertainty surrounding particular purchases has been reduced. Money also allows the emergence of a system of contracts, of financial intermediation and of credit creation. As the financial system becomes more sophisticated, the range of financial assets expands, and agents have to exercise judgement about the expected returns of financial assets compared with real capital. Liquidity preference is a significant element in making investment decisions.

The post-Keynesian theoretical analysis of the fundamental role of money in economic activity thus makes use of sequential time, uncertainty and expectations about the future. At the same time post-Keynesianism rejects the theoretical association of money with direct exchange, holding the view that barter cannot be shown to have prevailed anywhere or at any time. Since Walrasian general equilibrium analysis remains ultimately a theory of the barter economy, the post-Keynesian view amounts to a rejection of general equilibrium. By implication, the very principle of treating economic reproduction as the self-sustaining exchange of matter, which is merely facilitated by money, has been brought into question. Hahn (1982, p. 34) called this neoclassical principle the 'axiom of the absence of money illusion', namely that 'the objectives of agents that determine their actions and plans do not depend on any nominal magnitudes'. Davidson (1982, pp. 62–5), consistent with the rest of his approach, rejected this 'axiom of reals', thinking that he was also rejecting the 'neutrality' of money.[7]

10.1.2. Money, Uncertainty and Private Property

The post-Keynesian argument that uncertainty about the future and irreversible time are inescapable aspects of the human condition, is undoubtedly valid. However nothing in the reproduction of human societies necessitates that the primary method of confronting these should be the institution of money, and even more so of money contracts. Custom, law, hierarchy, political authority and social prestige are equally common social practices aimed at confronting irreversible time and uncertainty. Social responses to the latter can take several forms, including the customary holding of stocks of foodstuffs and raw materials, legal impositions on the division of output into production and consumption, and the distribution of unexpectedly diminished or increased output on grounds of hierarchy and social prestige. The substance of some of these social responses to uncertainty is not any different under capitalist conditions, for instance when stocks of agricultural products are formed, or when output is produced in excess of customary demand in order to serve as the material of future investment. The form taken by capitalist responses to uncertainty, on the other hand, is indeed dominated by monetary considerations. These responses can, for instance, appear as variations in the rate of interest or variations in the holding of money hoards. These monetary forms, however, reflect the specific social constitution of capitalism and are not an immutable condition of human existence.

Money, moreover, also increases the uncertainty surrounding economic activity. In economies organised through the market, the direct, often personal and customary nexus between producers and consumers is replaced by the indirect nexus of money. The relative certainty of distribution along religious, hierarchical, familial and other lines is replaced by the uncertainty of distribution founded on money incomes drawn from the precarious sale of commodities for money. Uncertainty becomes even greater when trading in money itself takes place, with its attendant speculation and fraud, and a specialist class of money dealers emerges that knows nothing about production and trade.

Even more fundamentally, the capitalist economy gives rise to uncertainty that is entirely specific to the underlying social relations of capitalism. Capitalist accumulation is founded upon the generation of surplus value through the exploitation of workers. The fundamentals of this process can be analysed on the 'real' basis of the labour theory of value, without necessarily implying that money is a neutral social phenomenon. Marxist economics, aware of the historical specificity and limitations of capitalism, demonstrates the inherent tendency of real accumulation to move cyclically, to generate crises, and so to intensify the uncertainty surrounding economic decision-making. It is not essential completely to deny the 'real' basis of capitalist reproduction in order to incorporate monetary phenomena in economic analysis. At the same time the capitalist mechanism of money, credit and finance can be shown to play a critical role in creating and enlarging the uncertainty specific to capitalism. Credit money in particular has profound repercussions on real capitalist accumulation, stimulating as well as disturbing it at different moments of its course.

We can explore the issue further by briefly considering Wray's (1990) influential book, which opens with an attack on the 'orthodox' view that money originates in barter. According to Wray, there is no evidence that barter has ever existed as a historical phenomenon of any significance.[8] Instead money arose when the institution of private property emerged. Wray's view is based on the work of Heihnsohn and Steiger (1987, 1989), who, as discussed in Chapter 2 above, argued that to associate money with barter is to be ignorant of anthropological research on money. Contrary to the economic analysis of commodity exchange, the foundation of economic transactions actually lies in the unilateral advance of property to others. For the owner of private property there is inevitable uncertainty about the return of the property plus a required increment. Consequently, for Wray money emerges as a unit of account that provides a secure base for the advance and return of property. In short, credit transactions are the original market phenomena, and money is a mere unit of account.

There is no historical evidence to support the view that money as means of account emerged prior to money as means of exchange, as was established in Chapter 2. That apart, the main theoretical problem with Wray's analysis is that private property is a historically specific term. Capitalist private property is founded on the ownership of the bulk of the means of production by a class not directly engaged in the process of production. Thus its underpinnings are qualitatively different from those of feudal private property, not to mention private property found in tributary Asian agrarian societies and the slave-owning societies of antiquity. It is simply meaningless to claim that the holders of these qualitatively different types of private property could enter into similar social relations generated by an undifferentiated 'advance' of their property. Private property is a complex notion that cannot serve as a theoretical foundation for the derivation of money. In effect Wray's procedure identifies all historically known forms of private property with the capitalist one.[9] In contrast to this approach, the process of commodity exchange, as the Marxist analysis of the origin of money stresses, does have a universality that transcends underlying social structures; whether they are produced by free peasants, slaves, artisans or wage workers, commodities are still things that are bought and sold. This also corresponds to the historical emergence of commodity transactions at the point of contact between different communities, irrespective of the particular relations of production within those communities.

Based on the view that money emerges to facilitate the advance of private property, Wray (1990, ch. 1) subsequently considers capitalist production, which involves the hiring of workers to produce goods for sale. The process takes time, and so the capitalist must advance means of subsistence plus raw materials at its beginning. Thus the capitalist must either use owned reserves or borrow from others, which, since the future is uncertain, implies that the capitalist must return the resources with an increment. Money appears to be the unit of account that facilitates the process:

> In summary, money is a balance sheet item, or a unit of account, which finances a flow of spending. It is created as one transfers purchasing power from the future to the present, and can be held in an uncertain world as insurance to meet expected and unexpected payment commitments because it is the generally recognised form of purchasing power and the universally recognised means of retiring debt (Wray, 1990, p. 13).

Wray's conclusion is consistent with the foundation of his analysis: not only credit precedes money but all money is credit money. This statement is simply erroneous, since ample evidence exists that both commodity and fiat money preceded credit money, and were very widely used until the early modern era. Commodity and fiat money are no one's debt, and they are not created through a balance sheet process. This fact presents insuperable difficulties for Wray's analysis, as the following contradictory statements make clear:

> Credit money was the first form of money, created as a unit of account. Markets were later developed, which led to the use of money as medium of exchange. As discussed in Chapter 1, the money of account came to be measured by commodity money (ibid., p 54).

But also:

Thus, credit money was nearly insignificant in ancient society, and became important only near the end of the premodern world (ibid., p. 31).

And:

It is interesting to note that once credit money has led to the development of commodity money, credit money ceases to be essential in precapitalist societies (ibid., p. 54).

The question of why money exists cannot be answered by general reference to uncertainty and the irreversibility of time. The post-Keynesian claim that the weakness of the neoclassical approach to the riddle of money is that it associates money with commodity exchange, is itself dubious. To have a place in economic reproduction, money must possess a special property relative to other goods; a property, moreover, that arises necessarily from the operations of commodity exchange itself. The weakness of neoclassical theory, rather, is that it assumes at the outset that commodities are directly exchangeable with each other. This encourages neoclassical theorists to attempt to derive money as a medium that facilitates the process of commodity exchange. But if commodities are directly and immediately exchangeable with each other, money can never have a special property in relation to them.

The Marxist theory of the forms of value, in contrast, accounts for the genesis of money on the basis of the essential character of the commodity, namely to request exchange with another commodity possessing a specific use value. As discussed in Chapter 2, the request turns the other commodity into the equivalent form of value, assigning direct exchangeability to the commodity that requests exchange. On this premise, it is possible to theorise the monopolisation of direct exchangeability by one commodity chosen by the others as the universal equivalent. For Marxist monetary analysis, money exists historically only in relation to other commodities, and it has a special position relative to useful commodity products in general. Money as the bearer of direct exchangeability is used broadly in a commodity economy, including as means of exchange, means of hoard formation and means of payment (the foundation of credit relations). From this vantage point, both the neoclassical and the post-Keynesian conceptions of money are narrow and unhistorical.

The logical derivation of money from the properties of commodity exchange is not at all premised on the historical existence of widespread barter. On the contrary, the derivation is perfectly compatible with the view that exchange was marginal to precapitalist societies in which money also had ritual, ceremonial and customary uses. To argue that money and exchange are inseparable is not also to claim that money emerges when hunter-gatherers meet in a state of nature (though some neoclassicals who believe in the timeless validity of their abstractions might think so). It is rather to claim that money is not fundamental to the reproduction of human society. In a complex and profound way, Marxism recognises that money is indeed a veil on human intercourse with nature. General equilibrium analysis makes a similar point but in a crass way, largely ignoring the influence money can actively exercise on economic reproduction. The post-Keynesian approach, on the other hand, attempts to supersede the difficulties of general equilibrium by embedding money into the fabric of all human society. To crack the nut of why commodity exchange must use money, post-Keynesianism uses the mallet of assuming that all human economic activity is necessarily mediated by money and credit.

10.2 MONEY SUPPLY ENDOGENEITY

10.2.1 Money Supply Endogeneity in Kaldor's Work

Kaldor advanced the first systematic exposition of the post- Keynesian theory of the endogenous supply of money. Kaldor (1982, p. 19) summarises the classical quantity theory of money, based on gold money, as the view that the 'value of money varies in inverse proportion to its quantity, the relationship depending on the demand to hold wealth in the form of money expressed as a proportion of income'. Actual money balances in the economy are given exogenously by the quantity of gold in existence. Moreover, since 'all the gold that is anywhere must be somewhere', if the actual balances are higher than the demanded balances, prices rise; if the actual balances are lower than the demanded balances, prices fall. Changes in the value of money bring the actual balances into conformity with the demanded balances. Kaldor argues that this doctrine is consistent with the proposition that the quantity of gold can vary: in the long run the value of gold conforms to the labour cost of production, as does the value of any other commodity. Furthermore, as long as paper money is strictly convertible into commodity money the money supply can be treated as exogenous, that is, it can be assumed that 'the supply of money is determined independently of the demand for it in the same way as when precious metals were the sole means of payment' (ibid., p. 44).

Recall here that Keynes opposed the quantity theory on the grounds that the impact of exogenous changes in the supply of money could be absorbed by the velocity of money rather than prices. Postwar monetarists, on the other hand, repeatedly attempted empirically to demonstrate the stability of the velocity of money, implying that exogenous increases in the supply of money tend to be translated into price increases.

In the course of his confrontation with Friedman, Kaldor became dissatisfied with the critique of monetarism based on the variable velocity approach. Kaldor (ibid., p. 22) opted for a critique of the quantity theory based on the argument that the direction of determination runs from income to money, and not the other way round. For Kaldor, the driving element of the quantity theory of money is the notion that the supply of commodity money (and convertible paper money) is independent of its demand. Kaldor broadly accepted that this holds for commodity and fiat money, but sought to disprove it for credit money. Consequently he claimed that the supply of credit money is not independent of its demand, since such money is created as a by-product of the advance of bank loans. For Kaldor, the vertical money supply curve of official postwar Keynesianism ought to be replaced by a horizontal one in interest-money space. The true independent variable is not the quantity of money but the rate of interest charged by the central bank.

If this is the case, and moreover if a broad definition of money is employed, there is no need to theorise the effect of changes in the rate of interest on the demand for money. Keynes' emphasis on liquidity preference was a 'red herring'. Changes in the velocity of money, furthermore, are at most a substitute for adjustment of the supply of money in response to the volume of money transactions. Thus Kaldor continues:

> When the response of the money supply is not complete – in other words when the money stock does not rise fully in proportion to the rise in expenditures – the velocity of circulation rises to make up the difference; in the opposite case it slows down. In other words, changes in the stock of money and changes in velocity are substitutes to one another; if the velocity of circulation *appears* stable it is only because the quantity of the money stock is *unstable* (ibid., pp. 28–9, emphasis in original).

In subsequent years this insight served as a foundation for the post-Keynesian theory of the endogenous supply of money and the relationship between money and prices, to which we now turn.

10.2.2   Banks and the Endogeneity of Money Supply

A theory of banking is necessary in order to support Kaldor's claims on the endogeneity of the supply of credit money. Lavoie (1984, 1985) has clearly stated the theoretical implications of money supply endogeneity for the operations of banks: contrary to the conventional view of the economics textbooks, loans make deposits and the central bank accommodates the loan advance by providing reserves.[10] In a series of papers, culminating in a major book, Basil Moore has provided depth to these arguments. Banks transform inputs of retail and wholesale deposit liabilities into outputs of retail earning assets (loans) and wholesale defensive assets (cash and securities) (Moore, 1988, ch. 3, 1989a). Banks charge a mark-up on the cost of their funds; they are price setters and quantity takers in the retail markets, and the opposite in the wholesale markets. The conclusion drawn by Moore is that the volume of loans made by modern commercial banks is determined entirely by their customers. Moore sought support for this view in, first, the overdraft facilities typically supplied by modern banks (half of which are normally unutilised, allowing borrowers to increase their debts at will), and second, the lack of marketability of retail deposits, which implies that banks cannot reduce their assets at will. Banks can reduce the volume of their loans only over a period of time by charging a higher rate of interest or requiring higher collateral.

Since they passively respond to loan requests by their customers, banks must subsequently take steps to sustain their reserve position. Moore (1988, ch. 2, 1986) argues that liability management by banks – mostly borrowing in the interbank markets – provides them with reserves that are independent of the central bank. When their ability to procure reserves independently has reached its limits, however, the banks seek to borrow from the central bank. Given the prior extension of loans by the banks, the central bank cannot refuse bank requests for reserves if it wishes to preserve orderly conditions in the credit system (ibid. ch. 5). Even more decisively, the central bank is in no position to reduce bank reserves through the sale of securities in open market operations, since banks cannot sell or quickly reduce their loan assets to bring them in tune with reduced reserves. Once a certain volume of bank loans has been advanced, the central bank must supply the reserves to sustain them. On the other hand the central bank can expand bank reserves by purchasing securities in open market operations or by directly lending to the banks. Bank reserves, far from being under the control of the authorities, are actually endogenously determined. What the central bank can set independently, however, are the terms under which it is willing to supply reserves: short-term interest rates are exogenously determined by the central bank, though 'within some range'. Moore (ibid., p. 266) identifies several of the determinants of that range:

> The range over which national central banks administer domestic nominal short-term rates may differ widely over time and among different countries. It will depend on the techniques of monetary policy, the sensitivity of economic behaviour to interest rate changes, the size and openness of the economy, the degree of capital mobility, the extent to which the central bank is willing to allow foreign exchange reserves and exchange rates to fluctuate, the expected domestic and foreign inflation rate, the willingness of the government to regulate and impose controls on the economy, and the extent to which policy is coordinated across countries. In open economies where capital is mobile the center point of this range may be expected to approximate average nominal interest rates currently ruling in foreign financial markets.

The implications of Moore's analysis for the supply of credit money are profound. Deposits are directly created as banks advance their loans, some remaining with the lending bank, some draining away as the borrowers use the funds to effect payments in their business transactions. As long as banks advance loans at a similar rate to each other, loss of deposits through the clearing reflux is balanced out by equivalent gains: when one bank loses some of the deposits created directly through lending, another bank acquires them. The total extant amount of credit money increases directly as a result of the advance of loans, a process necessarily supported by the advance of reserves by the central bank. Thus for Moore, as for Kaldor, the supply of money is horizontal in interest–money space:

> Any increase in the nominal supply of money will always be demanded. The quantity of nominal money demanded is thus always and necessarily equal to the quantity of nominal money supplied. The quantity of credit money supplied in turn responds

to changes in the demand for bank credit, and the demand for credit is simply the demand by borrowers for additional money balances (ibid., p. xiii).

To complete his macroeconomic schema Moore (1979, 1983) argues that money wages are determined exogenously, and they are inflexible downwards. Capitalist firms determine product prices on the basis of a mark-up over costs, wages being a very substantial part of the latter. The size of the nominal wage bill determines the volume of the demand on banks for working capital finance. The central bank accommodates the increase in the loans made by banks to provide working capital finance, and so sustains the concomitant increase in the supply of money. Inflation results from the upward pressure of money wages, the money supply rising in its wake.[11]

10.2.3   Post-Keynesian Critics of the Horizontal Money Supply

The horizontal money supply argument is not universally accepted by post-Keynesians. Rousseas (1986) offered an early critique, stressing the significance of the velocity of money and of financial innovation by banks and other institutions. For Rousseas (ibid., ch. 3), increases in the demand for money need not be accommodated fully by the central banks. They can instead be met by both utilising idle balances held by individuals, economising on transactions balances and financial innovation on the part of banks. Banks need not passively meet the loan requests of their customers, but might ration their loans. Too much emphasis should not be laid on overdrafts since they tend to remain 'unused' (ibid., ch. 4). Rousseas instead stresses the significance of the variability of velocity for the endogenous supply of money. Taken together, financial innovation, a partial rise in velocity resulting from economy in the use of transactions funds and mobilisation of idle funds, and partial accommodation by the central bank entail an upward sloping (though still endogenous) supply of money. For Rousseas (1989) the meaning of money supply endogeneity seems to be that money demand creates its own supply 'to a greater or lesser extent'. Moore, however, countered decisively that the 'horizontalist' position never claimed that the demand for money creates its own supply. Rather the demand for bank credit alters the quantity of money supplied. 'Endogenous money is perhaps better characterised as being credit driven' (Moore, 1989b, p. 483). Indeed for Moore the supply of money resulting from the demand for bank credit actually creates its own demand, as the resulting deposits are held somewhere in the banking system.

Nevertheless the upward-sloping money supply curve has continued to find adherents among post-Keynesians since it implies that the central bank can exercise quantitative restrictions on bank reserves and the supply of money.[12] Pollin (1991, 1993) has claimed that there are two strands to the post-Keynesian theory of the endogenous money supply. On the one hand there is the accommodationist side, represented by Moore and Kaldor, which holds that the central bank accommodates bank demand for reserves since it wishes to maintain orderly conditions in the financial system. The money supply is horizontal and the rate of interest is set by the central bank. On the other hand there is the structuralist side, represented by Rousseas and Weintraub (1978, ch. 5), which holds that the central bank can exert significant quantity constraints on the availability of reserves. To find reserves, banks are forced to borrow by issuing liabilities, such as certificates of deposit, and so alter the composition of their balance sheets. In spontaneously finding reserves, the banks tend to push up interest rates in order to attract asset holders to the less-liquid non-deposit instruments. Thus the money supply curve, though endogenous, slopes upwards in the interest–money space.[13]

Pollin's sympathies lie with the structuralist approach, and he emphasises the role of financial innovation in the determination of the upward slope of the supply of money. The institutional structure of the financial system tends to change as banks seek reserves: if the change is successful, it raises the liquidity of financial assets. Hence banks are able to find reserves without necessarily having to raise interest rates. Pollin (1993) distinguishes between two possibilities: first, financial innovation allows the money supply curve to remain horizontal until the effect of the innovations is exhausted and interest rates rise; second, financial innovation leads to a progressively lower slope of the money supply curve, tending towards a horizontal position. Which of the two prevails is essentially an empirical question and depends on the success of financial innovations. Pollin further argues that the spontaneous generation of reserves might not be entirely successful, in which case a liquidity crisis emerges and a financial crisis might be sparked. For Pollin, a strong point of the structuralist approach is that it naturally allows for the possibility of financial crisis.[14]

In a nutshell, the difference between the structuralist and the accommodationist approach refers to the extent to which the central bank can independently set the rate of interest. In response to Pollin's critique Moore (1991a, p. 406) stated that 'Interest rates are an *autonomous* policy instrument. Their level depends on how central banks choose to respond. It all depends. As a result, there can be no general theory of business cycles or economic growth' (emphasis in original). However when one bears in mind the statement by Moore on the limits to interest rate exogeneity quoted previously, the difference between the two approaches appears much less dramatic than at first sight. Indeed their similarity becomes evident as soon as international transactions are considered. Moore (1988, p. 271) has himself pointed out that under fixed exchange rates and with no capital controls, the ability of the central bank unilaterally to set interest rates is severely limited. Thus if the central bank faces the necessity of defending its foreign exchange reserves, the so-called autonomy of the rate of interest is heavily qualified. If exchange rates are flexible, on the other hand, the central bank possesses considerable power to set interest rates independently. Moore's argument about the exogeneity of the rate of interest as a policy instrument is at most a generalisation drawn from the narrow experience of the last quarter of century, during which time the central banks of the most advanced countries have not been under a severe obligation to defend their international reserves. The argument barely holds for central banks of smaller capitalist countries, which still need to defend their foreign exchange reserves. Moreover, insofar as exchange rates cannot be allowed to fluctuate without limit even for the advanced countries, the ability of the central bank unilaterally to set interest rates is again restricted.

The general retreat of monetarism has meant that far fewer economists now consider the reserves provided by the central bank as a policy instrument that ought to be tightly controlled. Goodhart's (1975, ch. 6) original argument, that attempts to control the reserves provided by the central bank will result in considerable volatility of interest rates has gained wide acceptability. It has also been conclusively demonstrated in empirical terms that the income velocity of money has been anything but stable since the beginning of the 1980s, (Friedman, 1988). Finally, it is now widely accepted that the most important policy instrument the central bank possesses to influence 'real' and monetary magnitudes in the economy is the short-term interest rate.[15] Post-Keynesian monetary theory can claim credit for its early advocacy of these ideas. Nevertheless the enormous weight attached to money supply endogeneity in post-Keynesian monetary analysis is actually an analytical retrogression. The large literature on the shape of the endogenous money supply curve has generated more heat than light. In this regard there are two important issues to be raised with respect to post- Keynesian monetary theory: first, the very meaning of endogeneity/exogeneity and second, determination of the exchange value of credit money.

10.2.4 Exogeneity/Endogeneity and the Form of Money

Exogeneity is a rather complex notion to define. There is exogeneity in the sense that a variable is determined outside a set of simultaneous equations; in the sense that an economic variable is, or can be, determined entirely at the will of state authorities; and in the sense that a magnitude is not determined within a set of economic relations.[16] Be that as it may, in the post-Keynesian literature supply exogeneity for commodity money usually means that supply is fixed for the relevant time period, while for fiat money it means that supply is unrelated to demand.

There is no doubt that supply exogeneity is a relevant concept for fiat money. The independence of the supply of money, and its arbitrary determination by the state, are ultimately the reasons why the quantity theory of money has some applicability to fiat money. As argued in Chapter 2, if the state continues to push fiat money into circulation, the rate at which commodity money is symbolised by fiat money will decline, leading to price increases. However supply exogeneity is entirely inappropriate for commodity money – the total stock of the latter cannot be taken as exogenously 'given'. Two reasons for this are immediately obvious. First, there is regular accretion of newly produced money metal to the existing stock, and equally regular loss of substance by metallic money through use. Second, the line between the monetary stock and the stock of the money metal existing as jewellery, plate and so on is very vague indeed. Given severe shortages, it is always possible to melt down and coin non-monetary, ornamental quantities of the money metal.

Assume for a moment, however, that a country contains only the monetary stock of the money metal, which is neither added to nor erodes through use. Is monetary theory justified in treating the money supply as given, and therefore all nominal magnitudes as ultimately conforming with the existing money supply? No, and the reason for this is hoarding. It is of course possible to treat money hoarding as a change in the income velocity of the total money stock. One can then oppose the quantity theory on the ground that increases in the quantity of the money stock are countermanded by falls in its velocity. However this would be to interpret the classical anti-quantity theory tradition in terms other than its own. The classical treatment of the velocity of money typically does not refer to the whole of the money stock but to that section of it which actually intervenes in circulation. Velocity pertains to money on the move (as distinct from money at rest – hoards), and is typically determined by non-exchange factors such as geography, the institutional make-up of the credit system, wage-payment customs and the phase of the business cycle. For critics of the quantity theory of money, hoarding (and dishoarding) of commodity money is a process that continually alters the quantity of money in circulation, that is, the quantity of money on the move. With purely metallic circulation, this entails continuous redivision of the total money stock, appropriately readjusting the quantity of money on the move to the needs of circulation. Given the continuous flows of money from the hoards to circulation and *vice versa*, we could even argue that the supply of commodity money to circulation, far from being exogenous, is endogenously determined through the process of hoarding.[17] In short, the endogeneity of the money supply is not a valid principle with which to differentiate between commodity and credit money.[18]

10.2.5   The Exchange Value of Endogenous Credit Money

There is, however, a more profound problem with respect to post-Keynesian monetary analysis, namely the stability of the exchange value of credit money, which the emphasis on money supply endogeneity tends to obscure. This is particularly apparent in Moore's work, based as it is on both denial of the independent demand for money and the belief that money supply creates its own demand.[19] As we have argued in Chapters 1 and 2, in all periods there is a definite quantity of money that is compatible with prices, values and velocities. To show that the process of loan provision by banks is necessarily related to real accumulation, and necessarily results in the creation of credit money (which Moore has done thoroughly), is not at all the same as showing that the resultant quantity of credit money is actually the quantity that is compatible with prices, values and velocities.

Credit money finds itself in someone's portfolio, and it might even be willingly 'held' in an individualist sense, but the quantity of such money is not thereby and necessarily in harmony with the other variables of capitalist accumulation. The existence of such harmony depends on the extent to which the previously advanced loans, which created the money in the first place, have actually been successfully used to generate surplus value and on the extent to which the surplus value created has actually been realised in commodity markets. Harmony also depends on the extent to which commercial credit is utilised by firms, the fluctuations of such credit and its articulation with bank credit. These phenomena must further cohere with the movement of real accumulation.

The endogeneity of the supply of credit money, that is, the fact that bank loans create money and that the demand for such loans is primarily determined by the process of real accumulation, is no guarantee that stability exists in the exchange value of credit money. In advanced capitalism the credit system provides the means of exchange, payment and hoarding, in the course of its operations, which are necessarily linked with the activities of capitalist producers and traders. The movement of credit is organically related to the movement of real capital accumulation, and reflects and exacerbates the latter's inherent instability. Whether business opportunities exist in the first place, whether capitalists are successful in the generation of surplus value, whether commodity capital is sold, and sold in time, are all issues that ultimately determine the demand for and repayment of credit. There is no stability in the process of real accumulation, and doubly so when the process is itself underpinned by credit. The quantities of money that are created and destroyed on the balance sheets of banks partly reflect this inherent instability. There can be no *a priori* guarantee that credit processes stably and harmoniously create a quantity of bank money that is compatible with commodity prices, values and velocities. Price instability originating in the monetary sphere is always possible.

The above has a bearing on the post-Keynesian analysis of inflation. If nominal wages are determined through institutional mechanisms, such as the bargaining procedures between unions and employers, and firms subsequently determine prices by a mark-up on costs, inflation is not caused by a rising supply of money. Consequently, confronted with the persistent inflation of the 1970s and 1980s, post-Keynesians strongly advocated the adoption of permanent incomes policies. As Weintraub (1978) made clear in his critique of monetarism, tight control of the money supply works to reduce inflation only through the socially costly method of raising unemployment. For the post-Keynesians, the credit system tends to accommodate cost-push inflation as it meets the 'needs of trade' for loans. The problem becomes particularly severe as the credit system does not consistently distinguish between loans justified by expanded activity and loans meeting the requirements of money wage increases. Davidson (1989) has called the former 'real' and the latter 'inflationary' bills, and claimed that a 'healthy' banking system can be subverted into one that does not distinguish between the two. For Davidson, the answer to these tendencies of the banking system appears to be a consistent government policy of full employment backed by permanent incomes policies.

The echo of Smith's distinction between 'real' and 'fictitious' bills is not accidental in this connection, and has important implications. As Thornton pointed out in his critique of Smith, if the credit system cannot systematically distinguish between the two types of bill, it is inevitable that banks should find it necessary to restrict reserves and loans through interest rate increases (as well as quantitatively) in the course of capitalist accumulation. The central bank, as discussed in Chapter 7, has often played this role in the history of capitalism, forcibly readjusting prices and the exchange value of credit money in the process. Thus as long as some relation of convertibility exists between commodity money and credit money, an anchor is provided for the value of credit money. The anchor can function even if it operates as a requirement to protect the reserves of the commodity money held by the banking system.

If, however, this restraint is removed, as has been the case since the collapse of the Bretton Woods system in our era, there is no anchor to guarantee the stability of the value of credit money. The untrammelled operations of the credit system might create quantities of credit money, willingly held at all times, that are not in harmony with real accumulation. The possibility exists of price inflation arising purely due to monetary factors, as well as of speculative bubbles involving stock exchange and other assets. In this respect the incomes policy proposed by post-Keynesians is not only irrelevant to inflation, but also inimical to workers' interests as it prevents the proper readjustment of nominal (hence real) wages.

Establishing the endogeneity of the supply of credit money, while important, is only one step in analysing the relation between money and prices. Endogenously created credit money can be profoundly destabilising in terms of both prices and real accumulation. Furthermore the role of the credit mechanism in fostering, as well as hampering, real accumulation requires a broader and more historically aware approach than that currently employed by post-Keynesianism. The tradition of Steuart and the banking school, broadened and more solidly based on Marx's insights, is absolutely necessary to analyse the profound financial instability of our own age. Furthermore, insofar as the latter originates in the endogenously created credit money, the central bank has broader tasks in relation to credit and real accumulation than the judicious setting of the rate of interest. Finally, the political economy of money and finance must also consider how the development of capitalism points to the greater socialisation of credit money, as well as its implications for the democratic and socially inspired control of credit and finance in the future. We turn to this task in the next chapter.

11 Money and Credit in a Socialist Economy

In its origin and functions money is the *nexus rerum* of the market economy. As the unit of account, the means of exchange and the absolute form of wealth, money is certainly indispensable to the organisation of a specifically capitalist market economy. The classical thinkers of Marxism largely assumed that in a socialist economy, which would exclude the market, money would disappear. In practice, however, Soviet and East European socialism retained a form of paper money with some rather restricted social functions. Goods and services were 'priced', though their 'prices' were not market-determined. It is important to examine the nature and functions of socialist money in order further to develop our understanding of those collapsed societies, as well as shape our own vision of a socialist system that transcends the capitalist market order, with all its instability and inequality. In general the nature and functions of socialist 'money' vary with the form of organisation of the socialist economy.

11.1 ABOLITION OR SOCIALISATION OF MONEY?

Should money be entirely abolished in a socialist society, or should it be retained and controlled? This is basically another expression of the fundamental issue of whether a socialist society should abolish or retain (and control) the market. The classical Marxist position has tended to be that both money and the market should be abolished, freeing society from the overweening and fetishistic power of money. In a socialist society, fully based on free association among its members, labour-time would serve as the unit of economic accounting. Thus the necessary social allocation of labour, and the distribution of products on the basis of individual labour contributions, would be made transparent. In Marx's (1867, p. 172) own words:

> We shall assume, but only for the sake of a parallel with the production of commodities, that the share of each individual producer in the means of subsistence is determined by his labour-time.

246

Labour-time would in that case play a double part. Its apportionment in accordance with a definite social plan maintains the correct proportion between the different functions of labour and the various needs of the associations. On the other hand, labour-time also serves as a measure of the part taken by each individual in the common labour, and his share in the part of the total product destined for individual consumption. The social relations of the individual producers, both towards their labour and the products of their labour, are here transparent in their simplicity, in production as well as in distribution.

The expectation that money and commodities would disappear in such a socialist society cohered with Marx's argument that 'only the products of mutually independent acts of labour, performed in isolation, can confront each other as commodities' (ibid., p. 132). On this premise, a community without independent and isolated producers appears to have no room either for money as the universal equivalent, or for commodities. Lenin (1921, p. 113) conveyed the substance of the classical Marxist argument with blunt clarity: 'When we are victorious on a world scale I think we shall use gold for the purpose of building public lavatories in the streets of some of the largest cities of the world'.

As has been argued throughout this work, however, Marx also provided a different insight into the origin of commodities and exchange, namely that 'the exchange of commodities begins where communities have their boundaries, at their points of contact with other communities, or with members of the latter' (Marx, 1867, p. 182). For most of the vast expanse of human history, communities have organised the fundamentals of their reproduction without relying on market relations, yet they have also contained forms of money and commodities. Commodity exchange has its origin in the relations between different communities; it represents a set of social relations essentially extrinsic to the labour process of the majority of past social formations. The historical specificity of capitalism derives from the fact that, under capitalist conditions, commodity relations penetrate and permeate the process of social reproduction, transforming into a commodity even the human capacity to work.[1] On the premise that money and the market were originally economic forms extrinsic to the core of social reproduction, the following two analytical positions are possible regarding their place in a socialist society.

First it could be claimed that a socialist society should achieve complete planned control over the metabolisation of nature by human beings, excluding money and the market from the core of economic reproduction.[2] Even so, to exclude money and the market from the core of social reproduction is not to abolish their socialist forms entirely. As is explained in the rest of this chapter, a socialist 'money' (distinct from the capitalist variety) could continue to play a significant economic role even in a planned socialist society based on free association.

Second it could be argued that a form of market socialism would prevail for significant periods of time, founded on the essentially extrinsic nature of money and the market relative to the underlying social relations of the labour process. Forms of the market economy might be employed as a coordinating device among relatively independent community organisations, firms and individual consumers. Under such conditions money would possess a very important social role, without necessarily disturbing the socialist character of the underlying labour process, as long as the means of production remained socially owned and democratically controlled by grassroots organisations.

11.2 'MONEY' IN A PLANNED SOCIALIST ECONOMY

11.2.1 'Labour Money'

The capitalist market order might be replaced by a socialist society completely based on free association, in which allocation of labour and distribution of the means of subsistence would be accounted for in terms of labour time. An hour of labour, for instance, might be called ten roubles. Certificates with the signification 'rouble' could be used to facilitate distribution of the means of subsistence and the allocation of the means of production and labour power to firms. Products could be 'priced' in terms of accounting roubles, 'prices' being proportionate to the labour embodied in the products, and incomes would be proportionate to hours worked. In effect the 'rouble' certificates would be 'labour money', representing the planned, conscious distribution of labour.

For Marx, labour money certificates should not be thought of as proper money, a point that is clear in Marx's critique of the Ricardian socialist John Gray. For Gray (1831, 1848), the origin of general economic instability, including overproduction crises, lies in the fact that inherently scarce gold is used as money. Construction of a harmonious and just economic order requires, transformation of the monetary system. Producers should be required to deliver their products to the warehouses of a national bank, where they will receive a certain amount of labour money expressing the labour embodied in their products. The labour money will function as a promissory note, enabling producers to claim other products held in the warehouses, of a value equivalent to that expressed by the labour money. Products will naturally exchange at prices proportionate to the labour time necessary to produce them.[3]

The essence of Marx's (1939, pp. 153–6) critique of this argument is that Gray did not explain why value is in practice measured in money (an extrinsic measure) rather than directly in labour-time (an intrinsic measure). Why is it that in practice all commodities have their value accounted for in terms of the money commodity instead of labour-time? For Marx, Gray was unaware of the very question itself because he assumed that the private labour contained in commodities is always and directly social labour. Thus Gray proposed that a national bank could issue labour money as if the private labour of commodities is directly social labour. This proposal, however, fails to recognise the fundamentally anarchical nature of the social relations that characterise commodity exchange and underpin capitalism. To be able to perform its assigned role, Gray's national bank would have to control production itself, as was implicitly admitted in Gray's own suggestion to transform private property in capital and land into national property. A bank that naively attempts to implement Gray's labour money without the prior restructuring of the process of social reproduction would certainly go bankrupt. The following two important issues arise in connection with Marx's critique of Gray.

First, Marx's stress on the necessary appearance of an extrinsic measure of value appears to suggest that labour time crystallised in the course of commodity production gives rise to the extrinsic measure of value. Put differently, because social production is undertaken privately by autonomous producers, private labour cannot be directly social; for the latter to be possible, money must emerge as the independent form of value. As has been argued throughout the present work, however, it is more meaningful to treat money and commodities as forms of circulation that arise at the point of contact of communities and are unrelated to the underlying relations of production. On any other basis, it is very difficult to conceive of a socialist economy that lacks privately undertaken production but has either socialist 'money' or proper money.

Second, Marx's critique of Gray implies that if capital and land were held socially and labour was directly social, it would be possible in practice to use labour money. Far from being dismissive of all schemes in favour of labour-money, Marx was sympathetic to that proposed by the utopian socialist Owen. For Owen (1821), labour money could be employed in an ideal society based on agricultural and manufacturing cooperatives and run on communal principles. Marx seems to have agreed that, provided the means of production are publicly owned and labour is directly social, labour money would be a feasible innovation, though it would not be proper money. He stated that:

> On this point I will only say that Owen's 'labour money', for instance, is no more 'money' than a theatre ticket is. Owen presupposes directly socialized labour, a form of production diametrically opposed to the production of commodities. The certificate of labour is merely evidence of the part taken by the individual in the common labour, and of his claim to a certain portion of the common product which has been set aside for consumption. But Owen never made the mistake of presupposing the production of commodities, while, at the same time, by juggling with money, trying to circumvent the necessary conditions of that form of production (Marx, 1867, pp. 188–9).

Assuming that labour money has been established in a socialist society, it is clear that its economic functions depend critically on the mode of income distribution. One mode of distribution might stipulate that no surplus should remain after the distribution of total income among workers. If, for instance, the result of eight hours' labour is expressed as 80 roubles, all workers who work eight hours a day would have the right to claim 80 roubles worth of the social product. Owen's aim in advocating social reform and labour money was, after all, to eliminate unearned income, ensuring full appropriation of the results of labour by the labourers themselves. There is a parallel here with the vision of a society that comprises small commodity producers owning their means of production and not hiring labour. It is possible that this shaped the original insight behind Marx's claim, cited above, that labour money in a socialist society would 'play a double part', that is, allocate labour and distribute income (ibid., p. 172).

Alternatively, the mode of distribution might specify that a common social fund be created to meet the needs of accumulation, communal consumption, insurance against disasters, and so forth. For instance individual workers who contribute eight hours' labour a day would receive, say, four hours as personal disposable income, the balance going towards the social fund. This mode of distribution evidently draws its inspiration from the creation and social regulation of surplus value in capitalist society.

Two approaches to labour cost accounting are relevant to these arrangements. One method is for the surplus part of a worker's labour to belong directly to a firm or central agency. The daily 'wages' (socialist, or s-wages) of the worker in the example used above would then amount to 40 roubles, or five roubles per hour. Another method is to stipulate that individual workers should themselves contribute a part of their income directly to the social fund. Daily wages would then amount to 80 roubles, or 10 roubles an hour, and firms might collect 40 roubles of surplus labour at source by deducting them from the wages. Though in substance the two methods amount to the same thing, it is possible that they have quite different implications for the relationship of the individual to society and for the structure of socialist prices.

11.2.2 Socialist 'Money' (S-Money)

In the socialist societies that emerged, lasted for several decades and subsequently collapsed in the Soviet Union and Eastern Europe, labour money was not instituted. This was despite the claim in Stalin's Constitutional Law that by 1936 socialism had been established and class antagonisms eliminated. 'Transparent and simple' economic relations, represented by labour time, never emerged in the Soviet Union. The Soviet rouble never functioned as labour money or as a labour certificate. It is vital to consider why this was so.[4]

A theoretical and practical difficulty of major significance in this respect was the reduction of heterogeneous and complex labour into homogeneous simple labour. In a capitalist economy the education and training necessary for complex labour result in a higher value of labour power, hence in higher wages, all other things being equal. Thus the generational reproduction of socially necessary varieties of skilled labour power is guaranteed through the accrual of private income. In principle, however, the value of labour power is not related to the living labour expended in the course of work. If, out of a common social fund, a socialist society were to meet the cost of training and educating skilled labour power, it would not be rational for skilled workers to receive higher levels of income simply because they have had higher education and training. To argue that they should, furthermore, is potentially to open the door to privilege and special advantages on the grounds that members of an elite possess exceptional abilities and skills that allow them to perform more labour in a given period of time compared with ordinary workers.[5]

A socialist society could adopt an egalitarian position as regards complex labour, treating the latter as the exercise of the fundamental human ability to work on the same basis as simple labour. Both simple and complex labour are manifestations of the common, universal human ability to work, and so possess an objective basis for their commensuration. Simple labour also covers a very wide variety of applications of the human capacity to work. Provided that education and training costs are socially met, it is reasonable to treat both complex and simple labour on the same footing, expressing them as abstract human labour in terms of simple hours of work. Once the fundamentally common human ability to work has been acknowledged in this manner, work that carries particularly onerous responsibilities might be accorded additional incentive payments, though not on the grounds that it contributes more labour to society than other work for any given period for time.[6] With labours made commensurate on the above basis, and assuming that a single product results from each process of production, the quantities of labour embodied can be determined by solving the simultaneous equations of the technical input–output characteristics of the system of reproduction.[7]

Though theoretically feasible, however, this solution is not particularly practicable. For one thing it would be next to impossible to collect appropriate information on the technical features of the process of production for hundreds of thousands of products. Solving the corresponding number of equations, moreover, would be a particularly arduous and time-consuming task. Both of these problems have a parallel in Hayek's (1935) argument, made in the course of the socialist economic calculation controversy, that it is probably not feasible to calculate solutions for general equilibrium models.

Recent developments in information technology, and the astonishing increase in the power of computers, might have already made the problem less intractable especially if only strategically important goods and services are included in the calculations. Alternatively a large number of final products could be excluded from the initial calculations as these do not enter as inputs in the production of other goods; their own labour costs can be gradually ascertained once the labour content of their inputs is known.

The quantities of labour embodied could also be estimated via a trial and error method. The level of s-wages would be set so that the entire product of living labour would be distributed, leaving no social surplus. In terms of the example used above, s-wages would be 80 roubles a day (or 10 roubles per hour), out of which individual workers would have to contribute 40 roubles a day to a social fund. Given that there is no social surplus (the equivalent of zero profit in the aggregate, under capitalist conditions), reproduction of the existing branches of production would require that prices be proportionate to the labour embodied in products. Were that not so, some branches of production would be unable to receive the necessary means of production and living labour to enable them to continue producing on the same scale. They would therefore be unable to meet the social demand for their products, indicating to the planning authorities that prices ought to be raised. Thus appropriate prices could be reached through a process of trial and error, eventually revealing the labour content of products in the proportions of relative prices. The trial and error method was originally proposed by Taylor (1929) and Lange (1936–7) in order to achieve equilibrium prices in the context of general equilibrium theory. The method could also be applied to reveal the labour embodied in commodities, given s-wages that take up the entire contribution of living labour.

In practice, however (and analogous to the absence of labour money), the Soviet central planning board assigned 'prices' (socialist, or s-prices) that were not accounted for in terms of labour time. If one adopts the view that money is strictly either labour money or market-based money, it follows that commodities and market-based money were present in the Soviet Union. Indeed a strand of official orthodox opinion in the Soviet Union, including Stalin himself, claimed that both commodities and money still existed in the country. Theoretical support was commonly sought in Marx's view, cited above, namely that money emerges only when the products of autonomous and independent producers confront each other as commodities. Presumably, only when all products were produced by state-owned firms under a comprehensive national plan would commodities completely disappear. Essentially it was claimed that the coexistence of nationalised firms, cooperative firms and agricultural cooperatives provided a social foundation for the continued presence of commodities in the Soviet economy. Still this argument could not explain why transactions among state-owned firms were conducted in terms of roubles and officially determined s-prices. Thus it was further argued by Soviet officialdom and its supporters that state-owned firms were relatively separate from each other as far as production was concerned, providing a basis for the existence of money and commodities.

However these old official Soviet views have never been convincing. Even if state-owned firms were relatively separate from each other, they were neither able to buy inputs and labour power, nor sell their output in open markets. Money and commodities, in the original sense discussed throughout this work, did not exist on any socially significant scale in the Soviet economy. This is probably one reason why the introduction of fully fledged market capitalism after the collapse of socialism in the early 1990s has proved so difficult, problematic and socially disruptive.

It is more instructive to approach the problem of Soviet prices and money by treating forms of money and prices as extrinsic to the core of social reproduction. From this perspective, Soviet money and prices had heavily restricted social functions: they were s-prices and s-money. The Soviet rouble was neither labour money nor market-based money; the false dichotomy between the two ought to be rejected. In a centrally planned socialist economy not fully based on the free association of producers, such as the Soviet Union, product prices need not be set at levels proportionate to labour embodied, or indeed bear any consciously planned relation at all to labour embodied. Under such a socialist price regime, money is not labour money, but equally it does not possess the comprehensive functions of market-based money. In general the money of such a socialist planned economy is best treated as s-money, an economic form with restricted but still broad functions.

The Soviet rouble, for instance, functioned as a unit of account but in the restricted sense of allowing the central planning board to set s-prices. As a unit of account it served to measure macroeconomic growth, and also allowed authorities and firms to calculate, and perhaps try to minimise, the costs of production.[8] Accounting roubles also facilitated the distribution of personal disposable income. The rouble further functioned as means of purchase and payment for the goods and services bearing officially determined prices. However, despite possessing roubles, firms could neither freely purchase production inputs (since the bulk of these was centrally allocated by the state supply agency), nor freely hire labour power. Rouble-holding consumers, furthermore, could not freely obtain demanded goods and services. The Soviet 'economy of shortage' was characterised by long queues, arduous searches for goods on foot and frequent shortages of demanded goods.[9] The functions of means of purchase and payment were thus severely restricted.

The restrictions on the functioning of money necessarily went together with the very slow (even non-existent) reallocation of resources and realignment of prices according to fluctuations in the volume of rouble-effected purchases. The prices of goods and services were fundamentally determined by the planning agency on the basis of costs, including wages. The products of several heterogeneous labours were indeed given a homogeneous form in terms of rouble prices, but the mechanism through which labours were evaluated was not that which operates in the context of the free market. In the latter, anarchically and subjectively set prices are repeatedly corrected as money functions as a means of purchase and simultaneously functions as a measure of value. Rouble-denominated wages, furthermore, were not determined in the same manner as the price of labour-power in a freely operating labour market. Rouble wages simply represented the state-determined distribution of personal claims to the social product. Even when wage payments were made through firms, the money largely returned to the state as workers purchased goods and services. Individuals could save (and hoard) fractions of their rouble-denominated income, but they could not universally employ the saved money in private transactions with the aim of generating money profit, nor could they employ it as capital by hiring labour power.

The rouble was also used as the international means of settlement among the nations of COMECON (Council of Mutual Economic Assistance), the latter being a system of planned international division of labour with the Soviet Union at its centre. Again, however, money did not act as the autonomous regulator of economic relations among these different states. A strong measure of centralised control was exercised over the international currency used by the Soviet Union and Eastern Europe, reducing it to mostly a unit of account and means of settlement in planned trade.[10]

In the course of history the forms of the market economy, particularly money and prices, have been articulated with a large variety of relations of production. In general, money and prices as pure forms of circulation can adopt different functions depending on the underlying social relations of production. Once incorporated into a centrally planned economy, s-money and s-prices appear to be subjected to severe restrictions but they still have important roles to play. The monetary experience of the Soviet Union is best interpreted as an attempt to socialise the organising functions of money on the basis of planning and public ownership of the means of production (while subject to severe weaknesses arising from the oppressive character of the Soviet state).

11.3   MONEY IN A MARKET SOCIALIST ECONOMY

Capitalism might be replaced by a market socialist economy based on public ownership of the means of production, rather than a socialist society incorporating comprehensive planning.[11] As well as a relatively freely operating market, a socialist market economy might contain the socially planned distribution of goods and services (under controlled prices) in the areas of economic activity in which conscious management would be deemed desirable. Insofar as the processes of the market would be employed in some less-controlled areas of the economy, money would, on the whole, retain its original functions. Money would, however, also assume an aspect of s-money, particularly in the controlled areas of economic activity. In the realm of international economic relations, furthermore, a market socialist country could choose among several available strategies, depending on its ability to compete internationally. For instance the country could opt for free international trade, confronting the fluctuations of exchange rates through its accumulated reserves of world money. Alternatively foreign trade could be tightly controlled and the available reserves of world money could be administratively rationed.

The functions of money in a market socialist economy would necessarily be more restricted than in a capitalist economy. It is open to the market socialist society, moreover, to exercise additional control over the operations of money by using a variety of monetary techniques. Capitalist countries have already acquired mechanisms and expertise to influence the operations of money, both domestically and internationally. Typically, such control is exercised in each capitalist country by an elite that operates as a group standing above society and specialising in money and finance. The essential interests of the capitalist class, connected to the specialist elite by a myriad of links, are carefully defended. This state of affairs is probably even more pronounced at the international level of control of money and finance.

A market socialist economy could use some of the accumulated knowledge and institutions of money management under capitalism, but also broaden the democratic basis of decision-making to include workers' and citizens' organisations. However, since it is the main nexus of a market economy, money cannot be managed through a system of decentralised decision-making. There is a fundamental difference here with the management of socialist firms. To manage money along socialist principles it is necessary to transcend partial interests and secure democratic representation. It is also necessary to possess accurate and abundant information about the economy, and to be capable of rapid decision-making. A significant degree of centralisation is inevitable in the management of money.

In this connection a market socialist society must also possess mechanisms for the appropriate resolution of political conflicts, particularly insofar as the latter are likely to have repercussions on the monetary mechanism. A market socialist economy would also find it necessary to widen the availability of economic information and to create more opportunities for the acquisition of economic knowledge. There is no doubt that assembling the mechanisms and the personnel capable of effective money management is a difficult task. Nevertheless a market socialist society need not confront this prospect with trepidation. After all it has taken capitalist society several generations, repeated trial and error and not a few disasters to acquire the present, and still highly imperfect and elitist, mechanisms of money management.

11.4 THE CREDIT SYSTEM AND INTEREST IN A SOCIALIST SOCIETY

A characteristic feature of Marx's treatment of interest is the claim that no material grounds underpin the determination of the average rate of interest. For the average rate of profit, on the other hand, such material grounds are provided by the existing technologies of production and real wages. In Marx's theory the average rate of interest varies between zero and the average rate of profit, according to the balance of the demand and supply of loanable money capital. This does not preclude the possibility of the rate of interest exceeding the rate of profit at certain points in the business cycle.

With respect to the social foundations of interest-bearing capital and the credit system, moreover, two approaches can be found in Marx's work, as explained in detail in Chapters 3 and 4. The first, in the line of the classical school, is to posit interest as the part of the profits of industrial capitalists that is paid to money capitalists for money loans made in the past. The credit system is thereby treated as a social mechanism that mediates the relations between two separate and distinct fractions of the capitalist class. The second, however, is to pose interest-bearing capital as socially transformed idle money generated in the course of the turnover of total social capital. Interest paid on loans is a form of redistribution of surplus value among industrial and commercial capitals. Analogously, the credit system is a set of mechanisms internal to the system of industrial and commercial capitals, which is aimed at the concentration and allocation of funds available for lending.

On the basis of the first approach, a socialist society would probably possess neither a credit system nor a rate of interest. All socialist currents are agreed that parasitic classes, such as money capitalists (more broadly, rentiers) and landowners, are entirely incompatible with socialism. The first approach appears to leave no room for the construction of a socialist credit system, particularly if abolition of money and the market is also advocated. The second approach allows for greater complexity in perceiving the role and place of the credit system in a socialist economy. Partly autonomous socialist firms might accumulate reserve funds, denominated in either labour money or s-money, in order more easily to expand their operations, replace their equipment or simply confront unpredictable events. Provided that some choice in consumption exists, individual workers might also create their own precautionary reserves to meet the exceptional requirements of marriage, foreign travel, sudden illness and so forth. In a socialist society a certain part of all these personal requirements would be met from social funds constructed prior to the distribution of individual income. Nevertheless there is no reason why individually held reserve funds should be entirely abolished. Nor is there any reason to expect that the accretion of such personal reserves per period would be exactly matched by their expenditure. On average, a balance of money-denominated idle reserve funds might well be held across a socialist society, providing an objective foundation for the construction of a credit system.

If the administrative allocation of goods and services were not fully comprehensive, some means of production could be transacted among firms. Interfirm credit, analogous to capitalist commercial credit, might then emerge. Firms in receipt of bills (denominated in labour money or s-money) that needed funds to pursue their operations might exchange the bills for money at a national bank that collected idle funds. Socialist firms in need of extra funds for expansion might borrow funds from the bank. Individuals might also borrow in order to increase the flexibility and smooth the time-profile of their expenditure. Thus a credit mechanism constructed on the basis of utilisation of idle funds could allow for the more flexible allocation of resources according to the spontaneously changing social needs. The further expansion of the credit system would itself be based on anticipation of future returns. If, on the other hand, there was fully comprehensive rationing of goods and services, little room would remain for the active role of credit. Even so the state could borrow idle funds from the national bank, or by issuing bonds, using them to sustain and expand accumulation. Insofar as the management of money would allow the state systematically and coherently to influence the general level of prices, mild inflation might reduce the real burden of interest payments (planned price increases could have the same effect). An extra source of accumulation funds could then be generated at relatively little cost to society as a whole.

The nominal rate of interest could be determined administratively by the central planning board as the strategically important price of loanable funds; alternatively the rate could be allowed to move within a certain band, reflecting the balance of supply and demand for loanable funds; or the rate could be allowed freely to find its own level. Even if its determination was free, the intervention of the public bank in the market for loanable funds would allow for the exercise of significant influence on the determination of the nominal rate of interest. Under most circumstances the real rate of interest would be kept positive in order to encourage individual saving and to avert indiscriminate and reckless borrowing by firms and individuals. The real rate of interest could also play a significant role in determining the pace of accumulation. It is probable that in determining their borrowing levels, relatively autonomous firms would compare the surplus expected from the expansion of operations to the burden of real interest payments. The rate of interest could thereby become a powerful macroeconomic tool in the hands of socialist authorities.

The significance of credit and interest in a socialist society varies directly with the importance of the market to that society. In this regard there can be no single model of market socialism based on some abstract combination of the market and the plan. Rather the breadth and depth of the functions of the market could be altered according to the wishes of the population. In the absence of fully comprehensive rationing, credit and interest could be manipulated to obtain more flexible adjustment of production and consumption, as well as to make more efficient use of resources. Credit and interest could also be manipulated to regulate the pace of economic growth, without recourse to direct command. In and of themselves, credit and interest are not plain money-making relations, nor are they necessarily antisocialist. Their socially beneficial functions can be freed from irrationality, and their tendency to encourage speculation and to disturb accumulation under capitalist conditions can be eliminated. In a socialist economy, interest could represent a further redistribution of economic surplus among individuals and firms along socially agreed lines, and could facilitate the rational utilisation of idle funds.

The collapse of Soviet socialism has made it clear that the critique of capitalism alone is not a sufficient theoretical and ideological foundation for the construction of a sustainable socialist economy. One path towards reconstituting the socialist vision of the future is offered by a reexamination of the forms and mechanisms of the capitalist economy: by extracting their rational core it is possible to obtain insight into the organisation of the future socialist society along more flexible lines than in the past. Capitalist money, credit and finance ought to be continually analysed on this basis.

In the course of the twentieth century capitalist money has been greatly transformed: from commodity (gold) money, anarchically originating in the operations of the market economy, it has become inconvertible bank money under the strong control of the state. The fact that such money is already partially managed demonstrates the plausibility of control over the *nexus rerum* of the market economy. Nevertheless the complete socialisation of money is probably impossible under capitalism, given the underlying anarchy in the operations of the economy. The transformation of the post-1973 crisis of capitalist accumulation into a period of rapid inflation, wild fluctuations of exchange rates and speculative bubbles is added confirmation of this point. Socialism must overcome economic instability resulting from the pursuit of profit and must socialise money, a task that is impossible for the capitalist economy.

Notes and References

Part I

1. Meek (1950) presents scholarly substantiation for the argument that the labour theory of value, and its logical implication that profit is surplus value, proved far too radical a foundation for mainstream economics.

1 Classical Political Economy of Money and Credit

1. See also Mill (1848, bk III, ch. 7).
2. Ricardo (1817, pp. 14–15) pointed out more clearly than Smith that corn and the money metals are not different in this respect.
3. Steuart's monetary theories continue to be neglected by modern research. Aspromourgos (1996) is typical of this, in an otherwise excellent book. An important exception is Green (1992).
4. Schumpeter (1954, pp. 296–7) remarked that this was an early and faulty notion of the numeraire. He did not state why it was faulty.
5. Steuart (1805) had a firm grasp of physical measurement. Essentially he approached the problem of value measurement as physics approaches the problem of the measurement of mass. All bodies have a definite mass, abstractly accounted for in grams; the closest practical approximation to the gram is the thousandth part of a certain mass kept at the BIPM in France.
6. James Mill (1826, pp. 294–5), probably reflecting Ricardo's opinion, criticised Hume for including a transmission mechanism in his account of the quantity theory.
7. This point has been much debated in the history of economic thought, but curiously enough the possibility of Steuart's opinions influencing Smith has been neglected, see for instance Eagly (1970) and Laidler (1981).
8. Green (1992, pp. 88–9) calls this 'the law of monetary circulation'.
9. Marx (1905, pt 1, ch. 3) explored this ambiguity in much more depth.
10. For more on this point see Lapavitsas (1996).
11. This brief historical account of Law's ventures is indebted to Buchan (1995).
12. A paper money mercantilist, as Heckscher (1931, vol. 2, p. 182) accurately described him.
13. Several classic accounts of the historical events and the bullion and banking controversies exist in English. For a sample of the different interpretations see, Fetter (1965), Morgan (1965), Viner (1937), Horsefield (1944, 1949), Silberling (1924a, 1924b), Rist (1940), Feavearyear (1931), Wood (1939) and Mints (1945).

14. For more than a century Ricardo was considered the main intellectual force behind the Bullion Report. There is no denying the very close affinity between the views of the report and those of Ricardo. However Fetter (1959) has established that Thornton actually provided the analytical foundations for the report.

15. It also led to some inevitable confusion about the price of goods measured in terms of bullion and in terms of paper money, as noted by Horner (1957, pp. 36–40) and Ricardo (1810, p. 60), with exasperation and relish respectively.

16. Viner (1937) has called consistent bullionism the Ricardo/Wheatley tradition, and his appellation has proved popular in subsequent literature. Viner's term, however, is seriously misleading. Ricardo was a giant of economic thought, Wheatley was an insignificant pamphleteer. Fetter's (1942) research into Wheatley's life and work does nothing to allay this impression.

17. In a candid moment John Stuart Mill (1848, p. 660) stated that the true but unacknowledged object of debate between the banking and the currency schools was how to deal with capitalist crises.

18. It is surprising that the first analytical biography of Tooke was Arnon's excellent book of 1991 (see also Arnon, 1984). Earlier, Robbins (1958) had sought to preserve Torrens' memory.

19. Torrens (1837, p. 7) had some doubts about this, but not enough confidence to stand up to Overstone.

2   Value and Money in Marx's Political Economy

1. Neoclassicism continues to disregard the historically specific character of capitalism, though on the basis of the marginalist subjective theory of value.

2. The ground here is particularly treacherous. It is, perhaps, fair to say that there are two major schools of interpretation of Marx's theory of value. There are theorists who essentially hold that Marx's theory of value refers to labour embodied in commodities in the course of production. See, for instance, Dobb (1940), Meek (1956) and Sweezy (1942). There are also theorists who argue that commodities are produced by private, concrete labour that becomes social and abstract (that is, value) only if and when commodities are exchanged with money. See Rubin (1927, 1928) and Reuten and Williams (1989). The approach of the Japanese Uno school argues that the substance of value is labour embodied in the course of production, but the forms of value can arise independently of, and prior to, the social establishment of the substance of value.

3. In a little more detail, the unfolding of the contradiction between use value and value takes place as follows. A commodity comes into existence as concrete labour time (use value), yet it can exchange only when it is recognised as universal labour time (value). It follows that in the process of exchange the commodity has to acquire an existence as value. Equivalently, commodities are particular things that are useful

for meeting particular needs, but to be exchanged they must confront each other simply as quantities of the same substance. It follows again that a commodity must acquire an existence as value. In short a commodity must have a dual existence as both value and use value in exchange, and yet, insofar as exchange is direct, a commodity has no adequate form as value. If the twin nature of the commodity was permanently split in two, and value acquired an adequate independent form in something other than the commodity, the contradiction could be resolved since the commodity would be a use value as itself and a value as that other.

4. The argument presented here is discussed in more detail in Itoh (1976).

5. Given the irreversible polarity between the commodity as the relative form of value and the commodity as the equivalent form of value, it is hard to see on what logical grounds Marx (1867, p. 157) simply reverses the expanded form of value in order to obtain the general form of value. In contrast the argument presented in this chapter claims that the instability of the expanded form amounts precisely to the temporary identification of exchangeability with one commodity. The commodity temporarily chosen as such thereby possesses an extra use value. The (shifting) possession of this extra use value allows one commodity to be chosen increasingly by the others and become the universal equivalent.

6. Our analysis explains the logical foundation for the advancing monopolisation of 'moneyness' by several commodities, but it does not fully establish why there should be complete monopolisation by one commodity. There is no satisfactory, purely logical, explanation of this phenomenon, whether neoclassical, Marxist or otherwise. But at least the Marxist approach provides a logical analysis of the spontaneous emergence of the process of monopolisation of exchangeability.

7. A point that has been strongly emphasised by the Japanese Uno school.

8. Several critiques of Engels' view exist, most notably Weeks (1981), Anderson (1983) and Shamsavari (1991).

9. The related problem of whether values can be directly accounted for in their substance, thereby setting prices in terms of hours of labour, also arises here. Why could not money be scraps of paper with hours of labour stamped on them? Marx (1939, pp. 153–9) extensively discussed this 'labour-chit' view of money and rejected it on the grounds that in an unconsciously organised economy of autonomous and competing capitalists, value had to achieve an independent form in another commodity. The measurement of value directly in labour time requires the existence of either a central planning agency or widespread communal association, which could directly estimate the labour time in products for society as a whole. This issue is more fully discussed in Chapter 11 below.

10. See Itoh (1988, pp. 91–2) for a development of this formula aimed at capturing the social chain of successive commodity exchanges.

11. Narrow means of exchange is characterised by constant movement. However, Marx (1859, p. 126) also recognised coin-in-suspension, that is, money momentarily resting in wallets, safes and pockets while still undertaking the function of narrow means of exchange.

12.	For a fuller discussion of Marx's specification of the quantity of circulating money, as well as of the relationship between the form of money and the performance of money's functions, see Lapavitsas (1991).

13.	See De Brunhoff (1973, pp. 64–72) for a discussion of hoarding and dishoarding in terms of the financing of capitalist accumulation. See also Lapavitsas (1994) for a further discussion of hoarding in Marx's analysis of capitalist reproduction.

14.	As De Brunhoff (1973, pp. 77–80) has pointed out, Marx's theory of credit is predicated upon his theory of money, it is a 'monetary theory of credit'.

15.	Naturally the same piece of money can be means of purchase and means of payment in succession, but this need not prevent us from analysing its movement separately. After all the determinants of money's velocity are different for the means of circulation and the means of payment, as is argued more fully in the rest of this section.

16.	Foley (1982, 1983) has argued that the distinction between the 'value of the money commodity' and the 'value of money' plays a critical role in Marx's theory of money. The 'value of the money commodity' is the labour embodied in a unit of money, while the 'value of money' is the labour represented by a unit of money, specifically the ratio of the fresh value added per period to the money price of the net product. Foley has used his concept of the 'value of money' very creatively in developing the 'new solution' to the transformation problem. However Foley's 'value of money' is labour commanded rather than labour embodied, and Marx (and Ricardo) clearly rejected such a definition of value.

	The approach adopted in this book is that monetary theory must first fully analyse the relationship between the exchange value of money and the value of the money commodity. In other words, monetary theory should demonstrate the complex and mediated manner in which the embodied value of the universal equivalent exercises a regulating influence on the exchange value of money. If the money commodity is banished from capitalist exchange, theory can turn to the pathological implications of that development for the exchange value of money.

17.	For a full discussion of Marx's critique of Ricardo's treatment of money in the world market see Lapavitsas (1996).

18.	Heihnsohn and Steiger (1987, 1989) have recently claimed that economic activity typically involves the advance of private property by one party on the understanding, and the promise, that the property's return, plus some gain, will take place in due course. The original role of money in this context is simply as an abstract unit of account that facilitates the advance and return of value among economic agents.

19.	The role of slavery in the Graeco-Roman world is a matter of intense scholarly debate, not least among Marxist scholars. The weightiest argument is undoubtedly that of St Croix (1981, chs 2, 3). While not denying the significance of free labour, he claims that slavery was the main source of the surplus appropriated by the Greek landed ruling class. Meiksins-Wood (1988, chs 3, 4), on the other hand, claims that free peasant labour, and not slavery, gave the Greek *polis* its distinctive character.

3 Interest-Bearing Capital: The Distinctive Marxist Approach

1. There are few Marxist analyses of interest-bearing capital created out of the savings of workers, but for an exploratory treatment see Harris (1976).

2. It is instructive to think of the circuit as a circular flow diagram (Fine, 1975, p. 47).

3. For a very clear presentation of Marx's treatment of interest-bearing capital as a commodity *sui generis*, and the relation between commodity prices and merchant capital profits, see Fine (1985–6). In this connection, however, it should be borne in mind that the 'peculiar' use value of generating surplus value does not accrue to all money; only money directly invested in the circuit of industrial capital (either at the beginning or as an addition) possesses it. Moreover this use value does not exist for the holders of idle money: they have to lend the latter in order to appropriate surplus value.

4. The antagonism between interest and profit of enterprise is not on a par with the antagonism between profit and wages. The former vanishes into thin air when the latter is sharpened. The production of surplus value is an absolute precondition for the formation of interest as a revenue.

5. Engels noted the error in Marx's demonstration (Marx, 1885, pp. 359–60). For a full analysis of the issue see Lapavitsas (1992).

6. The operating costs of commercial and money-dealing capital (mostly the costs of purchasing labour power) are net impositions on the total surplus value. Commodity prices therefore need not diverge from values on account of merchant's profit. Panico (1980, 1988) treated this issue erroneously, see Fine (1985–6, 1988). Panico's (1980, 1987) suggestion that the bankers' reserve of own capital could fall to zero was also not correct.

7. For a systematic summary of several of Marx's arguments on the social role of the credit system see Harvey (1982, pp. 260–72).

8. Harris (1981b) and Fine (1985–6) suggest that the systematic difference between the rate of interest and the rate of profit arises from the existence of barriers between financial and industrial capitalists, treated as fractions of the capitalist class. It is hard to see how such barriers could be sustained, however, as long as financial capitalists cannot dictate the actual use to which their loans are put. It is far less problematic to account for the difference between interest and profit in terms of the structurally different location of industrial and interest-bearing capital relative to the circuit of the total social capital. Despite the absence of barriers between the two areas, the mobility of capital cannot equalise the rate of profit and the rate of interest.

9. See also Lianos (1987) on the necessary fluctuations of the rate of interest in the course of the business cycle.

10. Marx certainly did not argue that 'it is impossible to make any generalisation about the behaviour of the rate of interest', as Robinson (1966, p. 69) suggested.

11. Though he further suggested that barter, and by extension purchase and sale, also arose out of gift giving, a conclusion contrary to what is claimed in this volume.

12. The great slave revolt of Pergamon in the second century BC appeared to aspire to the egalitarian 'City of the Sun'. While this might have been less a communitarian paradise and more a case of slaves enslaving their masters, there is no doubt that the depredations of Roman money lenders and tax farmers brought despair to both Greeks and others in Asia Minor within two generations (St Croix, 1981, p. 529; Green, 1990, pp. 393–4; see also Lekatsas, 1946).

13. Strictly speaking it is not money but an 'endowment' that is advanced since general equilibrium analysis faces formidable difficulties in logically incorporating money. There is, however, something decidedly unsatisfactory, not to say odd, about a first principles analysis of interest-bearing capital that does not explicitly recognise its monetary character.

14. Gertler (1988) offers an informative overview.

4 The Credit System

1. It is conceivable that, by assuming purely 'functioning' and 'monied' capitalists, Marx wanted to show that interest-bearing capital itself arises upon the grounds of modern capitalist production. However interest-bearing capital long preceded industrial capitalism, as Marx (1894, ch. 36) made clear. In his analysis of forms of market economy, preceding the analysis of capitalist production, Uno (1952, 1953) demonstrated that the forms of merchants' and interest-bearing capital could be derived by examining the transformation of money into capital. The ideally and problematically abstract presentation of interest-bearing capital prior to the analysis of the credit system could thus be avoided. See also Itoh (1988, chs 4.3, 8.2).

2. The leading area of capitalist accumulation in the era of emergent German and Japanese capitalism was chiefly heavy industries with huge fixed capitals that were normally beyond the means of individual capitalists. So-called direct finance through the capital market (the issuing of shares) was not a plausible option in these countries due to the insufficient number of private capital investors. As a consequence long-term industrial projects, which were potentially highly profitable, required industrial financing by banks.

    Banks could gather small amounts of idle money from large numbers of people, as well as taking advantage of the profitable opportunities present in the process of 'catching up' with the more advanced capitalist countries. However, in making loans for long-term fixed capital investment, German and Japanese banks became more closely linked with the fate of industrial firms. They went beyond 'sound banking', and often had to behave as senior partners or equity holders. This issue has been the subject of a long-standing debate in the political economy of credit and finance, some aspects of which are considered in Chapter 5.

The revival of contemporary Anglo-Saxon literature in this area can perhaps be traced to Gerschenkron (1962).

3. Marx also began to theorise the credit system by relying on the general features of English capitalism in the mid nineteenth century to provide an empirical basis for his abstractions. In this regard we can make the most of his original insights and contributions to the fundamental theory of the credit system, despite the fact that Marx (1894, pt 5) left a large part of his theoretical work on credit in a very unfinished and disorganised state.

4. It is assumed that there are no other credit relations, particularly credit given by banks. In the presence of a bank that could exchange a promissory note for money, it would indeed be easier for B to accept A's note. However commercial credit emerges spontaneously among capitalists and expands on its own grounds, independently of the existence of bank credit. At the same time, the separate study of commercial credit serves to establish the theoretical conditions for the necessary emergence of bank credit.

5. In ascertaining the relationship between the quantity of money and the price level, the tradition of the quantity theory of money tended to ignore the role of this form of credit money. The anti-quantity-theory tradition, on the other hand, tended to assume that the quantity of credit money was in harmony with the volume and value of commodity output, ignoring the possibility of overtrading financed by credit money.

6. The classic explanation for the decline of inland bills of exchange in England was advanced by King (1936). The bank amalgamation movement of the 1890s created large-scale branch banking, and the greater stability of the deposit base enabled banks to finance industry's circulating capital by means of overdrafts, obviating the need for bill-issuing. Nishimura (1971) has contested this view on the grounds that the decline was already apparent in the 1870s, long before the amalgamation movement. Nishimura proposed several partial reasons to explain the decline, including improvements in travel and communications, which lessened the need to hold inventories of raw materials, and hence reliance on bill discounting.

7. Typically, banknotes of the central bank, a form of credit money analysed below.

8. Marx (1885, ch. 6) discussed 'The Costs of Circulation' in three sections: 'Pure Circulation Costs', 'Costs of Storage' and 'Transport Costs'. In the first section, after buying and selling time and book-keeping, Marx considered money as a pure cost of circulation. In analysing the latter Marx argued that the value of gold (and silver) money is a pure cost of circulation. This argument should be broadened to include the costs of handling credit relations. The development of capitalism in the twentieth century has led to increasingly spare use of gold and silver as money; the cost to banks of handling credit money and credit relations in general, on the other hand, has gradually increased.

9. In this regard Panico's (1987) attempt, in the Sraffian tradition, to determine the general rate of interest from the material technical conditions of production is misguided. As argued in Chapter 3, no objective

material features of capitalist production are reflected in the rate of interest, other than the balance of demand and supply of interest-bearing capital. Analogously, there are no technical grounds for determination of the size of bank capital relative to its activities.

10. A tendency clearly exemplified by the so-called 'single banking' system in Britain in the mid-nineteenth century, under which most banks did not have branches.

11. Disregarding exceptional circumstances, for a long time the minimum face value of Bank of England notes was five pounds, much too large to be used for the payment of wages.

12. As Marx (1894, p. 656) observed, in England and Wales in 1844 local banknotes in circulation amounted to £8.63 million, together with Bank of England notes worth £21 million. Independent issuing banks were also active in Scotland and Ireland. In 1857 the total circulation of banknotes in Britain was £39 million while gold circulation was £70 million.

13. Similarly, the monitoring function of banks over customer firms, as discussed in Chapter 2, is necessarily hampered by the very nature of the capitalist market economy. The sanctity of private property fundamentally blocks out openness in economic activity, particularly with respect to future plans. Socialisation of the main means of production under conditions of democratic socialism, on the other hand, could bring about openness and make possible the social coordination of the future plans of firms. Monitoring the activities of firms and coordinating their future plans are easier to undertake under socialist conditions of production.

5 Joint-Stock Capital and the Capital Market

1. It cannot have been mere coincidence that the bubble of John Law's 'System' also emerged and burst at the same time in Paris. It is probable that the synchronisation of these phenomena was sustained by international speculative money flows between the two cities.

2. The average number of employees in British cotton factories did not increase substantially throughout the nineteenth century: the number was 137 in 1838 and 171 in 1871 (cited in Albritton, 1991, p. 130).

3. Even in 1884, by which time joint-stock companies had begun to proliferate again, the proportion of joint-stock companies among British cotton-weaving firms was only 5.2 per cent. The proportion was 18.8 per cent among the spinning firms (Tsuda, 1948, pp. 35–6).

4. Lenin combined Hilferding's insights with Hobson's (1902) stress on the significance of investment abroad for the absorption of surplus savings. Emphasis on the relationship between banks and industry to account for imperialism is also present in Bukharin's (1915) classic work.

5. This is very clear in the work of Baran and Sweezy (1966).

6. Uno (1952–3) claimed that the spread of joint-stock capital in industry ushered in the period of 'finance capital', the characteristics of which could not be analysed within the pure theory of capitalism. In opposition, Suzuki (1960–2), Iwata (1964) and Itoh (1981) have argued in

favour of broadening the historical basis of the abstraction employed to derive the basic principles of capitalism. By shifting the basis of the abstraction towards a period of capitalism later than the age of liberalism, the character of joint-stock capital can be accounted for more fully.

7. In his preface to the Japanese version of *A Future for Socialism*, Roemer (1997) underlined the significance of unbundling the property rights of productive assets under socialism. It should be noted that the unbundling of property rights already arises for joint-stock firms, though certainly within capitalist limits.

8. The complex relationship between property owners and managers of joint-stock firms makes it possible to alter the composition of the board of directors in favour of workers, consumers and local residents. For Marx (1894, p. 572), 'Capitalist joint-stock companies as much as cooperative factories should be viewed as transition forms from the capitalist mode of production to the associated one, simply that in the one case the opposition is abolished in a negative way, and in the other in a positive way.' Nevertheless a precondition for an alteration in the management structure of large companies in favour of workers and citizens organisations is that the political balance of power is broadly in favour of socialist forces.

9. Hilferding (1910, chs 11–14) discussed various motives for forming monopolistic cartels. With hindsight, Hilferding's view that the exclusion of commercial capital was a powerful motive for centralisation does not seem very persuasive.

10. The formulae in the text hold for the mathematically simple case of a perpetual stream of dividend payments of the same size. Under less stringent assumptions there is considerable complexity in the capitalisation calculations. Conceptually, however, there is no difference between the various calculations: they are all based on the simple notion of interpreting every regular payment of money as a payment of interest on some imputed capital. Marx called the imputed capital of shares, bonds and the like, 'fictitious' capital: 'The formation of fictitious capital is known as capitalisation' (1894, p. 567). In this context, there are two obvious ways of interpreting the term 'fictitious' capital. First, as for government bonds, the money sum does not generally represent capital value invested in producing surplus value. Second, as for company shares, the money sum often represents more capital than actually invested in the production of surplus value. Thus the collapse of financial asset prices in a crisis might be treated as the destruction of fictitious capital rather than of real capital productively employed. However, since the behaviour of asset prices in the course of the business cycle can be fully analysed by examining the relationship between expected dividends, capital gains and the market rate of interest, we will avoid employing the rather unclear term 'fictitious' capital in this book.

11. Given that share prices are generally determined by the capitalisation of expected dividends, that is by D^e/i, the expected share price at some point in the future, P_s^e, represents the capitalisation of dividends from that point in the future onwards. It follows that the formula D^e/i

implicitly contains expected capital gains and no new formula of share prices is necessary. However, to facilitate the discussion of the effect of expectations, it is preferable to include an explicit formulation of capital gains.

12. The development of microelectronic technologies in the late twentieth century has probably broadened the range of activities for which small and medium-sized private enterprises are appropriate.

13. The efficient market hypothesis treats the capital market as a securities market in a broad sense, including bond trading. The essence of its analysis, however, concerns the share market.

14. Hilferding (1910, ch. 11) rightly claimed that the profit of joint-stock capital participates in equalisation of the profit rate, together with the profit of private enterprise. He also recognised that equalisation of the profit rate is made more difficult by increases in fixed investment facilitated by joint-stock capital.

15. This was an important aspect of the depression of the 1930s, as explained in more detail in Chapter 6.

16. Neoclassical theory also stresses that monopoly prices are not arbitrarily raised; monopoly profit is maximised at the point at which marginal revenue equals marginal cost, except that, unlike perfect competition, marginal revenue is not constant but declines with output.

17. For a typical example, see the USSR Academy textbook Institute of Political Economy, *Political Economy* (1954, vol. 2, pp. 401–2).

6 Monetary and Financial Aspects of the Business Cycle

1. This note first appeared in the third German edition of the first volume of *Capital*, prepared for publication by Engels a short while after Marx's death in 1883. Nevertheless the note was actually written by Marx with the impending edition in mind, as subsequent German editions of *Capital* make clear. In the Penguin English translation of *Capital*, used throughout this work, it is mistakenly stated that the author of the quote was Engels and not Marx.

2. For more detail on the origins and significance of the different theories of crisis in Marx's own work, see Itoh (1980, ch. 4).

3. Fine and Harris (1979, pp. 77, 80) have claimed that the labour shortage theory is neo-Ricardian because it stresses class conflict that takes place in the sphere of distribution. However the approach of the Uno school is dynamic since it emphasises the changes taking place in the labour market in the course of capitalist accumulation. The work of the Sraffa school, on the other hand, is fundamentally static.

4. See in particular Uno (1952–3, 1953b) and Itoh (1973, 1988).

5. The industrial reserve army of labour during the age of the classic decennial cycle comprised the floating part (in the industrial centres), the latent part (in agriculture), the stagnant part (in domestic industry) and the *lumpen* or pauper part. Real wages typically rose at the centre of British industrial accumulation when the floating part became relatively scarce. In this respect Clarke's (1989, p. 142) stress on the 'secular

expansion in the size of the reserve army on a global scale since the very beginning of capitalism', which was intended as criticism of the labour shortage theory of crisis, is largely irrelevant.

6. In the age of the decennial business cycle the increase in the price of imported cotton, typically observed towards the end of the upswing, had similar effects to the rise in real wages since cotton could not be domestically reproduced in Britain. At the same time, the increased price of cotton was representative of the price movements of most other raw materials whose supply could not be promptly increased. Though the rise in the general price level partially mitigated the effect of the rise in real wages, the falling profit rate was not ameliorated for the cotton manufacturers as their raw material costs also rose.

7. During the age of the classical decennial cycle the time to maturity of bills of exchange was typically three months, and at most ten months. Consequently the acute phase of a crisis typically lasted for less than a year and mostly around six months.

8. In the course of the replacement of fixed capital a secondary boom and its subsequent collapse might also take place, especially in the capital goods industry. This intermediate crisis inevitably drives out of business those firms that fail to replace their fixed capital and innovate. Failure by these firms further promotes the restructuring of the generally excessive productive capacity.

9. The external drain of gold, which took place in the course of the decennial crisis in the era of English liberal capitalism, did not stop the fall in prices in the world market, and often became an internal drain. Marx (1894, p. 702) claimed that, 'with the possible exception of 1837, the real crisis has always broken out only after the exchange rates have moved, i.e. once the import of precious metal has the upper hand again over the export'. The fact that an internal drain of gold used to occur soon after the end of the external drain and immediately before the sharp fall in prices, also contradicts the simple quantity theory of money.

10. One of the earliest theoretical treatments of this question was offered by Senior (1829). Senior postulated that the social demand for the monetary metal (silver) comprised the demand for silver as an ordinary commodity (for ornaments, plate and so on) and the demand for silver as money. The opening and closing of the marginal silver mines was mostly determined by the demand and supply of silver as an ordinary commodity. The exchange value of silver was determined by silver's embodied value rather than the ratio of the quantity of circulating commodities to the quantity of silver money.

A rich debate on determination of the exchange value of money, spurred by a rising price level, took place among Marxists at the beginning of the twentieth century, involving Varga, Hilferding, Kautsky and Otto Bauer (*Neue Zeit*, 1911–13). The debate mostly concerned the special character of the social demand for gold (that is, whether gold demand is limitless as long as gold is the absolute form of wealth). The debate also considered the precise determination of the balance between social demand and supply of gold as money. The discussion served as a frame of reference for the analysis of price movements under a regime of inconvertible banknotes.

11. If the organic composition of the gold industry is below the social average, the fall in the rate of profit in gold production is even sharper as long as wages rise faster than commodity prices in the final phase of the upswing.

12. If the organic composition of the gold industry is below the social average, the rise in the profit rate of the gold industry is even sharper when wages fall more steeply than prices.

13. If productivity rises faster in the gold industry compared with other industries, the price level eventually rises (the exchange value of gold falls). Historically, the discovery of new gold mines has had just such an effect, as Vilar's (1976) work confirms, though how rapidly the effect appears depends on the concrete economic conditions of the time, and on the physical characteristics of the new mines. The discovery of alluvial gold in California in 1848–51 and in Australia a short while later, for instance, boosted effective demand and appeared to raise prices relatively rapidly. However it seems that the discovery of the South African mines in the 1880s had a more gradual but longer-lasting effect on the price level from the mid 1890s to the First World War.

14. Similarly to Kondratieff, Mandel also postulated that an abundance of loanable money capital was a precondition for the long upswing. Rowthorn (1980) has pointed out, however, that abundant loanable capital was virtually non-existent in most advanced countries immediately after the Second World War and could not have been a cause of the subsequent long upswing. The end of the long postwar boom, furthermore, was unrelated to a putative scarcity of loanable money capital. Indeed the subsequent vicious inflation appeared to indicate an excess supply of such capital. On the other hand it is likely that the existence of abundant loanable capital and low prices did contribute, if partially, to the upswing following the Great Depression of 1873–96. On the whole, the role of loanable capital is not particularly persuasive as a general cause of long waves.

15. Certainly as far as the *General Theory* is concerned. There is a long-running and largely inconclusive debate, considered briefly in Chapter 9 below, regarding the significance of the 'finance motive' for the demand for money. This is a rather vague notion of the liquidity demanded by firms in order to effect their investment plans.

16. There have been attempts to integrate Minsky's financial instability hypothesis into the modern Marxist analysis of business cycles; see Crotty (1993) and Yokokawa (1985, 1989).

7 Central Banking

1. It took the Bank of England, whose history provides the basis for our analysis, a century after its establishment in 1694 to emerge as holder of the centralised reserve of the banking system. At the time of the Napoleonic Wars the Bank's notes were the most credible means of obtaining

gold as far as other banks were concerned. It took an even longer time for the Bank to establish its short-term lending rate as the benchmark rate of the money market. The Usury Laws, a relic of the Middle Ages, set a ceiling of 5 per cent on the Bank's discounts until 1833.

2. 'Between the end of the Restriction Period and the beginning of the "Currency" and "Banking" controversy there occurred, almost without notice, a great change in the attitude of the Bank directors towards the regulation of their issues' (Morgan, 1965, p. 100).

3. This was precisely what Torrens and Overstone, the chief supporters of the Bank Act of 1844, had intended when they criticised Palmer's rule (Viner, 1937, pp. 224–9).

4. 'As the national debt is backed by the revenues of the state, which must cover the annual interest payments, etc., the modern system of taxation was the necessary complement of the system of national loans' (Marx, 1867, p. 921).

5. See also Andreades (1909, pt II, ch. I), who also argues that regulation of the paper currency and lowering the rate of interest upon the establishment of a national bank were perceived as needs of commerce.

6. The state connection of the Bank of England allowed it to secure privileges that increased its private profits. The most significant privilege was to be the only joint-stock bank allowed to issue notes in the vicinity of London, the commercial heart of the country. Thus the Bank lent money to the state at a profit and issued its privileged promises to pay at a further profit. The Bank's profits continually provoked complaints and calls for the nationalisation of its public activities. The Bank fiercely resisted the establishment of other joint-stock banks in London until 1833, even though the latter did not have the right to issue notes. One of its main weapons was to prevent the inclusion of these banks into the clearing mechanism. Joint-stock banks were not admitted into the mechanism until 1854 (Gilbart, 1834, vol. II, sec.XXXII).

7. Free banking is discussed in detail later in this chapter. As for social transformation effected through a nationalised central bank, it is important to consider Marx's (1939, pp. 154–8) devastating critique of the Saint-Simonist plan for a national bank issuing labour chits, as discussed in Chapter 11. In a nutshell, if the nationalised central bank is truly to break out of the limits of capitalist accumulation it will have to transform itself into a proper national planner and infringe upon capitalist property itself. Therefore the bank's activities will soon transcend the boundaries of the capitalist credit system. See also Marx (1894, ch. 36).

8. The emphasis of the classical school on the self-regulating properties of international economic relations, and its corresponding attack on mercantilism, actually obscured the inherently antagonistic nature of capitalist state relations.

9. In addition to price-oriented methods of altering the supply of its liabilities to banks, the central bank might also directly ration the supply. This method evidently has drastic implications for the ability of banks to satisfy the credit requirements of their own customers, and is not something to which central banks easily or normally resort. Direct rationing might also apply to the reserves of the central bank, a policy often

accompanied by direct quantity controls on the reserves and the lending activities of the banks themselves. Direct credit controls evidently limit the freedom of operation of the credit system.

10. 'A central bank is a banker's bank. It affords to the other banks of the community, the competitive banks, the same facilities as they afford to their customers.... These facilities being secured to them, the competitive banks are relieved from their responsibility for the provision of currency.... The real reason for that is not, as is sometimes supposed, that the central bank is usually a bank of issue, with the power of creating currency in the form of its own notes.... The Central Bank is the *lender of last resort*. That is the true source of its responsibility for the currency' (Hawtrey, 1932, pp. 116–17).

11. Though Arnon (1997) has argued strongly that Parnell accepted the need for some discretion and should not be seen uncritically as a precursor of the contemporary free banking school.

12. The historical absence of free banking regimes is acutely felt by theorists who wish to argue that such a system is somehow 'natural'. Much has been made in this respect of the supposed free banking regime in Scotland prior to the Act of 1844 (White, 1984, ch. 2). However it was understood at the time that Scottish banking could afford to operate with small and decentralised gold reserves mostly because the banks knew that they could ultimately obtain gold quite easily from the Bank of England. See Checkland (1975, pp. 432–3).

13. The ability of the reserve asset to function as a unit of account is a thorny issue that is not sufficiently discussed in the free banking literature. No matter what its past stability has been, the relative value of the asset could always change as the productivity of labour changes, thus inducing price instability. Under such circumstances the appropriate composition of the commodity bundle would be far from clear, and its ability to function as means of payment, that is, to settle past debt, would be perpetually in doubt.

14. Free banking advocates have devoted considerable effort to refuting this widely held opinion, but without particular success (see Dowd, 1993, ch. 6).

15. Timberlake (1984) argues that prior to the establishment of the Federal Reserve in 1907 the clearing house acted as lender of last resort and created the necessary money. In other words there was a spontaneous tendency towards centralisation of the bank reserve, and a rational basis for the use of this reserve within the clearing house. Timberlake (ibid., pp. 14–15) also argues that 'The Federal Reserve alternative, however, was critically different from the clearinghouse system. It introduced a discretionary political element into the monetary decision making and thereby divorced the authority for determining the system's behaviour from those who had a self-interest in maintaining its integrity'. However the centralised banking reserve is also the nation's main hoard, and this necessarily gives it a role in domestic circulation and international transactions. Rationality in that context has to have broader limits than 'the self-interest' of banks. The emergence of a central bank is a 'rational' step in this respect.

16. Hayek (1976a, pp. 64–5) skirted around this issue when he proclaimed 'the uselessness of the quantity theory', and seemed to think that there is no constant demand for money (as the quantity theory of money presumably argues) when the issue of money is free. However, whether the demand for money is constant or not, the possibility of having too much freely issued money relative to goods cannot be simply dismissed. In contrast, Smith (1936, pp. 33–5, 73–6) devoted considerable space to the question but without giving a definitive answer.

17. Glasner (1989, ch. 11) seems to believe that stabilising the domestic price level, by applying his proposal of competitive banking based on a labour/wage standard, would also solve the problem of unstable exchange rates. But the possible imbalances and conflicts between the total quantity of credit money and the international hoard of means of payment require explit treatment in their own right.

18. What Vera Smith (1936) called *bankmässige Deckung*.

8 Loss of Control over Money and Finance

1. A useful presentation of several views and arguments can be found in Marglin and Schor (1990).

2. This was an important aspect of the Regulation school's Fordist regime of accumulation. 'Regulation' here refers to the totality of social arrangements that make capitalist accumulation possible. The postwar period of high economic growth also resembles the upswing of a long wave of fifty years' duration. Mandel (1975) rightly stressed the importance of the Second World War in creating the appropriate conditions for a long upswing, and further claimed that a downswing was inevitable due to the difficulties intrinsic to capitalist accumulation itself.

3. Though the rate of interest on loans to firms is typically higher than the yield of government bonds, the latter is an acceptable rough estimate of the former.

4. Assuming that inflation affects the value of both invested capital and profits in more or less the same manner, the rate of profit, unlike the rate of interest, need not be discounted by the rate of inflation.

5. The profit share of manufacturing in the seven major capitalist countries declined by 14–26 per cent prior to the 1973 oil shock in 1973 (Armstrong and Glyn, 1986). The rise in wages (in terms of product prices) above the increase in productivity was instrumental to this phenomenon.

6. The Japanese yen, for instance, appreciated from 240 yen to the dollar in September 1985 to 120 at the beginning of 1988. This shocked the Japanese exporting industries and encouraged them to redouble their efforts in the domestic market.

7. Japanese household cash holdings as a proportion of real monthly income declined from roughly one third in 1972 to one fifth in 1988. This partly countermanded the tendency of the savings ratio to decline and allowed banks to find new sources of money capital.

8. Strange (1986) has aptly termed this development 'casino capitalism'.

9.   In Japan, for instance, total financial capital gains during 1985–9 were estimated at 1728 trillion yen, share prices contributing 569 trillion during 1986–9. Total capital losses in 1990–2, on the other hand, were estimated at 690 trillion yen, share prices contributing 490 trillion (Miyazaki, 1995, pp. 57–8). Compare these sums with the 387 trillion yen of the Japanese net national product in 1990.

10.   The Mexican crisis of 1994–5, necessitating substantial borrowing from the United States, was a timely reminder of the inherent difficulties of integrating such disparate countries as Mexico and the United States into a single free trade and investment zone. Financial speculation, often encouraged by US capital, appears to have intensified in the region. As for Asia and the Pacific, the heterogeneity of the countries involved is so pronounced as to make free trade zones, or monetary unification, all but impossible in the near future.

11.   The introduction of information technology has encouraged the emergence of electronic money in international transactions, a development that might appear to provide support for the free banking proposal. It is conceivable that some form of electronic money, which is not legal tender and does not ultimately rely on the supply of liabilities by the central bank, might become widely established in the world market. Such money could be generated by large financial institutions backed by assets that the issuers could easily, and relatively cheaply, sell in the international financial markets. The central bank's control over the supply of money would then be significantly diminished. This development, quite apart from being rather unlikely in the near future, would have contradictory implications. On the one hand it might lead to greater freedom in banking, but on the other it could actually provide a more solid and objective foundation for the establishment of a world central bank to control and regulate the new global money.

12.   For a more detailed discussion, see Haq *et al.* (1996).

9 The Rise and Fall of Keynesianism

1.   See Foley (1986) for a concise and illuminating statement of the importance of Say's law in economics. Foley formally considers the difference between Marx's and Keynes' opposition to Say's law, and finds the former (who relied on the hoarding decisions of capitalist firms) more persuasive than the latter (who stressed the hoarding decisions of speculators in the financial markets).

2.   Mill (1826, pp. 326–9) made this point clear in his lucid presentation of the Ricardian approach to Say's law.

3.   There is, however, a sense in which Say's law holds in some parts of Marx's analysis. Treated abstractly, the material reality of aggregate capitalist reproduction, as analysed by Marx (1885) in the schemata of reproduction, is untenable unless the hoarding of some section of the bourgeoisie is counterbalanced by equal dishoarding. In Marx's reproduction schemata, the whole of the output per period is taken up either as means of production or as means of consumption. For

Marx, however, this is simply a demonstration of the abstract possibility of autonomous aggregate capitalist reproduction. There is no presumption that capitalist accumulation possesses equilibrium tendencies towards the various states exemplified in the reproduction schemata, nor that full employment results. In fact actual reproduction entails constant negation of the balance between hoarding and dishoarding, as well as the existence of unemployment as a normal economic phenomenon.

4. See for instance Mill (1826, pp. 326–9).

5. In reply to Ohlin (1937a, 1937b), Keynes (1937) acknowledged that in the *General Theory* he had not considered money hoards held by capitalists in order to facilitate the completion of investment in progress. Such hoarding arose because of the 'finance' motive to liquidity preference. A 'revolving fund' of 'financial' hoards with regular dimensions exists for the whole of the capitalist class, held by banks and advanced to the investing capitalists. As long as savings equal investment *ex post*, enough funds are generated with the accrual of investment proceeds after the sale of output to repay the banks and replenish the hoard. Sudden jumps in investment by the capitalist class as a whole are impossible to finance, unless the banks provide extra credit.

    This is not a particularly well-thought-out notion, and Robertson (1937, 1938) rejected it as a guide to distinguishing between liquidity preference and loanable funds generated out of savings. Davidson (1965), on the other hand, has argued that by ignoring the 'finance' motive conventional Keynesianism has perpetuated the false dichotomy between the real and the monetary sector. For Asimakopulos (1983), in contrast, the 'finance' motive is problematic because it does not allow for the time it takes for the multiplier to operate and so generate the savings that will eventually replenish the 'revolving fund'.

6. Skidelsky (1983, ch. 6) offers an informative account of the importance of G.E Moore's ethical philosophy for the formation of Keynes' outlook.

7. Something that Harrod (1951, pp. 466–7) knew, despite his enormous respect and affection for Keynes: 'He seems, to my judgement, to stand rather in the same class as Adam Smith and Ricardo. In logical precision and penetration he was much superior to Adam Smith, in lucidity of writing to Ricardo.... While ... I put him in a class with Adam Smith and Ricardo, I express doubt whether his star, as an economist, was quite of their magnitude.' That is not to say, however, that our assessment of Keynes is the same as Harrod's.

8. For a full discussion of the analytical content of Patinkin's formulations see Harris (1981a, chs 4, 5) and Weeks (1989, ch. 6).

9. It is indicative of their approach to historical analysis that, according to them, an important reason for the interwar US depression was the premature death of Benjamin Strong, the governor of the Federal Reserve. Apparently Strong's wise counsel could have helped the Federal Reserve System prevent the collapse of US banking and the attendant contraction of the money supply of the early 1930s.

10. Moreover, for new classical economics the econometric work used to formulate policy is entirely without value since the econometric simula-

tions of the macroeconomy typically assume that the parameters of the models are invariant to changes in policy. The 'Lucas critique' (Lucas, 1976) claims that this is an incorrect assumption since agents adjust their behaviour to match the new environment created by policy. Economic policy is twice cursed: it is impossible to base on empirical foundations and it is ineffectual.

10   Post-Keynesian Monetary Theory

1. For early historical surveys of its development see Hamuda and Harcourt (1988) and Sawyer (1991).
2. For a sample of the range of issues now analysed from a post-Keynesian standpoint see Arestis (1992), Arestis and Chick (1992), Kregel (1989), Davidson and Kregel (1989), Davidson (1994).
3. Note, however, that Arestis (1996) has argued that coherence is beginning to emerge within the post-Keynesian current, deriving from the emphasis on institutionalism and its non-neoclassical methodology.
4. For a useful survey of post-Keynesian monetary theory see Cottrell, (1994).
5. It should be noted here that, if the Arrow-Debreu model has no use for money, it is clearly not the 'best developed model of the economy' insofar as this 'economy' is capitalism.
6. Dow (1985) has also discussed the methodological differences among the neo-Austrian, the neoclassical, the post-Keynesian and the Marxist schools. She distinguished between the 'Cartesian/Euclidean' axiomatic approach, typical of the neoclassical school, and the looser 'Babylonian' approach, which is multidisciplinary and typical of the post-Keynesian school. This might be a useful account of the output of the two traditions, but it is not a convincing general characterisation of the methodologies available to social science. Formal logic is not an optional extra for social analysis. The dialectical approach of Marxism is certainly not 'Babylonian', an unfortunate term that conveys confusion and lack of clarity. For more on the methodology of post-Keynesianism see Dow and Hillard (1995).
7. Drawing on Minsky (1984).
8. Wray (1990, ch. 1) argues that two approaches to monetary theory can be identified: the endogenous and the exogenous. This is reminiscent of the distinction between the banking and currency traditions in monetary theory. Wray should also have included Steuart and Smith in his 'endogenous' approach.
9. Wray (1990, p. 9) claims, bizarrely, that private property temporarily disappeared 'after the fall of Rome'.
10. Lavoie has also provided evidence for the continuing vitality of the anti-quantity theory tradition in the French-speaking world.
11. Similarly to Kaldor, Moore (1988, p. 15) argues that the endogenous and horizontal supply of money characterises credit money, rather than commodity and fiat money. Moore rejects liquidity preference (hoarding) as a critical factor in the allocation of wealth among real and

financial assets. For Moore (ibid., ch. 12), whenever the supply of credit money increases, borrowing units in the economy are deficit spending. In the aggregate, other agents are holding the increased deposits because they have sold without buying. The latter phenomenon he called 'convenience lending' by the selling units to banks (ibid., p. 315). The deposits created through lending are eventually held by someone; liquidity preference is not an important concept in this connection.

12. Wray (1990, chs 3, 6) supports the notion of the upward-sloping supply of money. Contrary to Moore, Wray also stresses the importance of liquidity preference, that is, the desire to hold shorter-term assets. A rise in liquidity preference, such as occurs in a financial crisis, might mean that the demand and supply of money actually fall. For Wray, when business expansion proceeds the balance sheets of firms become increasingly illiquid. The central bank may not provide the requisite liquidity for a period, making the supply of money temporarily vertical. However if financial stability is to be maintained, the central bank will eventually provide the necessary reserves, but at a higher interest rate. The supply of money slopes upwards in a series of steps.

13. More recently Dow (1996) has rejected the horizontal money supply curve on the grounds that banks systematically exercise credit rationing on the downswing of the business cycle. The increasing risks associated with loans force a rise in the liquidity preference of banks, and make them ration their advances. Dow stresses that this view relies on 'Keynesian' foundations compared with mainstream analysis, which also increasingly emphasises credit rationing by banks but on the basis of asymmetric information between banks and customers. See also note 15 in this chapter.

14. Pollin's emphasis on the structural determinants of the relationship between money supply and the rate of interest is welcome. However Pollin's work does not provide a systematic explanation of how financial innovation arises. What is the mechanism intrinsic to the operations of the financial system that leads banks and other financial institution necessarily to innovate? In the absence of such a theory, financial innovation appears in the model as a *deus ex machina*. Similarly, in the absence of such a theory, differentiating among accommodationism and structuralism can appear as primarily an empirical issue to be settled through recourse to econometric testing. In this respect, however, Moore (1991a) and Palley (1991) have argued strongly that Pollin's econometric tests are not conclusive. Pollin's argument, moreover, requires a more profound investigation of the role of credit money and the rate of interest in the course of real capital accumulation.

15. Though the mode in which interest rate policy is supposed to operate goes completely against Moore's analysis. The argument tends to be that interest rate changes by the central bank affect the profitability of commercial banks and so lead to quantitative restrictions in the supply of credit. Credit rationing by commercial banks is fast becoming the preferred 'transmission mechanism' for monetary policy within the IS–

LM model (Bernanke and Blinder, 1988; Friedman, 1995; Taylor, 1995).

16. For an informative discussion of the concept see Dow (1988).

17. The distinction between money on the move and money at rest, or 'active' and 'idle' money, is hard to pin down. Sayers (1960, p. 510) put the problem succinctly: 'But this distinction is at best misleading. No asset is in action as a medium of exchange except in the very moment of being transferred from one ownership to another, in settlement of some transaction, and no class of asset used in this way can logically be excluded from the class of active money. Between transactions all money is idle. Yet if activity is held to cover the state of being held in readiness against possible use in exchange, then all monetary assets are active all the time.'

This opinion, characteristic of the Radcliffe Report (1959), reflects Sayers's individualist standpoint. As far as social reproduction as a whole is concerned, which also contains a sphere of exchange into and out of which commodities regularly flow, the problem appears less intractable: the sphere of exchange must contain a quantity of money constantly on the move to facilitate commodity flows during any given period of time. Similarly, a quantity of money is at rest alongside circulation. Whether a particular element of the total money stock belongs to one or the other portion, and how that appears to its owner, are not important issues in this connection. For a stimulating discussion of money on the move and money at rest see Chick (1992, ch. 7).

18. For the classical quantity theory of money, furthermore, a country retains the amount of money appropriate to its commodity values, level of material output and money velocity – as long as governments and banks do not tamper with the monetary process. The rest of the available money is exported. In other words, commodity money is 'endogenous' money in the sense that its circulating quantity in a particular country is determined through the automatic operation of the process of exchange. In contrast credit money seemed to the quantity theorists to possess an evidently 'exogenous' aspect in that the banks, through easier terms of credit, appear to be able unilaterally to alter its circulating quantity.

19. Goodhart (1989, p. 33) found the following weakness in Moore's argument: 'Demand for money, in the sense of the optimal amount that I would want to hold in *equilibrium* in a given context, is *not*, the same thing as – or determined by – the credit-counterpart supply of money. The credit market is distinct and different from the money market... I agree that at any moment the actual supply of money is determined, under present circumstances, primarily in the credit market – as the credit-counterparts approach indicates – and that it is willingly accepted. But I deny that this actual stock is necessarily also demanded in the equilibrium sense outlined above' (emphasis in original).

In response Moore (1991b) sought recourse to a denial of the concept of the Walrasian auctioneer, but the reply he produced lacked his usual clarity. Goodhart (1991) rightly claimed that his point had remained fundamentally unanswered. Arestis and Howells (1996) also criticised Moore for rejecting the independence of the demand for money, relying on the ambiguous concept of 'convenience lending'.

11 Money and Credit in a Socialist Economy

1. This recognition is a cornerstone of the Uno school (Uno, 1950–2, 1980). As we have argued in chapter 2, it has allowed the Uno tradition to analyse commodities, money, merchant and interest-bearing capital as pure forms of circulation, that is, without reference to the substance of value or the specific social relations that characterise the underlying labour process.
2. Uno (1953a) appeared to accept this view when he rejected Stalin's claim that the law of value had a role to play in a socialist society. It is worth noting that Uno's critique was levelled prior to the commencement of de-Stalinisation in 1956.
3. For a more detailed discussion of Gray's views see Saad-Filho (1993).
4. One could perhaps argue that the Soviet Union had remained a transitional society, developing towards but not finally achieving socialism. This view, however, offers little insight into the theoretical and practical difficulties of establishing a monetary system based on labour money in a fairly developed planned economy, as the Soviet Union was after the Second World War.
5. The long-standing theoretical controversy regarding the reduction of heterogeneous concrete labour into homogeneous abstract labour has a bearing on this issue. Rubin (1928, chs 13, 14) asserted that the reduction is performed in the market through the process of commodity exchange. The problem then arises of establishing the commensurability of different kinds of labour in a socialist economy. Though Rubin introduced the concept of 'socially equalised labour' in addition to concrete and abstract labour, he did not offer a clear basis on which the various concrete labours could be reduced to socially equalised labour. Rubin's approach, moreover, does not allow for the necessary criticism of the arbitrary grading of labour that prevailed in the Soviet Union, securing privileges for state and Communist Party bureaucrats.
6. For further discussion on this point see Itoh (1988, ch. 6).
7. Assume n products produced in, respectively, n sectors of production. For the ith product, a_{ij} units of the jth product and l_i hours of living labour are technically necessary. Let the total of past and living labour embodied in a unit of the ith product be t_i hours. Then

$$a_{11}t_1 + a_{12}t_2 + \ldots + a_{1n}t_n + l_1 = t_1$$
$$a_{21}t_1 + a_{22}t_2 + \ldots + a_{2n}t_n + l_2 = t_2$$
$$\ldots$$
$$a_{n1}t_1 + a_{n2}t_2 + \ldots + a_{nn}t_n + l_n = t_n$$
$$(a_{ij} \geq 0, l_i \geq 0, i = 1, 2, \ldots, n)$$

There are n simultaneous linear equations, in n unknown t_i. The solutions are in terms of a_{ij} and l_i, which are the technical conditions of production. Okishio (1955) provided one of the earliest treatments of this problem.

8. In the interwar 'socialist economic calculation controversy' the critics of socialism claimed that, in the absence of a market for the means of production, it would be impossible to calculate and minimise the costs of production. However in the course of the resurgence of the neo-Ricardian and Marxist theories of value in the last three decades is has become clear that the calculation and minimisation of economic cost need not presuppose the neoclassical subjective theory of value and price. This point was not apparent to some of the defenders of socialism in the original controversy (Itoh, 1995).

9. Phenomena fully discussed by Kornai (1980).

10. Moreover, as far as the Eastern Bloc still engaged in trade with capitalist countries in the world market, it used gold, dollars and other currencies to make international payments. The historical fact that the Soviet Union was one of the largest gold producers in the world allowed the country more easily to acquire international reserves and, to an extent, underpinned its rapid industrialisation.

11. Market socialism is distinct from the mere social-democratic control of capitalism. The latter does not disturb the capitalist ownership of the means of production but merely attempts to effect the redistribution of income through tax and transfer policies.

Bibliography

Aglietta, M. (1979) *A Theory of Capitalist Regulation* (London: NLB).

Akerlof, G. (1970) 'The Market for "Lemons": Qualitative Uncertainty and the Market Mechanism', *Quarterly Journal of Economics*, vol. 84, pp. 488–500.

Akerlof, G. and J. Yellen (1985) 'Can Small Deviations from Rationality Make Significant Differences to Economic Equilibria?', *American Economic Review*, September.

Albritton, R. (1991) *A Japanese Approach to the Stages of Capitalist Development* (London: Macmillan).

Alesina, A. and Summers, L. H. (1993) 'Central Bank Independence and Macroeconomic Performance: Some Comparative Evidence', *Journal of Money, Credit and Banking*, vol. 25, no. 2.

Alesina, A. and G. Tabellini (1987) 'Rules and discretion with non-coordinated monetary and fiscal policies', *Economic Inquiry*, vol. 25.

Anderson, K. (1983) 'The "Unknown" Marx's "Capital"', *History of Political Economy*, vol. 15, no. 4.

Andreades, A. (1909, 1966) *History of the Bank of England*, 4th edn (London: Frank Cass).

Arestis, P. (1992) *The Post-Keynesian Approach to Economics* (Aldershot and Brookfield: Edward Elgar).

Arestis, P. (1996) 'Post-Keynesian economics: towards coherence', *Cambridge Journal of Economics*, vol. 20, no. 1 (January).

Arestis, P and V. Chick (eds) (1992) *Recent Developments in Post-Keynesian Economics* (Aldershot & Brookfield: Edward Elgar).

Arestis, P. and P. Howells, (1996) 'Theoretical reflections on endogenous money: the problem of convenience lending', *Cambridge Journal of Economics*, vol. 20, no. 5 (September).

Armstrong, P. and Glyn, A., Harrison, J. (1984) *Capitalism Since World War II*, (London: Fontana).

Armstrong, P. and Glyn, A. (1986) *Accumulation Profits, State Spending: Data for Advanced Capitalist Countries 1952–1983* (Oxford: Oxford Institute of Economies and Statistics.)

Arnon, A. (1984) 'The transformation in Thomas Tooke's monetary theory reconsidered', *History of Political Economy*, vol. 16, pp. 311–26.

Arnon, A. (1991) *Thomas Tooke: Pioneer of Monetary Theory* (London: Edward Elgar).

Arnon, A. (1997) 'Free and Not-so-Free Banking Theories Among the Classicals', *History of Political Economy*, forthcoming.

Asimakopulos, A. (1983) 'Kalecki and Keynes on finance, investment, and saving', *Cambridge Journal of Economics*, vol. 7, nos 3/4.

Aspromourgos, T. (1996) *On the origins of classical economics* (London & New York: Routledge).

Bagehot, W. (1873) 'Lombard Street', in N. St John-Stevas (ed.), *The Collected Works of Walter Bagehot*, vol. 9 (London: The Economist 1978).

284   *Bibliography*

Baran, P. and P. Sweezy (1966) *Monopoly Capital* (New York and London: Monthly Review Press).

Barro, R.J. and Gordon, D.J.B. (1983a) 'A Positive Theory of Monetary Policy in a Natural-rate Model', *Journal of Political Economy*, August, vol. 91, no. 4.

Barro, R.J. and Gordon, D. B. (1983b) 'Rules, Discretion and Reputation in a Model of Monetary Policy', *Journal of Monetary Economics*, vol. 12, July.

Bernanke, B. and A. Blinder (1988) 'Credit, Money, and Aggregate Demand', *American Economic Review*, May.

Bernanke, B. and M. Gertler (1989) 'Agency Costs, Net Worth, and Business Fluctuations', *American Economic Review*, vol. 79, no. 1 (March).

Borza, E. (1990) *In the Shadow of Olympus: The Emergence of Macedon* (Princeton, NJ: Princeton University Press).

Bowles, S. and R. Edwards (1985) *Understanding Capitalism* (New York: Harper & Row).

Boyer, R. (1986) *La Théorie de la Régulation* (Paris: Edition La Découverte).

Braudel, F. (1981, 1992) *The Structures of Everyday Life* (Berkeley and Los Angeles: University of California Press).

Brunhoff, S. de (1973, 1976) *Marx on Money* (New York: Urizen Books).

Buchan, J. (1995) 'Mississipi dreaming: on the fate of John Law', *New Left Review*, no. 210 (March/April).

Bukharin, N. (1915, 1972) *Imperialism and World Economy* (London: Merlin Press).

Checkland, S. G. (1975) *Scottish Banking: A History, 1695–1973* (Glasgow: Collins).

Chick, V. (1992) *On Money, Method, and Keynes*, selected essays edited by P. Arestis, and S. Dow (New York: St Martin's Press).

Clapham, J. (1944) *The Bank of England*, vols I, II (Cambridge. Cambridge University Press).

Clarke, S. (1989) 'The Basic Theory of Capitalism: A Critical Review of Itoh and the Uno School', *Capital & Class*, vol. 37 (Spring).

Clower, R. (1965) 'The Keynesian Counter-Revolution: A Theoretical Appraisal', in F. Hahn, and F. Brechling (eds), *The Theory of Interest Rates* (London: Macmillan).

Clower, R. (1967) 'A Reconsideration of the Microfoundations of Monetary Theory', *Western Economic Journal*, vol. 6 (December).

Cohen, E. (1992) *Athenian Economy and Society: A Banking Perspective* (Princeton, NJ: Princeton University Press).

Congdon, T. (1980) 'The Monetary Base Debate: Another Instalment in the Currency School vs Banking School Controversy', *National Westminster Bank Quarterly Review*, August.

Cottrell, A. (1994) 'Post-Keynesian monetary economics', *Cambridge Journal of Economics*, vol. 18, no. 6 (December).

Croix, G. E. M. de St (1981) *The Class Struggle in the Ancient Greek World* (London: Duckworth).

Crotty, J. (1993) 'Rethinking Marxian Investment Theory: Keynes–Minsky Instability, Competitive Regime Shifts, and Coerced Investment', *Review of Radical Political Economics*, 25(1).

Cukierman, A. (1992) *Central Bank Strategy, Credibility, and Independence: Theory and Evidence* (Cambridge, Mass: MIT Press).

Davidson, P. (1965) 'Keynes' finance motive', *Oxford Economic Papers*, vol. 17, no. 1.

Davidson, P. (1972a) *Money and the Real World* (London and Basingstoke: Macmillan).

Davidson, P. (1972b) 'A Keynesian View of Friedman's Theoretical Framework for Monetary Analysis', *Journal of Political Economy*, reprinted in *Money and Employment, Collected Writings of Paul Davidson* (Basingstoke & London: Macmillan, 1990).

Davidson, P. (1978) 'Why Money Matters: Lessons from a Half-century of Monetary Theory', *Journal of Post-Keynesian Economics*, reprinted in *Money and Employment*, Collected Writings of Paul Davidson (Basingstoke & London: Macmillan, 1990).

Davidson, P. (1982) *International Money and the Real World* (Basingstoke and London: Macmillan).

Davidson, P. (1989) 'Keynes and Money', in R. Hill (ed.), *Keynes, Money and Monetarism* (London: Macmillan).

Davidson, P. (1994) *Post-Keynesian Macroeconomic Theory* (Aldershot and Brookfield: Edward Elgar).

Davidson, P. and J. Kregel (eds) (1989) *Macroeconomic Problems and Policies of Income Distribution* (Aldershot and Brookfield: Edward Elgar).

Desai, M. (1981) *Testing Monetarism* (London: Pinter).

Diamond, D. W. (1984) 'Financial Intermediation and Delegated Monitoring', *Review of Economic Studies*, vol. 51, pp. 393–414.

Diamond, D. and P. Dybvig (1983) 'Bank runs, deposit insurance, and liquidity', *Journal of Political Economy*, vol. 91.

Dobb, M. (1940) *Political Economy and Capitalism* (London: Routledge & Kegan Paul).

Dow, S. (1984) 'Methodology and the Analysis of a Monetary Economy', *Economies et Societes*, vol. 18, *Monnaie et Production 1*, reprinted in *Money and the Economic Process* (Aldershot and Brookfield: Edward Elgar, 1993).

Dow, S. (1985) *Macroeconomic Thought* (Oxford: Blackwell).

Dow. S. (1988) 'Money supply endogeneity', *Economie appliquee*, vol. XLI, no. 1, reprinted in *Money and the Economic Process* (Aldershot and Brookfield: Edward Elgar, 1993).

Dow, S. (1996) 'Horizontalism: a critique', *Cambridge Journal of Economics*, vol. 20, no. 4 (July).

Dow, S. and J. Hillard (eds) (1995) *Keynes, Knowledge, and Uncertainty* (Aldershot and Brookfield: Edward Elgar).

Dowd, K. (1989) *The State and the Monetary System* (Hemel Hempstead: Philip Allan).

Dowd, K. (1993) *Laissez-faire in banking* (London and New York: Routledge).

Eagly, R. V. (1970) 'Adam Smith and the specie-flow doctrine', *Scottish Journal of Political Economy*, vol. 17, pp. 61–8.

Engels, F. (1981, 1894) *Supplement to Volume 3 of 'Capital'* (London: Penguin/ NLR).

Fama, E. (1970) 'Efficient Capital Market', *Journal of Finance*, vol. 25, no. 2, (May).

Fama, E. (1991) 'Efficient Capital Markets: II', *Journal of Finance*, vol. 46, no. 5, (December).

Feavearyear, A. E. (1931) *The Pound Sterling: A History of English Money* (Oxford: Clarendon Press).

Fetter, F. W. (1942) 'The Life and Writings of John Wheatley', *Journal of Political Economy*, vol. I, no. 3 (June).

Fetter, F. W. (1959) 'The Politics of the Bullion Report', *Economica*, vol. XXVI, no. 102 (May).

Fetter, F. W. (1965) *Development of British Monetary Orthodoxy, 1797–1875* (Cambridge, Mass: Harvard University Press).

Fine, B. (1975) *Marx's Capital* (London and Basingstoke: Macmillan).

Fine, B. (1980) *Economic Theory and Ideology* (London: Edward Arnold).

Fine, B. (1985–86) 'Banking Capital and the Theory of Interest', *Science & Society*, vol. XLX, no. 4 (Winter).

Fine, B. (1988) 'From Capital in Production to Capital in Exchange', *Science & Society*, vol. 52, no. 3 (Fall).

Fine, B. and L. Harris (1979) *Re-reading Capital* (London: Macmillan).

Finley, M, I. (1973) *The Ancient Economy* (London: Chatto & Windus).

Finley, M. I. (1981) *Economy and Society in Ancient Greece* (London: Chatto & Windus).

Foley, D. (1982) 'The value of money, the value of labour power and the Marxian transformation problem', *Review of Radical Political Economics*, vol. 14, no. 2.

Foley, D. (1983) 'On Marx's theory of money', *Social Concept*, vol. 1, no. 1.

Foley, D. (1986) 'Say's Law in Marx and Keynes', *Cahiers d'Economie Politique*, nos 10, 11.

Friedman, B. (1988) 'Lessons of Monetary Policy from the 1980's', *Journal of Economic Perspectives*', vol. 2, no. 3 (Summer).

Friedman, B. (1995) 'Does Monetary Policy Affect Real Economic Activity', *NBER Working Paper*, no. 5212, August.

Friedman, M. (1953) *Essays in Positive Economics* (Chicago, Ill.: University of Chicago Press).

Friedman, M. (1956) 'The Quantity Theory of Money: A Restatement', in M. Friedman (ed.), *Studies in the Quantity Theory of Money* (Chicago, Ill.: University of Chicago Press).

Friedman, M. (1968) 'The Role of Monetary Policy', *American Economic Review*', March.

Friedman, M. (1970) 'The Counter-revolution in Monetary Theory', IEA Occasional Paper No. 33, (London: Institute of Economic Affairs).

Friedman, M. (1981) 'Memorandum on Monetary Policy', presented to the Treasury and Civil Service Committee (London: HMSO).

Friedman, M. and A. Schwartz (1963) *A Monetary History of the United States, 1867–1960* (Princeton NJ: Princeton University Press).

Friedman, M. and A. Schwartz (1982) *Monetary Trends in the United States and the United Knigdom: Their Relation to Income, Prices and Interest Rates* (Chicago, Ill.: University of Chicago Press).

Fullarton, J. (1844) *On the Regulation of Currencies* (London).

Gale, D. and M. Hellwig (1985) 'Incentive Compatible Debt Contracts: The One-Period Problem', *Review of Economic Studies*, vol. LII, pp. 647–63.

Gerschenkron, A. (1962) *Economic Backwardness in Historical Perspective* (Cambridge, MA: Harvard University Press).

Gertler, M. (1988) 'Financial Structure and Aggregate Economic Activity: An Overview', *Journal of Money, Credit, and Banking*, vol. 20, no. 3 (August), pp. 559–88.

Gilbart, J. W. (1834, 1922) *The History, Principles, and Practice of Banking*, 2 vols, published in A. S. Michie, *Gilbart on Banking* (London: G. Bell).

Glasner, D. (1989) *Free Banking and Monetary Reform* (Cambridge: Cambridge University Press).

Goodhart, C. A. E. (1975) *Money, Information, and Uncertainty* (Basingstoke and London: Macmillan).

Goodhart, C. A. E. (1985, 1988) *The Evolution of Central Banks* (Cambridge, Mass: MIT Press).

Goodhart, C. A. E. (1987) 'Why do banks need a central bank?', *Oxford Economic Papers*, no. 39, also published in C. A. E. Goodhart, *The Central Bank and the Financial System* (London: Macmillan, 1995).

Goodhart, C. A. E. (1989) 'Has Moore become too horizontal?', *Journal of Post Keynesian Economics*, vol. 12, no. 1 (Fall).

Goodhart, C. A. E. (1991) 'Is the concept of an equilibrium demand for money meaningful? A reply to "has the demand for money been mislaid?" ', *Journal of Post Keynesian Economics*, vol. 14, no. 1 (Fall).

Gordon, D. R. Edwards and M. Reich (1982) *Segmented Work, Divided Workers* (Cambridge: Cambridge University Press).

Gray, J. (1831) *The Social System* (Edinburgh).

Gray, J. (1848) *Lectures on the Nature and Use of Money* (Edinburgh).

Green, P. (1990) *Alexander to Actium* (London: Thames & Hudson).

Green, R. (1992) *Classical theories of money, output and inflation* (Basingstoke: Macmillan).

Grierson, P. (1977) *The Origins of Money* (London: Athlone Press and University of London).

Grilli, V., D. Masciandaro and G. Tabellini (1991) 'Political and monetary institutions and public financial policies in the industrialised countries', *Economic Policy*, vol. 13.

Hahn, F. (1982) *Money and Inflation* (Oxford: Blackwell).

Hamuda O. and G. Harcourt (1988) 'Post-Keynesianism: From Criticism to Coherence', *Bulletin of Economic Research*, January.

Hansen, A. (1949) *Monetary Theory and Fiscal Policy* (New York: McGraw-Hill).

Hansen, A. (1953) *A Guide to Keynes* (New York: McGraw-Hill).

Haq, M., I. Kaul and I. Grunberg (eds) (1996) *The Tobin Tax* (London: Oxford University Press).

Harris, L. (1976) 'On Interest, Credit, and Capital', *Economy and Society*, May.

Harris, L. (1981a) *Monetary Theory* (New York: McGraw-Hill).

Harris, L. (1981b) 'Marx's Theory of Interest: A Comment', mimeo (Milton Keynes: Open University).

Harrod, R. (1951) *The Life of John Maynard Keynes* (London: W. W. Norton).

Harvey, D. (1982) *The Limits to Capital* (Oxford: Basil Blackwell).

Hawtrey, R. (1932, 1962) *The Art of Central Banking* (London: Frank Cass).

Hawtrey, R. (1938) *A Century of Bank Rate* (London, New York and Toronto: Longmans, Green).

288 *Bibliography*

Hayek, F. A. (1935) *Collectivist Economic Planning*, (London: Routledge & Kegan Paul).
Hayek, F. A. (1939) 'Introduction', *Thornton's Paper Credit* (London: Allen & Unwin).
Hayek, F. A. (1976a) *Denationalisation of Money* (London: Institute of Economic Affairs).
Hayek, F. A. (1976b) *Choice in Currency* (London: Institute of Economic Affairs).
Heckscher, E. (1931, 1994) *Mercantilism* vols 1, 2 (London and New York: Routledge).
Heihnsohn, G. and O. Steiger (1987) 'Private Ownership and the Foundations of Monetary Theory', *Economies et Societes*, no. 9.
Heihnsohn, G. and O. Steiger (1989) 'The Veil of Barter: The Solution to the Task of Obtaining Representations of an Economy in which Money is Essential', in J. Kregel (ed.), 1989.
Helphand, A. (Parvus) (1901) *Die Handelskrisen und die Gewerkschaften* (Munchen: Ernst).
Hicks, J. (1937, 1967) 'Mr Keynes and the "Classics"', *Econometrica*, vol. V, no. 2 (April), reprinted in *Critical Essays in Monetary Theory* (Oxford: Clarendon Press).
Hicks, J. (1967) 'Thornton's *Paper Credit*', in *Critical Essays in Monetary Theory* (London: Oxford University Press).
Hilferding, R. (1910, 1981) *Finance Capital* (London: Routledge & Kegan Paul).
Hobson, J. (1902) *Imperialism* (London).
Horner, F. (1957) *Economic Writings of Francis Horner*, ed. F. W. Fetter (London: London School of Economics).
Horsefield, J. K. (1944) 'The Origins of the Bank Charter Act, 1844', *Economica*, vol. XI, no. 44 (November).
Horsefield, J. K. (1949) 'The Bankers and the Bullionists in 1819', *Journal of Political Economy*, vol. LVII, no. 5 (October).
Hume, D, (1752, 1955) 'Essays, Literary, Moral and Political', in E. Rotwein (ed)., *Writings on Economics* (Edinburgh: Nelson).
Institute of Political Economy, USSR Academy (1954) *Political Economy* (Japanese translation) (Tokyo: Godo-shuppan).
Itoh, M. (1973) *Credit and Crisis* (in Japanese) (Tokyo: University of Tokyo Press).
Itoh, M. (1976) 'A Study of Marx's Theory of Value', *Science & Society*, vol. 40, no. 3 (Fall), also published in *Value and Crisis* (London: Pluto Press, 1980).
Itoh, M. (1980) *Value and Crisis* (London: Monthly Review Press) (New York: Pluto Press).
Itoh, M. (1981) *The Theory of Value and Capital* (in Japanese) (Tokyo: Iwanami-shoten).
Itoh, M. (1988) *The Basic Theory of Capitalism* (London: Macmillan, Totown: Barnes and Noble).
Itoh, M. (1990) *The World Economic Crisis and Japanese Capitalism* (London: Macmillan, New York: St. Martin's).
Itoh, M. (1995) *Political Economy for Socialism* (London: Macmillan, New York: St. Martin's).

Iwai, K. (1996) 'The Bootstrap Theory of Money: A Search- Theoretic Foundation of Monetary Economics', mimeo, University of Tokyo.

Iwata, H. (1964) *World Capitalism* (in Japanese) (Tokyo: Mirai-sha).

Jaffee, D. M. and T. Russell (1976) 'Imperfect Information Uncertainty and Credit Rationing', *Quarterly Journal of Economics*, vol. XCI, pp. 651–66.

Kaldor, N. (1970) 'The New Monetarism', *Lloyds Bank Review*, July.

Kaldor, N. (1980) 'Monetarism and UK Policy', *Cambridge Journal of Economics*, December.

Kaldor, N. (1982) *The Scourge of Monetarism* (Oxford: Oxford University Press).

Kaldor, N. (1985) 'How Monetarism Failed', *Challenge*, May–June.

Kautsky, K. (1901–2) 'Krisenteorien', *Neue Zeit*, XX-2.

Kautsky, K. (1911) 'Finanzkapital unf Krisen', *Neue Zeit*, XXIX-2.

Kautsky, K. (1913) 'Die Wandelungen der Goldproduktion und der wechselnde Charakter der Teuerung', *Neu Zeit*, supplement to no. 16 (January).

Keynes, J. M. (1936, 1973) *The General Theory of Employment, Interest, and Money* (London: Macmillan).

Keynes, J. M. (1937) 'Alternative theories of the rate of interest', *Economic Journal*, vol. XLVII, no. 2.

Keynes, J. M. (1973) 'The General Theory of Employment', in *The Collected Writings* of J. M. Keynes (London: Macmillan, pp. 109–23).

Kindleberger, C. (1984) *A Financial History of Western Europe* (London: George Allen & Unwin).

King, W. (1936) *History of the London Discount Market* (London: Routledge).

Kiyotaki, N. and R. Wright (1989) 'On Money as a Medium of Exchange', *Journal of Political Economy*, vol. 97 (December).

Kondratieff, N. (1935) 'The Long Waves in Economic Life', *Review of Economics and Statistics*, vol. 60.

Kornai, J. (1980) *Economies of Shortage* (Amsterdam: North-Holland).

Kregel, J. (ed.) (1989) *Inflation and Income Distribution in Capitalist Crisis* (Basingstoke: Macmillan).

Kydland, F. and E. Prescott (1977), 'Rules rather than Discretion: The Inconsistency of Optimal Plans', *Journal of Political Economy*, June.

Kydland, F. and E. Prescott (1982) 'Time to Build and Aggregate Economic Fluctuations', *Econometrica*, November.

Laidler, D. (1981) 'Adam Smith as a monetary economist', *Canadian Journal of Economics*, vol, XIV, no. 2 (May).

Lange, O. (1936–7) 'On the Economic Theory of Socialism' in B. Lippincot (ed.), *On the Economic Theory of Socialism* (University of Minnesota Press, 1938).

Lapavitsas, C. (1991) 'The Theory of Credit Money: A Structural Analysis', *Science & Society*, vol. 55, no. 3.

Lapavitsas, C. (1992) 'A Model of Money Hoard Formation in the Circuit of Capital', Working Paper No. 8, School of Oriental and African Studies, University of London, March.

Lapavitsas, C. (1994) 'The Banking School and the Monetary Thought of Karl Marx', *Cambridge Journal of Economics*, vol. 18, no. 5 (October).

Lapavitsas, C. (1996) 'The Classical Adjustment Mechanism of International Balances: Marx's Critique', *Contributions to Political Economy*, vol. 15.

Lavoie, M. (1984) 'The Endogenous Flow of Credit and the Post Keynesian Theory of Money', *Journal of Economic Issues*, vol. 18, no. 3 (September).

Lavoie, M. (1985) 'Credit and Money: The Dynamic Circuit, Overdraft Economics, and Post Keynesian Economics', in M. Jarsulic (ed.), *Money and Macro Policy* (Boston: Kluwer-Nijhoff)

Law, J. (1705, 1966) *Money and Trade Considered* (New York: Kelley).

Leijonhufvud, A. (1967) 'Keynes and the Keynesians: A Suggested Interpretation', in R. Clower (ed.), *Monetary Theory* (London: Penguin).

Leijonhufvud, A. (1968) *On Keynesian Economics and the Economics of Keynes* (London: Oxford University Press).

Lekatsas, P. (1946, 1978) *The City of the Sun* (in Greek) (Athens: Kastaniotis).

Leland, H. and D. H. Pyle (1977) 'Informational Asymmetries, Financial Structures and Financial Intermediation', *Journal of Finance*, vol. 32, pp. 371–87.

Lenin, V. I. (1921, 1966) 'The Importance of Gold Now and After the Complete Victory of Socialism', in *The Collected Works of Lenin*, vol. 33, (Moscow: Progress Publishers).

Lianos, T. (1987) 'Marx on the Rate of Interest', *Review of Radical Political Economics*, vol. 19, no. 3, pp. 34–55.

Long J. and C. Plosser (1983) 'Real Business Cycles', *Journal of Political Economy*, February.

Lucas, R. (1972) 'Expectation and the Neutrality of Money', *Journal of Economic Theory*, April.

Lucas, R. (1973) 'Some International Evidence on Output–Inflation Trade-offs', *American Economic Review*, June.

Lucas, R. (1976) 'Econometric Policy Evaluation: A Critique', in *The Phillips Curve and Labor Markets*, ed. K. Brunner and A. Meltzer (Amsterdam: North Holland).

Luxemburg, R. (1913, 1951) *The Accumulation of Capital* (London: Routledge & Kegan Paul).

Mandel, E. (1975) *Late Capitalism* (London: NLB)

Mandel, E. (1980) *Long Waves of Capitalist Development* (Cambridge: Cambridge University Press).

Mankiw N. and D. Romer (eds) (1991) *New Keynesian Economics* (Cambridge, Mass.: MIT Press).

Marglin, S. and J. Schor (eds) (1990) *The Golden Age of Capitalism* (Oxford: Clarendon Press).

Marx, K. (1859, 1970) *Contribution to the Critique of Political Economy* (Moscow: Progress Publishers).

Marx, K. (1867, 1976) *Capital*, vol. I (London: Penguin/NLR).

Marx, K. (1885, 1978) *Capital*, vol. II (London: Penguin/NLR).

Marx, K. (1894, 1981) *Capital*, vol. III (London: Penguin/NLR).

Marx, K. (1905, 1969) *Theories of Surplus Value*, pts 1, 2, 3 (London: Lawrence & Wishart).

Marx, K. (1939, 1973) *Grundrisse* (London: Penguin/NLR).

Mattick, P. (1969) *Marx and Keynes* (London: Merlin).

McCallum, B. (1995) 'Two Fallacies Concerning Central Bank Independence', *American Economic Review*, Papers and Proceedings, vol. 85, no. 2.

McCallum, B. (1997) 'Crucial Issues Concerning Central Bank Independence', *Journal of Monetary Economics*, vol. 39.

Mauss, M. 1954, *The Gift. Forms and Functions of Exchange in Archaic Societies* (London: Cohen & West)

Meek, R. (1950) 'The Decline of Ricardian Economics in England', *Economica*, vol. XVII, no. 65 (February).

Meek, R. (1956) *Studies in the Labour Theory of Value* (New York: Monthly Review Press).

Meiksins-Wood, E. (1988) *Peasant-Citizen and Slave* (London & New York: Verso).

Menger, K. (1892) 'On the Origins of Money', *Economic Journal*, vol. 2, (March).

Mill, J. (1808, 1966), 'Smith on Money and Exchange', in *James Mill: Selected Economic Writings*, ed. D. Winch (Edinburgh and London: Oliver & Boyd).

Mill, J. (1826, 1966), 'Elements of Political Economy', in D. Winch (ed.), *James Hill, Selected Economic Writings* (Edinburgh and London: Oliver & Boyd).

Mill, J. S. (1848, 1965) *Principles of Political Economy* (Toronto: University of Toronto Press).

Millet, P. (1991) *Lending and Borrowing in Ancient Athens* (Cambridge: Cambridge University Press).

Minsky, H. (1975) *John Maynard Keynes* (New York: Columbia University Press).

Minsky, H. (1982) *Can 'It' Happen Again: Essays on Finance and Instability* (Armonk, NY: M. E. Sharpe).

Minsky, H. (1984) 'Frank Hahn's Money and Inflation: A Review Article', *Journal of Post Keynesian Economics*, vol. 6.

Minsky, H. (1985) 'The Financial Instability Hypothesis', in *Post Keynesian Economic Theory* P. Arestis and T. Skouras (eds) (Armonk, NY: Sharpe).

Mints, L. (1945) *A History of Banking Theory in Great Britain and the United States* (Chicago, Ill.: University of Chicago Press).

Miyazaki, Y. (1992), *Complex Depression* (in Japanese) (Tokyo: ChuoKoronsha)

Miyazaki, Y. (1995), *Twilight of National Economies* (in Japanese) (Tokyo: Asatin-Shinbun-Sha)

Modigliani, F. (1944) 'Liquidity Preference and the Theory of Interest and Money', *Econometrica*, January.

Moore, B. (1979) 'The endogenous money stock', *Journal of Post Keynesian Economics*, vol. 2, no. 1 (Fall).

Moore, B. (1983) 'Unpacking the post Keynesian black box: bank lending and the money supply', *Journal of Post Keynesian Economics*, vol. 5, no. 4 (Summer).

Moore, B. (1986) 'How Credit Drives the Money Supply: The Significance of Institutional Developments', *Journal of Economic Issues*, vol. 20, no. 2 (June).

Moore, B. (1988) *Horizontalists and Verticalists: The Macroeconomics of Credit Money* (Cambridge: Cambridge University Press).

Moore, B. (1989a) 'A simple model of bank intermediation', *Journal of Post Keynesian Economics*, vol. 12, no. 1 (Fall).

Moore, B. (1989b) 'On the endogeneity of money once more', *Journal of Post Keynesian Economics*, vol. 11, no. 3 (Spring).

Moore, B. (1991a) 'Money supply endogeneity: "reserve price setting" or "reserve quantity setting"?', *Journal of Post Keynesian Economics*, vol. 13, no. 3 (Spring).

Moore, B. (1991b) 'Has the demand for money been mislaid? A reply to "has Moore become too horizontal?"', *Journal of Post Keynesian Economics*, vol. 14, no. 1, (Fall).

Morgan, D. (1994) 'Bank Credit Commitments, Credit Rationing, and Monetary Policy', *Journal of Money, Credit, and Banking*, vol. 26, no. 1 (February), pp. 87–101.

Morgan, E. V. (1965) *The Theory and Practice of Central Banking*, 1797–1913 (London: Frank Cass).

Morgan, E. V. and W. A. Thomas (1962) *The Stock Exchange: Its History and Functions* (London: Elek Books).

Muth, J. (1961) 'Rational Expectations and the Theory of Price Movements', *Econometrica*, July.

Neue Zeit (1911–13) The Debate on Gold as Money, 30 bd.1–7, 31 bd.1–16, November 1911–January 1913.

Nishimura, S. (1971) *The Decline of the Inland Bills of Exchange in the London Money Market, 1855–1913* (Cambridge: Cambridge University Press).

Norman, G. W. (1833) *Remarks Upon Some Prevalent Errors with Respect to Currency and Banking* (London).

OECD *Historical Statistics*, several issues (Paris: OECD).

Ohlin, B. (1937a) 'Some notes on the Stockholm theory of savings and investments II', *Economic Journal*, vol. XLVII, no. 2.

Ohlin, B. (1937b) 'Alternative theories of the rate of interest – rejoinder', *Economic Journal*, vol. XLVII, no. 3.

Okishio, N. (1955) *Value and Prices* (in Japanese), Research in Economics, Kobe University, March.

Overstone, Lord (S. Lloyd Jones) (1840a, 1857) 'Effects of the Administration of the Bank of England', in *Tracts, etc., on Metallic and Paper Currency*, ed. J. R. McCulloch (London).

Overstone, Lord (1840b, 1857) 'A Letter to J. B. Smith', in McCulloch (ed.), ibid.

Overstone, Lord (1840c, 1857) 'Remarks on the Management of the Circulation and on the Condition and Conduct of the Bank of England and of the Country Issuers during the Year 1838', in McCulloch (ed.), ibid.

Overstone, Lord (1840d, 1857) 'Effects of the Administration of the Bank of England. A Second Letter to J. B. Smith Esq. McCulloch (ed.)

Owen, R. (1821) *Report to the County of Lanark* (Glasgow).

Palley, T. (1991) 'The endogenous money supply: consensus and disagreement', *Journal of Post Keynesian Economics*, vol. 13, no. 3 (Spring).

Panico, C. (1980) 'Marx's analysis of the relationship between the rate of interest and the rate of profit', *Cambridge Journal of Economics*, vol. 4, pp. 363–78.

Panico, C. (1987) *Interest and Profit in the Theories of Value and Distribution* (London: Macmillan).

Panico, C. (1988) 'Marx on the Banking Sector and the Interest Rate: Some Initial Notes for a Discussion', *Science & Society*, vol. 52, no. 3 (Fall), pp. 310–25.

Parnell, H. (1827) *Observations on Paper Money, Banking, and Overtrading* (London: Ridgway).

Parnell, H. (1832) *A Plain Statement of the Power of the Bank of England and of the Use It Has Made of It* (London: Ridgway).

Patinkin, D. (1965) *Money, Interest and Prices*, 2nd edn (New York: Harper & Row).

Persson, T. and Tabellini, G. (1993) *Designing Institutions for Monetary Stability*, Carnegie–Rochester Conference Series on Public Policy, December, 39.

Phillips, A. W. (1958) 'The Relation Between Unemployment and the Rate of Change of Money Wage Rates in the United Kingdom, 1861–1957', *Economica*, November.

Polanyi, K. (1944) *The Great Transformation* (Boston: Beacon Press).

Polanyi, K., C. Arensberg and H. Pearson (eds) (1957) *Trade and Markets in Early Empires* (Glencoe, Ill.: Free Press).

Pollin, R. (1991) 'Two theories of money supply endogeneity: some empirical evidence', *Journal of Post Keynesian Economics*, vol. 13, no. 3 (Spring).

Pollin, R. (1993) 'Money Supply Endogeneity: What Are the Questions and Why Do They Matter?', in E. Nell and D. Deleplace (eds), *Money in Motion: The Circulation and Post Keynesian Approaches* (London: Macmillan).

Radcliffe Report (1959) *Report on the Working of the Monetary System* (London: HMSO).

Reden S. von (1994) 'Ancient Money: Institution and Symbol. The Greek Polis as a Case Study', paper presented at the international conference on Economic Thought and Economic Reality in Ancient Greece, Delphi, Greece, 22–26 Sep.

Reuten, G. and M. Williams (1989) *Value Form and the State* (London: Routledge).

Ricardo, D. (1810, 1951) 'The High Price of Bullion', in P. Sraffa and M. Dobb (eds), *Works and Correspondence of David Ricardo*, vol. III (Cambridge: Cambridge University Press).

Ricardo, D. (1811, 1951) 'Reply to Bosanquet', in P. Sraffa, and M. Dobb, (eds), ibid.

Ricardo, D. (1816, 1951) 'Proposals for an Economical and Secure Currency', in P. Sraffa and M. Dobb (eds), ibid., vol. IV.

Ricardo, D. (1817, 1951) 'On the Principles of Political Economy and Taxation', in P. Sraffa and M. Dobb (eds), ibid., vol. I.

Ricardo, D. (1951) 'Letters', in P. Sraffa and M. Dobb (eds), ibid.

Rist, C. (1940) *History of Monetary and Credit Theory from John Law to the Present Day* (London: Allen & Unwin).

Robbins, L. (1958) *Robert Torrens and the Evolution of Classical Economics* (London: Macmillan).

Robertson, D. (1937) 'Alternative theories of saving and investment – rejoinder', *Economic Journal*, vol. XLVII, no. 3.

Robertson, D. (1938) 'Mr Keynes and "finance"', *Economic Journal*, vol. XLVIII, no. 2.

Robinson, J. (1942, 1966) *An Essay on Marxian Economics* (London & Basingstoke: Macmillan).

Roemer, J. H. (1997) *A Future for Socialism* (Japanese edition) (Tokyo: Aoki Shoten).

Rogoff, K. (1985) 'The Optimal Degree of Commitment to an Intermediate Monetary Target', *Quarterly Journal of Economics*, November, vol. 100, no. (4).

Rogoff, K. (1989), 'Reputation, Coordination, and Monetary Policy, in *Modern Business Cycle,* ed. R. Barro (Oxford: Blackwell).

Rousseas, S. (1986) *Post Keynesian Monetary Economics* (Armonk, NY: M. E. Sharpe).

Rousseas, S. (1989) 'On the endogeneity of money once more', *Journal of Post Keynesian Economics*, vol. 11, no. 3 (Spring).

Rowthorn, B. (1980) *Capitalism, Conflict, and Inflation* (London: Lawrence & Wishart).

Rubin, I. (1927, 1978) 'Abstract Labour and Value in Marx's System', *Capital & Class*, Summer.

Rubin, I. (1928, 1975) *Essays in Marx's Theory of Value* (Montreal: Black Rose Books).

Saad-Filho, A. (1993) 'Money, Labour, and "Labour-Money"', *History of Political Economy*, Vol. 25, no. 1.

Samuelson, P. (1947) *Foundations of Economic Analysis* (Cambridge, Mass.: Harvard University Press).

Sargent, T. and N. Wallace (1975) 'Rational Expectations, the Optimal Monetary Instrument and the Optimal Money Supply Rule', *Journal of Political Economy*, April.

Sargent, T. and N. Wallace (1976) 'Rational Expectations and the Theory of Economic Policy', *Journal of Monetary Economics*, April.

Sawyer, M. (1991) 'Post-Keynesian Macroeconomics', in D. Greenaway, M. Bleaney and I. Stewart (eds), *Companion to Contemporary Economic Thought* (London: Macmillan).

Sayers, R. (1957) *Central Banking After Bagehot* (Oxford: Clarendon Press).

Sayers, R. (1960) 'Monetary Thought and Monetary Policy in England', *Economic Journal*, vol. 70, no. 280 (December), reprinted in H. Johnson (ed.), *Readings in British Monetary Economics* (Oxford: Clarendon Press, 1972).

Schumpeter, J. A. (1939) *Business Cycles*, 2 vols (New York: McGraw-Hill).

Schumpeter, J. A. (1954) *History of Economic Analysis* (London: Routledge).

Selgin, G. (1988) *The Theory of Free Banking* (Totowa, NJ: Cato Institute/ Rowman & Littlefield).

Senior, N. (1829) *Three Lectures on the Value of Money* (London: Fellows).

Shamsavari, A. (1991) *Dialectic and Social Theory: The Logic of 'Capital'* (Braunton: Merlin Books).

Silberling, N. (1924a) 'Financial and Monetary Policy of Great Britain During the Napoleonic Wars', *Quarterly Journal of Economics*, vol. XXXVIII (February).

Silberling, N. (1924b) 'Financial and Monetary Policy of Britain During the Napoleonic Wars', *Quarterly Journal of Economics*, vol. XXXVIII (May).

Skidelsky, R. (1983) *John Maynard Keynes: Hopes Betrayed, 1883–1920* (London: Macmillan).

Smith, A. (1776, 1904) *The Wealth of Nations*, ed. E. Cannan, vols. I and II (London: Methuen).

Smith, V. (1936, 1990) *The Rationale of Central Banking* (Indianapolis: Liberty Press).

Sowell, T. (1974) *Classical Economics Reconsidered* (Princeton, NJ: Princeton University Press).

Steuart, J. (1767, 1805) 'An Inquiry into the Principles of Political Economy', in *Works, Political, Metaphysical, and Chronological, of the Late Sir James Steuart*, vols I, II, III, IV (London).

Steuart, J. (1805) 'A Plan for Introducing an Uniformity of Weights and Measures within the Limits of the British Empire', in *Works*, vol. V, ibid.

Stiglitz, J. (1985) 'Capital Markets and the Control of Capital', *Journal of Money, Credit, and Banking*, vol. 17, no. 2 (May).

Suzuki, K. (1960–2) *Principles of Political Economy* (in Japanese), 2 vols (Tokyo: University of Tokyo Press).

Sweezy, P. (1942, 1968) *The Theory of Capitalist Development* (New York: Monthly Review Press).

Taylor, F. (1929) 'The Guidance of Production in a Socialist State' in B. Lippincot (ed.), *On the Economic Theory of Socialism* (University of Minnesota Press, 1938).

Taylor, J. B. (1995) 'The Monetary Transmission Mechanism: An Empirical Framework', *Journal of Economic Perspectives*, Fall.

Thompson, W. E. (1978) 'A view of Athenian banking', *Museum Helveticum*, vol. 36, pp. 224–41.

Thompson, W. E. (1982) 'The Athenian Entrepreneur', *L'Antiquite classique*, vol. 51, pp. 53–85.

Thornton, H. (1802, 1939) *An Enquiry into the Nature and Effects of the Paper Credit of Great Britain* (London: Allen & Unwin).

Timberlake, R. H. (1984) 'The Central Banking Role of Clearinghouse Associations', *Journal of Money, Credit, and Banking*, vol. 16, no. 1.

Tobin, J. (1970) 'Money and Income: Post Hoc, Ergo Propter Hoc?', *Quarterly Journal of Economics*, May.

Tooke, T. (1826) *Considerations on the State of the Currency* (London).

Tooke, T. (1829) *A Letter to Lord Grenville* (London).

Tooke, T. (1844, 1959) *An Inquiry into the Currency Principle* (London: London School of Economics).

Tooke, T. (1840) *History of Prices, 1838–39*, vol. III (London).

Tooke, T. (1848) *History of Prices, 1839–1847*, vol. IV (London).

Torrens, R. (1812) *An Essay on Money and Paper Currency* (London).

Torrens, R. (1837) *A Letter to the Right Hon Lord Melbourne* (London).

Torrens, R. (1847) *On the Operation of the Bank Charter Act of 1844 as it Affects Commercial Credit* (London).

Torrens, R. (1857) *The Principles and Practical Operation of Sir Robert Peel's Act of 1844*, 2nd edn (London).

Townsend, R. (1979) 'Optimal Contracts and Competitive Markets with Costly State Verification', *Journal of Economic Theory*, vol. 21, pp. 265–93.

✓ Trotsky, L. (1941) 'On the Curve of Capitalist Development', *Fourth International*, May.

Tsuda, T. (1948) *The Development of Cotton Capitals in the World* (Nagoya: Reimei Shobo).

Tugan-Baranowsky, M. (1913) *Les Crises Industrielles en Angleterre* (Paris: Jiard & Brieve).

Uno, K. (1950–2) *Principles of Political Economy*, 2 vols (in Japanese) (Tokyo: Iwanami-shoten).

Uno, K. (1953a) 'The Economic Law and Socialism' (in Japanese), *Shiso*, October.

Uno, K. (1953b) *Theory of Crisis* (in Japanese) (Tokyo: Iwanami-shoten).

Uno, K. (1980) *Principles of Political Economy* translated from a Japanees 1964 version by T. Sekine (Brighton: Harvesten, Atlantic Highland: Humanities).

Varga, E. (1937–8) *World Economic Crises*, 2 vols (Japanese translation) (Tokyo: Keio-shobo).

Vilar, P. (1976) *A History of Gold and Money* (London and New York: Verso).

Viner, J. (1924) *Canada's Balance of International Indebtedness, 1900–1913*, (Cambridge, Mass.: Harvard University Press).

Viner, J. (1937) *Studies in the Theory of International Trade* (New York: Harper).

Walsh, C. (1995) 'Optimal Contracts for Central Bankers', *American Economic Review*, March, vol. 85, no. 1.

Weeks, J. (1981) *Capital and Exploitation* (Princeton, NJ: Princeton University Press).

Weeks, J. (1989) *A Critique of Neoclassical Macroeconomics* (New York: St. Martin's Press).

Weintraub, S. (1978) *Keynes and the Monetarists* (New Brunswick and New Jersey: Rutgers University Press).

White, L. (1984) *Free Banking in Britain* (Cambridge: Cambridge University Press).

White, L. (1989) *Competition and Currency* (New York and London: New York University Press).

Wicksell, K. (1898, 1965) *Interest and Prices* (New York: Augustus Kelley).

Wicksell, K. (1935) *Lectures on Political Economy*, vols I, II (London: George Routledge).

Williamson, S. (1986) 'Costly Monitoring, Financial Intermediation, and Equilibrium Credit Rationing', *Journal of Monetary Economics*, 18 September, pp. 159–79.

Wilson, J. (1859) *Capital, Currency, and Banking* (London: The Economist).

Wood, E. (1939) *English Theories of Central Banking Control, 1819–1858* (Cambridge, Mass.: Harvard University Press).

Wray, R. (1990) *Money and Credit in Capitalist Economies* (Aldershot and Brookfield: Edward Elgar).

Yokokawa, N. (1985) 'Theories of Value and Reproduction', unpublished PhD thesis, University of Cambridge.

Yokokawa, N. (1989) *Value, Employment, and Crisis* (in Japanese) (Tokyo: Shakaihyoron-sha).

Index